WELSH
HISTORIC
MONUMENTS

A Guide to
Ancient and Historic Wales

•

Dyfed

Sian Rees

London : HMSO

•

© Text copyright Sian Rees 1992
First published 1992
ISBN 0 11 701220 3
Applications for reproduction should be made to HMSO

Front cover: Pembroke Castle, by Augustus W Calcott, RA (by kind permission of M Ivor Ramsden)
Back cover: Pentre Ifan burial chamber (no. 4)

Other volumes in the series:
Glamorgan and Gwent

Forthcoming:
Gwynedd
Clwyd and Powys

Series Editor: Sian E Rees

While the information contained in this book is to the best of our knowledge correct at time of publication, the publisher and author can accept no responsibility for any inconvenience which may be sustained by any error or omission. Readers are also reminded to follow the Country Code when visiting the countryside monuments in this book.

HMSO publications are available from:

HMSO Publications Centre
(Mail, fax, and telephone orders only)
PO Box 276, London, SW8 5DT
Telephone orders 071-873 9090
General enquiries 071-873 0011
(queuing system in operation for both numbers)
Fax orders 071-873 8200

HMSO Bookshops
49 High Holborn, London, WC1V 6HB 071-873 0011 (counter service only)
258 Broad Street, Birmingham, B1 2HE 021-643 3740
Southey House, 33 Wine Street, Bristol, BS1 2BQ (0272) 264306
9–21 Princess Street, Manchester, M60 8AS 061-834 7201
16 Arthur Street, Belfast, BT1 4GD 0232-238451
71 Lothian Road, Edinburgh, EH3 9AZ 031-228 4181

HMSO's Accredited Agents
(see Yellow Pages)

and through good booksellers

Printed in the United Kingdom for HMSO
Dd 293652 C40 7/92 68772

Contents

Preface

During the time that I worked in Dyfed as Inspector of Ancient Monuments, my primary task was concerned with the conservation of the historic sites of the county. I firmly believe that one of the best methods of conservation is to awaken in people an awareness of the unique contribution that ancient sites make, enriching our landscape by their quiet presence. With that aim in mind, this series of four regional guides was conceived, covering, in turn: Dyfed; Glamorgan and Gwent; Gwynedd; and Clwyd and Powys. Each volume describes 150 well-preserved monuments which are accessible to the public. The volume on Dyfed covers the area roughly equivalent to the old counties of Cardiganshire, Carmarthenshire and Pembrokeshire.

The time-span covered by the volumes is from the first appearance of man in the Old Stone Age to the 16th century AD. The 16th century heralded many changes which suggested it as an appropriate end to a guide devoted to ancient monuments rather than to townscapes and general landscapes. Speaking somewhat casually, it marked the end of serious use of the castle in Wales, the end of the monasteries, and, with the Acts of Union of 1536–43, the political merging of Wales with England.

Inevitably there are many omissions from the book, sometimes made very reluctantly. Churches in use are not included as, despite their obvious interest and appeal, they are neither ruins nor monuments, and their very number is such that they need a guide of their own. The remains of industrial sites are a particular casualty of the cut-off date, as the vast majority of the more spectacular date from later than the 15th century. There are other sites of which the very fragility of the archaeological remains, or of the wildlife within them, render visits inadvisable. Yet more sites were left out because they were remote and difficult of access. The main omissions, however, were the many monuments which lie inaccessible to the public on private land, many of which are very fine. For this reason, an appendix has been added, listing well-preserved sites for which special permission must be obtained before visiting, or which are especially difficult of access.

Ancient sites are a tangible link with our past; they are our only link with the remotest past before literacy gave us a written history. And for the events of that written history, later sites are the stage, scenery and backdrop to the action that took place. To see these monuments makes our past come alive, if we can only clothe their stones and earthworks, battlemented walls and traceried windows with our imaginations. If this book helps the visitor to do this, its main objective will have been achieved.

How to Use the Book

The introduction to the book gives an outline of the physical characteristics of Dyfed. The main gazetteer is then ordered into period-based chapters, so that monuments of a class fall together, and each chapter is preceded by a brief description of the history and monuments of that period in Dyfed. Each site is given a number to aid its identification on the location maps.

Location

The monuments are ordered numerically in the gazetteer, and each is given the name by which it is normally known, which generally, but by no means invariably, is that found on the Ordnance Survey 1:50,000 maps. The nearest readily identifiable town or village is also given, from which the access directions start. The site type, a rough indication of its date, the Ordnance Survey 1:50,000 map number, and the site's six-figure national grid reference are also given. It is hoped that the directions alone will enable those without the 1:50,000 map to find the sites, but road and path signs, house names and the position of lay-bys change so rapidly that it is always safer to have the relevant map, if at all possible.

To locate a site on an Ordnance Survey map, first get the appropriate 1:50,000 map, the number of which is given on each entry (e.g., OS 157). Then look at the grid reference for the site, which consists of two letters and six figures (e.g., SM 750255). The letters at the beginning of the reference can usually be ignored as long as the correct map is being used, as they are a large-scale reference for the appropriate 100km grid square. Then take the first three numbers, which refer to the numbers on the top or bottom of the map; the first two of these will indicate the western line of the 1km square in which the site lies. The third will measure in tenths how far eastward within that square the site lies. Repeat the procedure with the second group of three numbers, which refer to the numbers on the right or left side of the map and increase in value northwards. Although this may sound complicated, after doing a few trial searches there should be no problem with easily locating any given site.

Accessibility

A guide to the accessibility of each site is given by the following:

U   Unrestricted, i.e., access at any reasonable time free of charge.

R   Restricted, i.e., access is restricted by opening hours and/or entry charge. If this symbol is used, an explanation is usually given at the end of the access direction.

Cadw standard hours

Many monuments maintained by Cadw are unrestricted, while a few operate under the 'key keeper' system by which the key may be collected from a nearby shop or house. The opening hours of the six or seven monuments with admission charges do vary slightly from site to site and according to the time of year. It is safe to assume, however, that where 'Cadw standard hours' is indicated, a monument will be open from Monday to Saturday and often part of Sunday during main daylight hours, except for Christmas Eve, Christmas Day, Boxing Day and New Year's Day. Full details of opening hours may be obtained from Cadw on request.

Monuments owned by other bodies may have similar opening times to Cadw throughout the year, in which case the phrase 'standard hours' is used. Where monuments are only open in the summer, this is indicated, with, wherever possible, a contact point, as opening dates may vary from year to year.

Disabled visitors

An attempt has been made to estimate how accessible each monument may be for disabled visitors. The entries are rated 1 to 4, this number appearing directly after the U or R at the head of each entry.

1   Easy access for all, including wheelchairs.

2   Reasonable access for pedestrians but limited access for wheelchairs.

3   Restricted access for disabled, but view of site from road or car park.

4   Access for able-bodied only.

It is also an unfortunate fact of life that monuments tend to get covered with bracken in high summer so that some almost disappear. This has been indicated.

Abbreviations

These occur especially in the access directions:

CCW	Countryside Council for Wales
km	kilometre
L, LHS	left, left-hand side

m	metre
ml	mile
NT	National Trust
OS	Ordnance Survey
PO	Post Office
RSPB	The Royal Society for the Protection of Birds
R, RHS	right, right-hand side
tel	telephone

Welsh Place-Names

Any visitor to Wales will soon realise that the spelling of Welsh place-names can vary considerably, different versions of the same name being found on maps, road signs and in publications. Many Welsh place-names are compounded of two or more elements which are sometimes written as separate words, sometimes linked with hyphens and sometimes run into one. This series has attempted to use the most commonly found version of place-names, though the use of hyphens has been avoided wherever possible.

Safety

Anyone who makes periodic visits to ancient monuments will be aware of the hazards which different sorts of sites present to the unwary. Every visitor to sites in category 4 should have sensible footwear and clothing; in exposed areas, or even on country paths, sudden rain can make a walk a flounder, and mists equally suddenly can make apparently familiar terrain look strange and baffling. A pocket compass is always a good idea. Best of all, tell someone where you are going and when you expect to return.

Ruins that are officially open to the public, looked after by Cadw, the National Trust or private trusts, however hard those bodies try, may still be hazardous, especially for children, who should be supervised on higher areas of monuments and told cautionary tales about the dangers of climbing on walls. Most monuments in categories 1, 2 and 3 are perfectly suitable for children of all ages as long as parents are aware of the hazards and avoid them. Many category 4 sites, though requiring longer walks, will also be quite suitable for older children, probably depending more on the psychological make-up and disposition of the child than on age or physique. The promise of a picnic can do wonders for enticing the most unenthusiastic young visitor, and many monuments have areas for picnics nearby.

Country Code

It is, of course, most important to observe the Country Code when visiting the majority of the monuments in the book, which are situated on public footpaths through private land. Keep dogs on leads, always shut gates securely and open and shut them rather than climbing over. Keep to paths, do not drop litter and avoid any action that could start a fire. If you keep to these rules, monuments in private hands will continue to be cherished and visitors welcomed.

Further Information and Useful Addresses

A number of the monuments described in the gazetteer are owned or maintained by Cadw: Welsh Historic Monuments, a body with the statutory responsibility for protecting, conserving and presenting the 'built heritage' of Wales on behalf of the Secretary of State. Many more of the sites listed in the book have been 'scheduled', or given statutory protection by the Secretary of State. Lists and maps of scheduled ancient monuments are produced by Cadw and a series of guidebooks provide detailed descriptions of the monuments it maintains. Further information can be obtained by contacting Cadw at: Brunel House, 2 Fitzalan Road, Cardiff CF2 1UY, tel: 0222 465511.

The Pembrokeshire Coast National Park Authority maintains a long-distance footpath around the coast of the south-western peninsula from St Dogmaels on the north to Amroth on the south. It is largely thanks to this footpath that so many of the characteristic Iron Age coastal promontory forts are accessible to the public. The Authority also maintains several ancient monuments in the National Park, including Carew Castle and St Govan's Chapel. The information offices run by the National Park are a mine of information about accommodation and boat trips to the islands, to mention but two subjects of especial importance to users of this guide. The address is: The Pembrokeshire Coast National Park Authority, County Offices, Haverfordwest, Dyfed SA61 1QZ, tel: 0437 764591 ext. 5135.

The National Trust has substantial holdings of the most important areas of natural beauty, including a great many ancient monuments, particularly those belonging to the prehistoric periods. Of especial importance are the gold mines and Roman fort at Dolaucothi, which the National Trust owns and presents to the public. The south Wales headquarters of the National Trust are at: The King's Head, Bridge Street, Llandeilo, Dyfed SA19 6BB, tel: 0558 822800.

The Dyfed Archaeological Trust is the body responsible for maintaining a Sites and Monuments Record, a list of all known monuments in Dyfed. It carries out rescue excavation and survey work on sites which are threatened with development or erosion. The Trust may be contacted at: The Old Palace, Abergwili, Carmarthen, Dyfed SA31 2JG, tel: 0267 231667.

The following museums have material from ancient sites in Dyfed:

The National Museum of Wales, Cathays Park, Cardiff.

Carmarthen Museum, The Old Palace, Abergwili, Carmarthen.

The Castle Museum, Haverfordwest.

Scolton Museum, Scolton Manor, Haverfordwest.

Tenby Museum, Castle Street, Tenby.

Ceredigion Museum, Aberystwyth.

While all possible attempts have been made to ensure that the accessibility of monuments is as described, unforeseen circumstances can alter access quite suddenly; monuments may sometimes have to be closed for short periods for repair work, and sadly, footpaths, even well-established ones, do disappear from time to time. Discretion must therefore be exercised during visits and no liability can be accepted for errors in the information supplied.

Introduction

It is probably the coastline of the far south-west of Wales that lingers longest in the visitor's memory. It is fractured with countless inlets from the great sheltered waters of the Cleddau at Milford Haven to tiny, secret bays protected by rocky crags. Through these harbours settlers gained access to the rich soils of the low-lying south-western peninsula. Further north and east the coastline is less craggy; the undulating, low coastal plateaux of south Carmarthenshire are, none the less, well supplied with major rivers, the Taf, the Tywi and Cothi and the two Gwendraeth rivers, and the wide estuaries of these rivers and the prized alluvial soils of their valleys inevitably had a major impact on early settlement pattern, routeways and territorial demarcation. Further north, Cardigan sits at the mouth of the great Teifi river, and its fertile valley from there way inland to Tregaron is marked by prehistoric settlement and medieval castles alike. The coastal plain of Ceredigion, with its fine pasture land, has no major river valleys, but only smaller inlets and streams, with the exception of the Rheidol and Ystwyth which emerge at Aberystwyth, and the great Dyfi estuary which marks the northern boundary of the county.

Inland from the coastal plateaux and away from the valleys, Dyfed is essentially mountainous. Even in the generally low-lying south-western peninsula, the ridge of the Preseli hills, although rising to a mere 540m, effectively divides the area into two – the flatter arable south and the hill country of the north. This always had, and still has, a dramatic effect on settlement pattern. In central areas of the county, however, the foothills which skirt the coastal plateaux, and through which the fertile valleys pass, give way to the Cambrian Mountains which stretch into adjacent Powys, and which, by their extent, height and remoteness, and their thin, acid soils, always formed a formidable barrier to passage and settlement. Even from early prehistory, when climatic conditions were warmer, evidence of man's activity is not dense, though standing stones and funerary cairns found on the fringes of the uplands suggest that these areas were far from deserted. It is the mountains that have helped to mould the Welsh character, independent and stoical and, above all, difficult to organise into a single unity but equally difficult to conquer and rule.

As the topography of Dyfed moulded settlement and movement, its rocks and soils dictated both architectural techniques and farming practices. The oldest rocks in Dyfed are the weathered igneous tuffs and granites which make up the Preseli hills in the north of the south-western peninsula. The Preselis were of great importance early in prehistory as a source of the precious spotted dolerite, a good raw material for the prized polished stone axes of the Neolithic, and the famous bluestones of the inner stone setting at far-away Stonehenge. Elsewhere, Dyfed is made up of rather younger rocks, the Ordovician grits and shales of the coastal plateaux, the Silurian rocks of the mountainous interior and, younger still, the old red sandstone, millstone grit and carboniferous limestone of the south. The band of limestone runs east to west along the south-west coast and this, for instance, made practical a type of architecture which demanded a plentiful supply of tough stone while tolerating its tendency to break into small slabs. The vaulted buildings so characteristic of medieval Pembrokeshire were the result, as were the thick, earth-filled stone field walls called 'Pembrokeshire hedges'. The old red sandstone of the far south-west gave rich red soils ideal for arable agriculture, and the mild maritime climate still makes the area famous for early harvests. The millstone grit of mid-Pembrokeshire, quarryable into larger blocks, makes reasonable building stone, and can be seen as the main stone in medieval buildings in such places as Haverfordwest, while the Pembrokeshire slate from the Preselis was useful for roofing. Further north, the plentiful, but easily fractured shales were utilised in the durable, grey buildings of Ceredigion. The alluvial soils of valley sides and glacial drifts of the coastal plateaux favoured mixed farming regimes, while the adjacent foothills have always been used primarily to support cattle. Inland, the grits and shales of the mountains now give only thin acid soils where flocks of sheep reign unchallenged, and the available stone is poor. It is used in small, irregular slabs in the isolated farmhouses, barns and dry field-walls which still dot the sheltered hillsides where the concrete block bungalow has not yet totally taken over. Wales in general is a country of low agricultural potential with a predominantly pastoral farming tradition. Inevitably this is a generalised picture, and, wherever possible throughout history, mixed farming would be undertaken on farms striving for self-sufficiency, even if cultivation was on a very small scale, harnessed to pastoralism, to provide some grain for human consumption and fodder for animals.

The other main influence upon man's behaviour, that of climate, has altered at different times, most dramatically, of course, during the Ice Ages of our remote past. That the rainfall of modern Wales is surplus to requirement is a truism, and to many the very name of the country is synonymous with rain. The flora and fauna and the use to which the land may be put are, of course, profoundly affected by this major element, along with the fact that the country sits within the belt of westerly winds. However, during warmer periods in the past, more favourable conditions have from time to time allowed farming, deforestation, quarrying and other activities over most parts of Dyfed. Indeed, at times of rising population or economic pressures, or of even minor climatic improvement, cultivation would expand higher up the hills so that as late as the early 19th century there might be quite extensive arable farming at high altitudes. The vegetational landscape that we know in the country today is largely a result of this interference and exploitation of the land by man. This is quite clear in the south and west where the present-day field systems cover the countryside. It is perhaps less clear in the uplands of the Cambrian Mountains, where, none the less, the vast tracts of moorland are at best a semi-natural response to man's activities.

The complex two-way process of topography, geology and climate affecting man's exploitation of land, and the activity of man himself affecting the vegetation, has resulted in the richly varied landscape that is our inheritance today. The ideal way to study the history of a county must therefore be to look at this landscape in its entirety. Such a luxury is not given to the holidaymaker and even the specialist frequently needs to examine in detail one site at a time, be it a castle, cairn or standing stone. This guide is designed to help them, but inevitably while it selects and describes specific monuments it also to some extent isolates them from their landscape. When visiting historic sites it is important, therefore, always to bear in mind the relationship between man and environment which has created each one of the monuments around us.

1

The Earliest Prehistoric Periods

The earliest traces of man's activity that archaeologists have found in Wales belong to the period known as the Palaeolithic or Old Stone Age, during the later stages of the Pleistocene Ice Age. The Ice Age was not, of course, one continuous cold era, but rather a succession of cold, sometimes glacial periods interspersed with warmer interglacials. Even the cold phases were themselves interrupted by shorter warm periods known as interstadials, and it was possibly during one of these interstadials within the 'Anglian' glaciation that man first appeared in Britain around 450,000 BC. Population numbers must always have been very small, and people were ever on the move, following game animals which were themselves affected by the changes in climate over this almost incomprehensibly long time. At some periods, Britain would have been one with the continental landmass of Europe, while at other warmer times the rise in sea level would have caused Britain to be an island.

The first evidence of man found on a site in Wales is later, and probably belongs to an interglacial which began around 250,000 BC. Even for this stage, human remains are extremely rare. Many areas of the country were subsequently covered with ice during the later cold period, and the ice action must have scoured away or obscured traces of earlier settlement. Even so, groups of hunters must still have been few in number. At just one site in Wales, in a cave at Pontnewydd near Denbigh in Clwyd, human remains probably belonging to the forerunners of Neanderthal man and stone artefacts including hand-axes and scrapers have been discovered, dating to about 225,000 BC. The model suggested for the lifestyle of Palaeolithic man is of groups of hunting and collecting peoples following game over great distances and making periodic visits to the parts of the peripheral area of the European landmass that would later become Britain. They may well have used caves and rock shelters for temporary settlement as they followed their quarry. The type of game hunted varied, of course, depending upon the climate of the time, but at Pontnewydd horse seems to have been the most important. Bones of wolf, bear, lion, rhinoceros and deer were also found, and some of these, too, may have been killed for food or, more probably, for their skins.

During the fluctuating cold and warm phases which characterised the onset of the final 'Devensian' glaciation *Homo sapiens sapiens* is the sole human type encountered, Neanderthal man having died out before 30,000 BC. Several cave

Reconstruction drawing of a cave settlement, 70,000 BC

sites in Wales, including Hoyle's Mouth near Tenby (no. 1) and Paviland in Gower, have yielded artefacts dating to this time, which is called the Early Upper Palaeolithic. To this period belongs the extraordinarily rich burial at Paviland Cave in Gower, where a male body was buried, daubed in red ochre and surrounded by ivory rods and rings. The ice sheet of the final glaciation stopped short of parts of what is now the south coast of Dyfed and Glamorgan, and it is just possible that the caves in this limestone belt were used as shelters for summer hunting parties even during the colder periods, and as base camps perhaps for exploiting reindeer grazing areas further north during periods of warmer weather.

The ice of the Devensian glaciation began to retreat around 15,000 BC and gradually population spread northwards as elk, horse, reindeer, deer and other small mammals returned to Britain to take advantage of the new forests of birch and pine. Evidence for man's activity now becomes more commonly found, and during this period, the Late Upper Palaeolithic, several caves in south-west Wales were evidently used for shelter. Their excavation has produced quantities of bone tools, and finely worked stone blades and scrapers of 'Creswellian' type.

As the climate continued to ameliorate, the post-glacial pine and birch forests became established and widespread, and attracted wild cattle, deer and wild pig.

Reconstruction drawing of a settlement of hunting and gathering people, 7000 BC

In response, the artefacts manufactured by man about 10,000 years ago seem to undergo a considerable change: flint tools become much smaller and archaeologists refer to a 'microlithic' industry, apparently designed to provide sharp stone tips and barbs for wooden spears or arrows, the bow and arrow now being widely used as a hunting tool for the first time. There is a remarkable increase in the amount of bone and antler tools found on settlement sites, and new forms of stone axe were introduced, used for the clearance of forest prior to settlement. This new phase in man's history has been called the Mesolithic or Middle Stone Age.

The climate continued to improve and consequently the sea level rose; gradually Britain became cut off from Europe, first by marshes and then, by 6000 BC, by the sea. The forests changed with the increasing warmth and oak, elm, lime and alder became the dominant species. The population increased, especially, it seems, in coastal areas. Excavations on later Mesolithic sites at various places in Britain show hunters and collecting people becoming more expert at forest exploitation, the manipulation and management of wild animals such as red deer, at hunting a greater variety of smaller animals, sea birds and wildfowl, at fishing and collecting shellfish and edible plants and nuts. The way of life was almost certainly still nomadic, though settlements appear to have been used and reused on a seasonal basis. Settlement sites are occasionally discovered which suggest that occupation was in tents made of skin and timber, and the tool types found on these later Mesolithic sites are different, with small geometric microliths becoming common forms. By the end of the Mesolithic, it seems that the population was becoming more settled, less mobile, and that even some sort of exchange system had evolved, allowing the transfer of precious raw materials from source areas to other areas further afield.

Mesolithic artefacts have been found in some numbers in Dyfed, concentrated in coastal sites in the far south-west. But physical remains of settlements have not yet been discovered, even at the rich site at the Nab Head (no. 3), where great quantities of microliths and shale beads have been found.

1
Hoyle's Mouth Cave, Tenby
Old Stone Age cave
25,000 BC? 11,000–8000 BC and later
OS 158   SN 112003   U2

From Tenby, take A4139 towards Pembroke for 0.8ml (1.2km). Turn R opposite Kiln Park Garage towards Penally, then R on to Trefloyne Lane. After 0.3ml (0.5km), park and take path on LHS of road, following it to R at fork, through wood, 50m to cave. Visit in summer months; bats use cave in winter

Savory 1973

The majority of the natural caves to be found in Dyfed lie within the hard grey carboniferous limestone which runs in a band east–west from Tenby to Pembroke. These caves are of prime importance for the evidence that they hold for man's earliest activity in the area during the Palaeolithic period (Old Stone Age). Subsequent communities also used them, and finds from the Mesolithic and Neolithic (Middle and New Stone Ages) and succeeding periods as late as medieval times suggest that they continued to provide useful temporary shelter to man through the millennia.

The Hoyle, or Hoyle's Mouth Cave is situated in sloping woodland overlooking the valley of the Ritec stream, which must at one time have been a deep sea inlet. The mouth of the cave is about 4m in height and leads to the main cavern, which divides to form a short eastern and a longer narrow western passage, the latter running about 40m into the hill. It was one of the first caves in Wales to attract scientific attention, largely because of the interest taken in it by the Revd G N Smith, rector of Gumfreston, in the mid-19th century. The early excavations carried out by Smith and others, together with more recent excavations in 1969 and 1986, have uncovered a considerable number of flint artefacts which show that the cave was used by man probably as early as the Early Upper Palaeolithic and certainly in the succeeding Later Upper Palaeolithic. Finds from later times, including Mesolithic flint tools and Iron Age and Roman pottery, have also been uncovered, though the pottery may derive from the site of a separate late prehistoric settlement thought to lie somewhere above the cave.

The Palaeolithic stone tools from Hoyle's Mouth, which include flint blades, points, burins and scrapers, belong principally to the 'Creswellian' type, though one 'Aurignacian' burin from the preceding Early Upper Palaeolithic has also been found. They are among the earliest man-made objects to have been discovered from extant sites in Dyfed,

Hoyle's Mouth Cave

though stone artefacts of Aurignacian type have also been found at Paviland Cave in Gower, and excavations at the now-destroyed Coygan Cave near Carmarthen have produced Middle Palaeolithic 'Mousterian' hand-axes. Bones of mammoth, hyaena and bear from Hoyle's Mouth form an important collection of Late Glacial fauna. This is not necessarily contemporary with the use of the cave by man, though some reindeer bone also uncovered during the excavations may well be connected with human occupation.

A number of other caves in the locality were inhabited during the Upper Palaeolithic and similar Creswellian tools have been found at nearby Little Hoyle, at Priory Farm, Pembroke and at Nanna's Cave, on Caldey Island (see Appendix). The artefacts from Hoyle's Mouth are now widely scattered, housed in Bristol City Museum, Bolton Museum, the National Museum of Wales, Cardiff and, happily, in the museum at Tenby, rather more convenient for the visitor to the cave.

2
The Wogan, Pembroke
Middle Stone Age cave
8000 BC–12th century AD
OS 158   SM 982017   R2

The cave is within Pembroke Castle, and may only be visited together with it. Directions as for Pembroke Castle (no. 112). Cave is down steps at far end of castle. Standard hours, entry charge

King 1978; Pembroke Castle Guidebook

The spectacular cave known as the Wogan is a massive single chamber some 10m high within the carboniferous limestone rock on which Pembroke Castle now stands. It has a high natural mouth which opens in the rock face overlooking the Pembroke River, is relatively well-lit, and spacious. It is not surprising that the cave has a long history of use by man. Flint tools have been found here from time to time which may suggest its occupation at least during the Mesolithic period (Middle Stone Age) and probably in later prehistoric periods as well.

After the construction of the medieval castle directly overhead, the cave might have presented a weak point in the defences if allowed to remain open. Consequently, the mouth was largely blocked up by a massive stone wall in the 12th century and an access stair to the cave from the castle was constructed. The cave was probably used as a boathouse.

Finds from the Wogan may be seen at Tenby Museum. The curious name of the cave is probably derived from the Welsh 'ogof' (or 'cave').

3
The Nab Head, Marloes
Middle Stone Age site and Iron Age promontory fort
7000–3000 BC and later 1st millennium BC
OS 157   SM 790108   U2

From Haverfordwest, take B4327 Dale road W for 8ml (12.8km). At crossroads, follow road to St Brides for 3ml (4.8km) to T-junction and take St Brides Beach road to R. Park at chapel. Walk L (W) along coast path for 1ml (1.6km) to promontory fort, from which site visible

Wainwright 1971; David 1989

There is no doubt that the Nab Head was a place of considerable importance in the

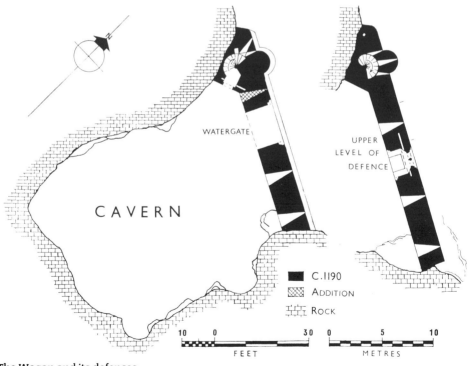

WATERGATE

CAVERN

UPPER LEVEL OF DEFENCE

■ C.1190
▨ ADDITION
▥ ROCK

```
10   0            30   0        5        10
FEET                METRES
```

The Wogan and its defences

Figurine and shale beads from the Nab Head

generally, such objects of adornment are very rare in the British Mesolithic. Beads from the Nab Head may have belonged to a number of items of jewelry, perhaps deposited in burials. Alternatively, as the beads were being manufactured here, they may have had some purpose related to trade.

Stone implements from the Nab Head include microliths, awls, scrapers and axes, all similar to tools found at the Mesolithic site at Daylight Rock on Caldey Island. Other finds include the so-called 'bevelled pebbles', soft stone pebbles formed into convex scoops sometimes interpreted as scoops for scraping the flesh of shellfish from their shells. Radiocarbon dates suggest an early date in the Mesolithic of about 7000 BC for the main Nab Head occupation; other tools, such as the bevelled pebbles, imply a reoccupation later in the period, after 6000 BC.

Finds from the Nab Head may be seen at the museums at: Scolton (Haverfordwest) which houses the famous statuette, Tenby and Abergwili (Carmarthen) and the National Museum of Wales (Cardiff).

The adjacent promontory fort, built much later in the Iron Age, is a good deal more spectacular as a site on the ground. It lies on an irregular rocky headland and is formed by a defensive series of one prominent inner, and two slighter outer, banks and ditches which cut off the promontory from the mainland to the east. The single entrance in the centre of the system is well preserved but the northern end of the defences has been removed by coastal erosion. Small-scale excavations in 1971 revealed, in the interior of the fort, a circular stone hut 10m in diameter with a single entrance and a hearth. A section cut through the inner defensive bank showed it to have had two phases of building and to have been constructed behind a stone revetment.

Mesolithic (Middle Stone Age), though, unfortunately, as is usual with sites of this date, nothing can now be seen above ground. In the early Mesolithic, when the sea level was considerably lower, the rocky promontory overlooked an inland valley, perhaps just over 1ml (2km) from the sea.

While no structures associated with settlement have ever been found here, excavations and casual finds have brought to light a large variety of artefacts. Most important among these is what is probably the only carving in the round known from a Mesolithic context in the British Isles. It is a small object of shale and has been variously interpreted as a Venus figurine or a phallus. Also of extreme interest are the perforated shale beads which have been found on the site; over 500 have been discovered through the years, and the fact that some of these are unfinished suggests that beads may have been manufactured here. Similar shale beads have come from two nearby sites but

2
The First Farmers

In the middle of the 4th millennium BC, a great change took place. The first agricultural communities arrived in Britain from the Continent bringing with them the seedcorn and flocks and herds which would alter man's lifestyle and his relationship with his environment for ever. They introduced into this country domesticated wheat and barley, cattle, sheep and goats, the wild progenitors of which had originated in the Near East. The settlers may have come directly from north Germany or north-west France and may have only come in small numbers, for, as has been described, the native Mesolithic hunter-gathers were by now more settled and were already tending towards regionalism and the manipulation of their environment. These native peoples may well have been quickly able to adopt these new techniques, which seem to have spread over a wide area of Britain in a fairly short period of time. The earliest farming settlements favoured the lighter, fertile soils of coastal areas and river valleys.

The spread of agriculture must have revolutionised social groupings, as in this period, known as the New Stone Age or Neolithic, settled communal life was all important. This is reflected in the first large-scale 'public' monuments which still stand in our landscape, raised by communal effort and evidently regarded as an important facet of life. Wales has a large number and variety of stone-built (or 'megalithic') funerary monuments. Stone tombs within long trapezoidal cairns are a feature of south-east Wales, for example, while the splendid late passage graves of north-west Wales belong to another well-defined group. The Neolithic tombs of Dyfed, numerous, small and disparate, are not so easily understood but some, at least, seem to belong loosely to two large groups of tombs which are concentrated around the Irish Sea coasts: firstly, 'portal dolmens', found in Cornwall, west Wales and north and eastern Ireland, and secondly, simple 'passage graves' found in west Wales, western Scotland and eastern Ireland.

Portal dolmens often have asymmetric chambers, and the front two stones of the chamber seem to have been designed as an important 'door' into the tomb, as they are often covered with a wedge-shaped capstone with the thick side at the portal end to accentuate the effect of the high front. Related to the Irish Sea long cairns, portal dolmens tend to be set in rectangular cairns. Passage graves, on the other hand, usually have polygonal symmetrical chambers with no obvious front. The tombs get their name from the stone-lined passage which leads into the grave.

Frequently the slighter passage stones have fallen and no trace of the passage survives above ground. The surrounding cairn is often found on excavation to have been circular.

A few of the Dyfed tombs have closer associations with the large family of tombs known as 'court tombs' of northern Ireland and south-west Scotland. These are stone-chambered 'gallery graves' set in long cairns, and Pentre Ifan (no. 4), Bedd yr Afanc (no. 9) and Garn Turne (no. 17) may have affiliations with this group. The final group of tombs, the so-called 'sub-megalithic' tombs, is not, strictly speaking, a true type, but more an opportunistic use of available materials, where natural boulders or slabs, often of truly enormous size, have been formed into capstones by cutting the chamber into the ground below, and propping up the capstone while work was in progress, with a series of small sidestones. This type of tomb is, of course, most commonly found among rock outcrops.

The tombs are very difficult to date, but it seems as though the passage graves were erected early in the Neolithic while the portal dolmens continued in use throughout the period. Both cremation and inhumation were practised. The tomb builders certainly seem to have been influenced more from the Irish Sea area than from the east.

Reconstruction drawing of a farming scene, 4000 BC

Very few settlements belonging to the Neolithic period have been discovered in Dyfed. Remains of houses have been found only at Clegyr Boia (no. 60) and Rhos y Clegyrn (no. 34), while ephemeral traces of Neolithic occupation were found at Coygan Camp. However, rectangular timber houses and drystone field walls dating to this period have been discovered elsewhere in Britain and Ireland, and their excavation tells us about the cultivation techniques employed by Neolithic farmers, the crops of emmer and einkorn wheat and barley that they grew and the cattle, pigs and sheep that they kept. However, hunting, fishing and the gathering of wild fruits and berries continued as an important means of obtaining food.

The difference in the wealth of settlements found in southern England compared with Wales is too great to be an accident of preservation or discovery. Perhaps the less favourable conditions for agriculture in Wales caused a greater emphasis on animal husbandry and pastoralism, which favoured smaller farming groups with less resources or less cultural necessity to produce the large, public ritual or settlement sites found elsewhere.

One area of Dyfed, at least, however, was of particular importance in the Neolithic period: Carn Meini in the Preselis is thought to have been a source of the prized spotted dolerite, used for the manufacture of polished stone tools. Polished stone axes appear to have had a ritual or ceremonial role over and above their vital importance as woodworking tools for forest clearance. The ability of Neolithic people to manufacture such high-quality items as these axes leads to the supposition that specialists in stonework, and perhaps in woodwork and other crafts, could by now be supported by the agricultural communities.

After about 2500 BC, the importance of monumental tomb building appears to decline, and many tombs were blocked up and abandoned. In southern England settlements fell out of use, and many areas of Britain earlier cleared of their forests for agricultural land reverted to scrub. New styles of pottery and flintworking appear, and the first round barrows and cairns were built for the burial of individuals rather than communities. Henges were a new type of ceremonial enclosure constructed at this period: circular non-defensive enclosures, with the bank built outside the ditch, and with one or more entrances. They are rare in Wales generally and the few henges that are known in Dyfed are unfortunately on private land and inaccessible to visitors.

Nineteenth-century drawing of Pentre Ifan burial chamber

4
Pentre Ifan, Newport
Neolithic burial chamber
4th millennium BC
OS 145   SN 099370   U2   Cadw

1.5ml (2.4km) E of Newport on A487, turn S on to signed road. Follow signs over crossroads, 1st R, past turning on LHS and track on RHS to gate on RHS. Signed footpath 150m to site

Grimes 1949; Cadw Guidebook; Lynch 1972

The magnificent burial chamber of Pentre Ifan (or 'Ifan's Homestead') is justly celebrated as one of the most impressive megalithic monuments in Wales. The enormous weight of the capstone is given an extraordinary feeling of lightness by the tapering, pointed sidestones. It stands isolated on the upper slopes of a ridge, crowned by Carneddau Meibion Owen to the south-west, and commands extensive views over the Nevern Valley. The rather unusual north–south orientation of the tomb may be related to the desire of the builders for the monument to face the hilltop.

The open-sided rectangular chamber has four uprights, three of which support the massive wedge-shaped capstone. Three stones stand at the southern end, and together form an apparent doorway, or front, to the tomb; this 'doorway' is itself framed by a curving facade of upright stones. Excavations carried out by Professor Grimes in 1936–7 and 1958–9 showed that both chamber and facade were originally rather different. The chamber, which was built in a shallow pit (dug, perhaps, to level the naturally sloping ground), had had two additional sidestones on the west; one was found prostrate (where it still lies), while the other had disappeared and the marks of the stone-hole alone remained. The facade originally was formed by four uprights, two on either side of the door or portal, but, of these, one survived only as a stump and another had disappeared entirely.

The gaps between the facade stones and the chamber sidestones, and the entire east side of the chamber, may have been filled with drystone walling, or with shallow-seated sidestones which have now disappeared – both methods are known to have been used by the tomb builders. The apparent 'doorway' on the south could not in fact have been used for access to the tomb, as the massive portal stone was tightly wedged in place; it was more symbolic – the gateway into the afterlife, perhaps. Access to the tomb for successive interments would presumably have been via the gaps between the sidestones. The stones of the chamber are all of local igneous rock and bear no signs of tooling, though the portal stone has one faint decorative 'cupmark' pecked into its surface.

The excavation of the site revealed slight traces of a trapezoidal cairn of boulders, about 40m in length, which originally would have at least partially covered the chamber. The wider, southern end of the cairn curves in to form a forecourt which was carefully blocked with rows of tightly wedged, pitched stones. This blocking may have been removed before, and then systematically rebuilt after, each successive use of the tomb, or it may have been positioned just once, to close the tomb at the end of its life.

Within the cairn were a number of enigmatic features. East of the chamber was a slumped stone, probably once upright but deliberately felled before the cairn was built; in front of it was a pit within which were signs of burning. Further north were two square slab-lined pits and along each side of the cairn towards the south was an irregular line of small stone-holes, one of which still had its upright stone in position. The function of the stones is uncertain. Similar, but more closely-packed lines of stones have been interpreted as revetment stones at other chambered tombs, but the space between the stones makes this interpretation unlikely here; presumably they were either simple markers, or, along with the slab-lined pits, were connected with burial rites or the consecration of the tomb.

The tomb, as now laid out for display, incorporates a number of modern features. The stone lines are shown by modern markers, stumps of stones have been placed to show the position of the missing sidestone on the south-west of the chamber and the inner facade stone on the west, and the cairn has been built up to show its probable original shape and length. The result is an apparent 'ditch' around the cairn, though the cairn originally had no ditch.

As no trace of burials was found, we do not know whether cremation or inhumation was practised here, but we may safely assume that so large a tomb would have been used for collective burial over many years. The number of artefacts discovered in the tomb was disappointingly small: a few sherds of plain brown round-bottomed pots were uncovered, along with some flint pieces, including a triangular arrowhead. Grimes has suggested that Pentre Ifan was a simple one-period construction similar to other 'court cairns' in north-eastern Ireland. A more recent analysis, however, suggests that it may be a two-period structure: an original portal dolmen tomb with short rectangular cairn bordered by the upright stones and a massive portal, later embellished by a lengthened cairn and an elaborate facade and forecourt.

5
Carreg Coetan Arthur, Newport
Neolithic burial chamber
4th millennium BC
OS 145   SN 060393   U1   Cadw

On E side of Newport, take Moylegrove road. 100m on LHS, leave car at roadside at

Carreg Coetan Arthur burial chamber, during excavations

entrance to Carreg Coetan Estate. Walk 20m to site. Signposted

Cadw Guidebook

This small but well-preserved chambered tomb lies on the estuary of the River Nyfer on low-lying flat land near the sheltered Newport Bay. It is one of a number of tombs which lie clustered along the fertile slopes of the Nevern Valley. In common with most of these, it defies attempts to categorise it firmly within the classes of chambered tombs in Wales, though the appearance of a blocked entrance on the higher, south-eastern side of the chamber suggests at least an influence by the portal dolmen tradition. The large megaliths of which the tomb is composed are almost certainly local erratics, carefully selected for shape and size, but not apparently fashioned or tooled. The massive wedge-shaped capstone is supported by only two of the four sidestones which stand about 1.5m high at the front.

Excavations in 1979 and 1980 revealed that the chamber had been surrounded, and presumably partially covered, by a circular cairn composed of redeposited sandy glacial drift subsoil and revetted by a ring or kerb of boulders about 11m in diameter. Only one small segment of the cairn survived, and on the old ground surface below it lay round-bottomed Neolithic pots with out-turned, heavily incised rims, made of a coarse fabric tempered with large pieces of quartz. The pots probably served as cremation urns, as, within and around the broken sherds, were quantites of charcoal and pieces of the cremated bone of adult humans. They lay on a surface which had been carefully laid with small slabs of stone. Also outside the chamber, but unassociated with the cremated bone, was found a considerable amount of Neolithic pottery of a burnished brown corky fabric. A fragment of polished axe, flint knives and scrapers were also found.

The tomb was dated by a series of four radiocarbon dates to about 3500 BC (corrected date). The tomb was probably open for a number of years to serve the Neolithic farming community who settled in the area in the 4th millennium. Access to the tomb was presumably through the apparently original spaces between the sidestones, though these may have been blocked by drystone walling between successive interments of the cremated remains of the dead.

The 'coetan' part of the name of the tomb refers to the old game of quoits, and is often associated with burial chambers in England and Wales. In this particular case, King Arthur, who also frequently appears in the place-names of historic sites, is supposed to have played the game using the 'carreg' (stone) of the tomb.

6
Cerrig y Gof, Newport
Neolithic burial chamber
4th–early 3rd millennium BC
OS 157   SN 037389   U1

From Newport, take A487 W towards Fishguard for 1ml (1.6km) and park on road just beyond river. Site in field on RHS of road, through gate. Private owner kindly allows access. Ensure field gate is left shut

The name of this site signifies 'Rock of the Smith', a reference, presumably, to the anvil-like appearance of the capstones. Cerrig y Gof is a very curious, complex burial chamber, consisting of five small box-like chambers arranged radially within a circular mound, 17m in diameter and 0.3m high. Each grave has between two and six sidestones which vary greatly in size from chamber to chamber and, while one has lost its capstone entirely, four retain theirs albeit in dislodged positions. The chambers all have their open end facing outwards, and all five are roughly the same size, so that there is apparently no main chamber. Only one chamber, that on the south-east, retains its structure relatively intact and may reflect the original form of the others. It has one large back stone, one large pair of sidestones and then a smaller pair towards the front. The open end of the

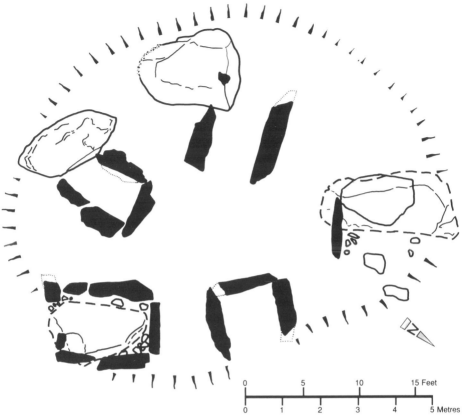

The five burial chambers of Cerrig y Gof

chamber is then restricted by two small stones set within the opening, like doorposts.

The tomb is an oddity in the Nevern Valley group, and indeed is without close parallel in Wales. Richard Fenton, the 19th-century Pembrokeshire antiquarian, dug into each of the chambers and found charcoal, particles of bone, pebbles and 'pieces of urns of the rudest pottery'. He was of the opinion that a 'cromlech' had once stood in the centre of the mound, but his explorations there revealed nothing 'indicative of sepulture'. Antiquarian descriptions of the site suggest that there were originally other standing stones around the mound.

7
Trellyffaint, Nevern
Neolithic burial chamber
4th–early 3rd millennium BC
OS 145   SN 082425   U2

From Nevern (E of Newport) turn L (signposted to Nevern Castle). After 0.5ml (0.8km), fork R, then 1.5ml (2.4km) later, turn L at T-junction. After 0.5ml (0.8km), leave car at Trellyffaint Farm gate on LHS of road. Owners kindly allow access across private fields. Go through metal gate on RHS of farm entrance and walk across

Trellyffaint burial chamber

field, cross ditch at culvert, go through gate and follow sheep track obliquely across field to far gate. Site in next field across cattle track

Trellyffaint chambered tomb is situated on a gentle slope about half-a-mile (0.8km) from the sea. It is a double tomb, consisting of a main chamber and a smaller, perhaps later, chamber, lying side by side, rather than one behind the other as at St Elvis (no. 16). The main rectangular chamber has a small capstone supported on two large stones on the south and another which closes the back or north side. A smaller upright stands on the east, but the slumped stone which lies against this is a broken piece from the capstone. The capstone only covers the back part of the chamber, and the tomb may originally have had two capstones. On the upper surface are carved 35 'cupmarks', small round saucer-like depressions about 5cm across, with one elongated oval hollow on the broken piece. Cupmarks have also been found on a flat slab, possibly the capstone of another, now vanished burial chamber, in a field at Trefaes, Moylegrove, only 2ml (3.2km) from Trellyffaint.

Of the smaller rectangular chamber only three sidestones survive, but their position suggests that, like the main chamber, it probably faced south-west. The two chambers seem to have been enclosed in a long mound orientated north-west/south-east, though the barely visible remains of this could have been altered by the cultivation of the surrounding field. The higher, more massive paired stones on the south-west of the main chamber give an apparently deliberate feel of a 'front' to the tomb. This feature, and the insignificant part played by the non-load-bearing sidestones, has led to classification of the tomb within the portal dolmen tradition of the Irish Sea area.

Trellyffaint means 'Home of the Toads' and is said to refer to the story related by Giraldus Cambrensis about a man named Sisillus Long Leg, who lived hereabouts and who was apparently persecuted and eventually eaten by large numbers of toads.

8
Llech y Dribedd, Moylegrove
Neolithic burial chamber
4th–early 3rd millennium BC
OS 145   SN 101432   U2

From Nevern, take B4582 E towards Cardigan for 2.3ml (3.7km), and turn N (L) at 1st crossroads, towards Moylegrove. After 2ml (3.2km), past 2 crossroads, turn L at T-junction. After 0.7ml (1.1km), park at farm track on LHS of road signed Pen-lan Farm. Tomb in field over stile at end of track (ignore farm entrances to L to Pen-lan and R to Trefwrdan)

Llech y Dribedd is similar in its position to the tomb at Trellyffaint (no. 7) only 2ml (3.2km) away, and lies on the same high coastal plain 400m from, but 183m above, the sea. However, unlike Trellyffaint, it is built of the massive pillar-like uprights characteristic of the Nevern Valley tombs. Perhaps because the choice of stones in the immediate area was poorer, the rather squat, dumpy uprights and the extraordinary thickness of the capstone give the tomb, at least in its present-day form, a somewhat cumbersome, unartistic look. Originally, of course, it would

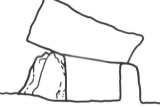

0 — 5 — 10 Feet
0 — 1 — 2 — 3 Metres

Llech y Dribedd burial chamber

upright stated as being present in a description of the tomb of 1693.

The name of the tomb translates as 'Tripod Stone', a fairly straightforward reference to the appearance of the chamber.

9
Bedd yr Afanc, Eglwyswrw
Neolithic burial chambers
4th–early 3rd millenium BC
OS 145   SN 109346   U4

From Eglwyswrw, take A487 W towards Newport for 0.5ml (0.8km), then B4329 SW towards Haverfordwest. After 2.8ml (4.5km) park in pull-in on LHS at bridge. Walk up track to Bryn Glas to L, past stream and house, through gate on to open moor, to L over stream, for 300m to site (inconspicuous)

Grimes 1939; Lynch 1972

have appeared taller, as the floor of the chamber must lie considerably below the modern ground level.

The wedge-shaped capstone measures 3m by 2.8m, and at its thickest end rests on two squat uprights. The capstone tapers in thickness, but only to a blunt square end which is supported by the only other upright still in position, rather smaller in size than the other two. This accentuates the wedge shape of the capstone to create an apparently deliberate look of a higher open front at the south-east, suggesting that the tomb belongs to the portal dolmen tradition of the Irish Sea area. The sides of the tomb are open and may have originally been closed with non-load-bearing sidestones, or with drystone walling. The stone which now lies prostrate on the south side of the chamber may be the fourth

Bedd yr Afanc burial chamber, the passage

The long, low cairn of this tomb is about 18m long and 10.6m wide, and is orientated east–west. Within the cairn is a 'gallery grave', or long, simple, parallel-sided structure open at one short end. The main part, the passage, has an entrance on the east and is composed of about 10 pairs of upright stones up to 0.5m in height. It leads to a small circular chamber at the west end, delimited by seven boulders of roughly similar size. No capstones survive.

Bedd yr Afanc, which was excavated in 1939, is the most inland of the Nevern Valley group of chambered tombs, but is quite distinct and apparently unrelated to the other members. It is unusual in its remote, upland, boggy setting, and in its form, which may point to influence from the Irish long cairn tradition. It also differs from gallery graves in general, in that its long gallery is open rather than being divided into sections as is normal within this category of megalithic tomb.

The name of the tomb translates as 'the grave of the monster', the 'afanc' in Welsh folklore being a monster who lived in lakes or rivers and who exercised malevolent powers against local people, particularly by causing flooding. Hence the word is now often translated as 'beaver'.

10

Garn Wen, Goodwick
Neolithic burial chambers
4th–early 3rd millennium BC
OS 157   SM 948390   U2

From NW end of Goodwick harbour (Fishguard) on A40, take road signposted to Llanwnda. Up this steep road, take 1st sharp turning to R (New Hill), and drive 100m to dead end in Harbour Village. Park by phone box, and walk

Garn Wen burial chambers, the southernmost tomb

around houses on to common behind. Site on footpath, immediately behind houses

Garn Wen burial chambers belong to a group of megalithic tombs all with similar characteristics and situated in the splendid scenery of the Strumble Head peninsula. The line of three fine burial chambers runs north–south below the rock outcrop of Garn Wen immediately to the west. They are all surrounded by round cairns which have become very overgrown with brambles and bracken, but the tombs are none the less quite easy to find. The normal approach is from the south, and the tombs are therefore described from south to north.

The first is probably the best preserved of all three. An enormous capstone rests partly on the three low sidestones and partly on the ground. The chamber is about 1m in height, and is open on the west. One large upright stone, 1.2m high, stands isolated a little way to the west, and there are other smaller stones on this side which may be associated either with the chamber, or with its low round cairn.

The massive capstone of the second tomb is supported on the north side of the chamber by three small sidestones; other small upright stones nearby are probably associated with the chamber. The chamber, surrounded by a small round mound, is open on the short east and west sides and is about 1m high on the inside.

One tall sidestone supports the capstone of the third tomb on the south side of the chamber. On the other sides, the capstone has slumped on to the ground. The chamber has an internal measurement of 4m by 1.6m and is 0.7m high. It is open on the short east and west sides, and is surrounded by a round cairn.

The three burial chambers are characteristic of the group of sites concentrated around Strumble Head – which includes Garn Wnda (no. 11), Garn Gilfach and Penrhiw (see Appendix) – in their use of large flat slabs for construction, and in their situation, nestling below prominent natural rock outcrops.

Garn Wnda burial chamber

11
Garn Wnda, Llanwnda
Neolithic burial chamber
4th–early 3rd millennium BC
OS 157   SM 932392   U4   NT

From Goodwick (Fishguard) on A40, take road to Llanwnda. At approach to village, park and walk up track on LHS past Ymyl y Graig then strike up slope to L towards rock outcrop of Garn Wnda. Site is just below outcrop, on its near (W) side, on moorland

The massive capstone of this tomb is supported on the west (downhill) side by one pointed sidestone while on the east it rests on the ground. A second sidestone forms the south wall of the chamber, which is deep and apparently partially rock-cut. This type of tomb, where the capstone is only partially supported on sidestones, but rests mainly on the ground or on the semi-subterranean chamber wall, is called a 'sub-megalithic earthfast tomb'. Tombs in this class are sometimes difficult to distinguish from naturally fallen boulders, but in the case of this tomb, its man-made origin is beyond doubt. A very similar tomb lies only 1ml (1.6km) further west, at Garn Gilfach (see Appendix).

Excavations were carried out at Garn Wnda late last century under the capstone of the tomb, and a small urn containing calcined bones was discovered. The urn apparently 'was of coarse manufacture and crumbled to pieces'.

12
Trellys, St Nicholas
Neolithic burial chamber
4th–early 3rd millennium BC
OS 157   SM 906349   U4

4.5ml (7.2km) SW of Goodwick on A487 St Davids road, take minor road N (R) toward St Nicholas for 0.6ml (1km). Park by Tre-llys-draw

Farm, and walk through gate up footpath opposite (unmarked), up slope for 0.5ml (0.8km) through two fields into moorland above. 'Path' (overgrown by thick gorse) leads to site, by drystone wall on other side of field

A visit to this tomb in the spring, when the gorse which covers the hillside is in flower, makes the difficulty of access seem unimportant. A large capstone rests apparently most lightly on two tall sidestones with pointed tops. The uprights are 2m apart and, being opposite one another, give the chamber a rectangular look, but otherwise the tomb is unclassifiable.

Around the chamber are slight traces of a round mound about 0.4m in height, which may be the remains of the original cairn. Earlier descriptions of the tomb mention an erect stone standing nearby on the west but this has now disappeared. The tomb is known locally as Ffyst Samson.

Nineteenth-century drawing of Trellys burial chamber

13
Carreg Samson, Mathry
Neolithic burial chamber
4th–early 3rd millennium BC
OS 157   SM 848335   U2

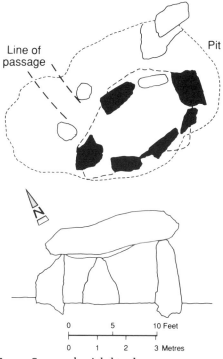

On A487, 5.8ml (9km) SW of Fishguard, turn N (R) into Mathry. Take RH turn to Abercastle (2.3ml, 3.7km), taking R turn at fork, and straight across crossroads. Take Trevine road from Abercastle and park in road at 1st farm turning on RHS (Longhouse). Walk down farm track (turn R at farmhouse) to tomb

Lynch 1975

Carreg Samson burial chamber

The tomb is situated on gently sloping land at the head of a narrow creek above the sheltered Abercastle harbour. It has a particularly impressive appearance as the chamber is composed of no less than six large, pointed uprights, three of which support the massive, rather symmetrial capstone. The polygonal chamber is 2m high with an internal measurement of 3.5m by 1.7m. Excavations in 1968 suggested that on the north-west side of the chamber there had been at least one and possibly two further stones on either side of a passage, which presumably led from the perimeter of the cairn into the chamber. This helps classify this tomb within the widely scattered, rather disparate group of passage graves of western Britain, and the excavator drew parallels between this tomb and the passage graves of Hanging Stone, (no. 18) and Dolwilyn (no. 22). The excavations also showed that the gap between the sidestones on the north had originally been filled by a seventh upright. Three of the sidestones and the capstone are of a conglomerate stone incorporating seams of quartz.

An especially interesting fact revealed by the excavations was that the whole of the chamber had been constructed in a pit, 8m by 5m and at least 80cm deep. It is possible that the boulder later used as the capstone was a naturally occurring erratic, and had been visible on the surface of the ground prior to the construction of the burial chamber. The pit was apparently about the shape and size that would result had a hole been excavated around the stone to dig it out for its utilisation within the burial chamber. No trace of any surrounding cairn was discovered, so its original shape or size remains uncertain; however, there was some inconclusive evidence for it having been composed of the clay subsoil, as was the cairn found at Carreg Coetan (no. 5).

The excavation of the site revealed that the burial rite practised at the tomb had been cremation; sherds of pottery from a single round-bottomed pot of the dark-brown hard 'corky' fabric, also discovered at Clegyr Boia (no. 60) and Carreg Coetan (no. 5), were found in the chamber.

Nineteenth-century drawing of Coetan Arthur burial chamber

14
Coetan Arthur, St Davids
Neolithic burial chamber
4th–early 3rd millennium BC
OS 157   SM 725280   U2   NT

From St Davids, take minor road signposted to Whitesands Bay (1.5ml, 2.4km). Park in beach car park and walk N along coastal path for 0.7ml (1.1km). Follow path as it turns to R past St Davids Head. Tomb a few metres to RHS of path

Coetan Arthur lies on the open moorland above the cliffs of St Davids Head, in an area rich in archaeological monuments. The partly collapsed chamber consists of a large capstone supported on one side by a sidestone about 1.5m high, but with the other side now resting on the ground. Two other sidestones lie prostrate beneath the capstone.

The small polygonal chamber is surrounded by the remains of a round cairn of small stones, and a line of stones on the west leading from the perimeter of the cairn to the chamber has been tentatively interpreted as a passage. Only excavation could prove this, but if correct it would suggest that this tomb may be a member of the small group of Dyfed passage graves. On the other hand, it has been argued that this is not a collapsed chamber at all but is actually in its original form and thus belongs to the sub-megalithic group of tombs. The monument was explored in 1899, but the report states that nothing was found.

The name of the tombs, translated as 'Arthur's Quoit', refers to the game of quoits said to have been played in the Dyfed landscape by legendary figures such as King Arthur (also no. 5 and perhaps no. 20) and the Devil (no. 19).

15
Garn Llidi, St Davids

Neolithic burial chamber

4th–early 3rd millennium BC

OS 157   SM 735279   U4   NT

From St Davids, take minor road to Whitesands Bay (1.5ml, 2.4km). Park in beach car park, then walk back down road to 2nd track on L marked No Through Road. Walk down this lane, forking R past Upper Porthmawr Farm, 400m to open common. Skirt Garn Llidi peak, keeping it to R, and tombs nestle on N slope below outcrop

The two sub-megalithic burial chambers lie in rock-strewn, open moorland on the sloping ground north-west of Garn Llidi, at the westernmost point of the ridge. They are similar to the tomb at Garn Wnda (no. 11), both in their 'sub-megalithic' (partly subterranean) form, and in their siting, just below rock outcrops.

The western chamber has a large capstone supported on the west by one sidestone. The other long side had been supported originally by another sidestone of roughly the same length, but this has collapsed. On the short sides are a number of smaller stones which may have formed part of the chamber walls. The chamber appears to be partly rock-cut. The tomb faces downhill.

A smaller chamber lies 2m further east. Its capstone is supported on one sidestone and elsewhere it rests on the ground adjacent to the rock-cut chamber wall. Three other uprights survive on the north, north-west and west. The chamber is partly subterranean and has an internal height of 0.5m.

Garn Llidi burial chambers, eastern tomb

16
St Elvis, Solva
Neolithic burial chamber
4th–early 3rd millennium BC
OS 157   SM 812239   U2   NT

On A487, 2.7ml (6km) W of St Davids, 0.6ml
(1km) E of Solva, turn S down a track
signposted St Elvis Farm. Leave car in NT car
park a little way down track, and walk another
600m past St Elvis farmhouse. Tomb on
pathway to S of, and visible from, farmhouse

The burial chamber lies on flat ground, 400m
from the sea. It has been disturbed in the past
by being incorporated into a hedgebank, and
one of the sidestones has been used as a
gatepost. Now that the bank has been
removed, the tomb lies at the junction of two
farm tracks which have inevitably eroded the
adjacent area to give the impression that the
megaliths are surrounded by a long stony
cairn; this impression may not be entirely

illusory, and only excavation could reveal
whether a real mound connects the two
chambers of this apparently double tomb.
Another indignity was suffered by the tomb in
1890 when, apparently, the tenant farmer
blasted and carted away two of the
supporting stones of the eastern chamber,
after he had dislodged both capstones.

Despite these past disturbances, the site is
an impressive one, with one large chamber on
the east and perhaps the remains of a much
ruined westerly one. The main chamber
consists of a large capstone supported on the
south by a small sidestone, has an internal
measurement of 4m by 4m and is 1m high. It
is open on the east, while the other sides are
closed by several small boulders lying at
ground level.

The second group of megaliths consists of
two large sidestones with a massive capstone
lying between. The site is characteristic of the
St Davids Peninsula and Strumble Head
tombs (nos. 10–11 and 14–16) in its utilisation
of the large slabs which are the most readily

St Elvis burial chamber

Garn Turne burial chamber

available forms of natural boulders in this area. This form of construction tends to give tombs a wider, rather flat look. The two chambers and slab-like construction of the tomb are reminiscent of Trellyffaint (no. 7), but without excavation it remains unclassifiable within the main groups of tomb construction in the south-west.

17
Garn Turne, Wolf's Castle
Neolithic burial chamber
4th–early 3rd millennium BC
OS 157 SM 979272 U2 Dyfed
Wildlife Trust

From Wolfscastle, go N on A40 towards Fishguard for 1ml (1.6km) and turn R towards Ambleston. After 0.7ml (1.1km), turn R at T-junction and, after 1.2ml (1.9km), tomb on L (N) of road, over stile, just before crossing of 2 farm tracks

The chambered tomb lies in rock-strewn moorland immediately below the Garn Turne rock outcrop. The large chamber has collapsed, but the massive capstone can be seen to lie on two or three prostrate sidestones, one of which has broken into two large pieces. The back of the capstone rests· on the earth.

A particularly interesting feature of this cairn is a large V-shaped forecourt on the north-east, formed by a number of massive uprights which diminish in size as they are distanced from the chamber. Though very much more ruined, this is reminiscent of the facade at Pentre Ifan (no. 4) and the similarity might suggest that Garn Turne, like Pentre Ifan, may have had a long cairn. Indeed, with the eye of faith, one can pick out the shape of a long mound among the litter of stones that surrounds the chamber, but only excavation could show whether or not this is genuine. An outlying upright stone stands a little way from the main tomb on the south-east.

Nineteenth-century drawing of Hanging Stone burial chamber

18
Hanging Stone, Rosemarket
Neolithic burial chamber
4th–early 3rd millennium BC
OS 158   SM 972082   U2

From A477 Haverfordwest–Neyland road between Johnston and the Toll Bridge, take any road to E marked Rosemarket. From Rosemarket, take Haverfordwest road N to outskirts of village, and turn R to Sardis. 1ml (1.6km) along this road (ignore 1 L turning), in Sardis, drive R down Thurston Lane for 400m (ignore fork to R). Site signposted on LHS over stile and 100m along path, past some barns, by a hedgebank

The polygonal chamber of this tomb is formed by a large capstone supported by three uprights, two in the open field and one in the hedgebank within which part of the site lies incorporated. In the hedge may be seen a large stone which may be a second capstone, and three uprights which some authorities have suggested may be a passage through a surrounding cairn to the chamber. This tomb has accordingly been classified as belonging to the passage grave family along with Carreg Sampson (no. 13). A description of 1864 tells of drystone walling being present between the uprights, but as no such walling remains today, we cannot be sure whether it was likely to have been an original feature or a more modern addition. Nothing visible remains of the surrounding cairn either, though it is conceivable that the hedgebank is protecting parts of a mound.

Devil's Quoit burial chamber

19
Devil's Quoit, Angle
Neolithic burial chamber
4th–early 3rd millennium BC
OS 157   SM 886008   R2   NT

Site is on B4320, 6ml (9.6km) W of Pembroke, 2.5ml (4km) E of Angle, in sight of the B4319 turning to Castlemartin. Tomb is visible from roadside, in sandy burrows on S (LHS) of road. Tenants of Middle Hill Farm (next farm on RHS past B4319 turning) kindly allow access, but like to know who is visiting, so ask at farm first. Then go through gate by bungalow and walk L along far fenceline to tomb

This small chambered tomb lies about 400m from the sea, in the low-lying Broomhill

Burrows, an extensive area of sand dunes in the ownership of the National Trust. The large wedge-shaped capstone is supported on the east by two massive sidestones, which form this side of the chamber and give it an internal height of about 1m. On the west, a third sidestone has fallen so that the capstone rests slumped on the prostrate stone. The blown sand in the area has obscured the contours of the ground, so that there is now no evidence of any surrounding cairn. The appearance of the chamber as being in a hollow is almost certainly also due to the sand, blown on to the site subsequent to the construction of the tomb. The tomb in its present condition is unclassifiable.

20
King's Quoit, Manorbier
Neolithic burial chamber
4th–early 3rd millennium BC
OS 158   SS 059973   U2

From A4139 Tenby–Pembroke road, take B4585 S to Manorbier. Park in beach car park, and walk to beach. Walk along beach to L (S), and join coast path to climb slope to site on LHS

King's Quoit lies on open moorland above the sea cliff with spectacular views overlooking Manorbier Bay. It is a low, fairly inconspicuous tomb, consisting of a large capstone supported by two small sidestones; one of these forms one of the long sides on the west, while the other smaller stone forms the northern end of the chamber. Another stone, which probably served as the southern end-stone of the chamber, lies at the south-east corner. The chamber has an internal height of 0.8m and is partially below ground level, one side of the capstone being supported by earth alone. The site has been classified as belonging to the sub-megalithic group of chambered tombs.

21
Morfa Bychan, Pendine
Neolithic burial chambers
4th–early 3rd millennium BC
OS 158   SN 222075   U4

At Pendine, 4.5ml (7.2km) W of Laugharne on A4066, park at W end of Pendine Beach and join coastal footpath up steep slope by Cliff Snack Bar. Follow footpath for 1,200m, past Gilman Point Fort (no. 74) and down steep-sided valley to bay. Cross a chippings track and follow signed track obliquely up valley side. At top, turn L to follow fenceline along track to a rocky terrace on LHS. Walk along terrace towards sea, with rock outcrop to RHS. The 4 tombs run in line N–S amid bracken and gorse

Ward 1918, p 64

This line of four fine burial chambers rewards the necessary hunt among the bracken and rock outcrop on the coastal ridge above Ragwen Point on which they lie. Their low megalithic chambers, composed of a cluster of uprights, their flat, massive capstones and oval/round cairns of small boulders suggest

Nineteenth-century drawing of King's Quoit burial chamber

Morfa Bychan burial chambers, detail of chamber of southernmost tomb

that the tombs belong to, or are at least influenced by, the passage grave tradition. Though the usual approach is from the north, the southern tombs are the easiest to find and the descriptions therefore follow the tombs from south to north.

1 An oval cairn of boulders surrounds a closed, grave-shaped chamber, consisting of nine uprights (see illustration). There are three sidestones on each of the long sides, and one and two at the short west and east ends respectively. Although there is no obvious entrance, all the sidestones being closed together, the stone on the west may have been chosen or fashioned to form a small opening or 'window'. The capstone is dislodged and lies on the south, propped on the southern sidestones.

2 A roughly circular cairn of small boulders lies 40m to the north and within this lies an irregular oval-shaped chamber, composed of

seven uprights with roughly pointed tops. The capstone lies displaced on the south. The two or three upright stones on the west may belong to a related structure, but may be purely natural.

3 A low cairn of stones lies 75m to the north again, and 9m south of the prominent natural outcrop called 'The Druid's Altar'. It is probably the ruined remains of another similar, though probably smaller, tomb. No capstone is evident, but a number of upright sidestones still stand.

4 The fourth tomb, 80m north again, consists of a partly subterranean, rectangular chamber, formed simply by underpinning a massive natural slab with small boulders. The chamber thus formed lies in the centre of a low round cairn, and there is a short passage connecting the chamber with the perimeter of the cairn. This tomb is the only one of the four to have the capstone in position.

Three of the four tombs have been explored, the most northerly by Treherne in 1910, when he uncovered the partly subterranean stone-lined entrance on the south-east, and a slab door-stone covering the entrance. The two southern tombs were opened by Ward in the same year. Some good flint artefacts and a hammerstone were discovered in the southernmost tomb, which was the more intact of the two. A paved surface, probably the original chamber floor, and parts of the circular stone cairn were uncovered. The artefacts uncovered during the excavations are now in the National Museum of Wales (Cardiff).

22
Dolwilym, Efailwen

Neolithic burial chamber
4th–early 3rd millennium BC
OS 145   SN 170256   R2

This tomb is in private property and for permission to visit, write to Fountain Forestry,

Dyfed

Brecon Road, Hay-on-Wye, Powys. From
Efailwen on A478, turn E on to Llanglydwen
road. In Llanglydwen, park near bridge, walk
into Station Yard (office hours only), and cross
stile. Follow track along river for 1ml (1.6km).
Cross stile, take next track on LHS up hill to
clearing in wood, Follow track sharp L, site
short way along path

Dolwilym burial chamber stands in sparse
beech woodland adjoining a forestry
plantation, on sloping ground above the River
Taf. It is also known as Gwal y Filiast ('Lair of
the Greyhound') and Bwrdd Arthur ('Arthur's
Table').
　　Four sidestones support the large wedge-
shaped capstone. The tomb now presents an
open front on the downhill, southern side, but
a description in 1872 states that it originally
had five or six sidestones, rather than the four
that were then present. The gap on the south
may, therefore, have been filled by a
sidestone which has now disappeared.
However, a description of 1695 states that
even at that time only four uprights
supported the capstone, so the existence of

further sidestones cannot be proved. The
1872 description refers to the tomb being
surrounded at a little distance by a circle of
isolated stones, but no such feature is now
evident. Two small stones, or perhaps stumps
of stones, lie on the uphill side of the tomb.
These have been interpreted as a sill for a
passage, and this feature combined with the
polygonal shape of the chamber has led to the
suggestion that this tomb may have been a
passage grave. This could only be finally
proved or disproved by excavation.

23
Twlc y Filiast, Llangynog
Neolithic burial chamber
4th–early 3rd millennium BC
OS 159　SN 338161　R4

*From Carmarthen, take A40 towards St Clears.
5.5ml (8.8km) along this road, turn L and drive
to Llangynog. Just past Llangynog sign, stop at
Bancyffynon Farm on RHS for permission
(owners kindly allow access on request). Drive
through village and park, just past school, on
RHS. Walk through iron kissing-gate, down
field and cross bridge. Climb over RH bridge
rails and follow river for short distance to tomb*

Savory 1956

This tomb, in its low-lying, rather boggy
position by the side of a brook, can become
overgrown with bracken and brambles. The
small trapezoidal chamber is defined by three
sidestones and has an open south side. The
capstone has been displaced and rests partly
on the ground outside the chamber and
partly on the west sidestone.
　　Excavations in 1953 showed that the
chamber had originally been enclosed within
an oval cairn, 18m long and 9m wide, and
built of large stone blocks. Also, at a high level
within the cairn material, there was a
suggestion of a very disturbed funnel-shaped
forecourt lined with boulders which led to an
antechamber on the south of the chamber.

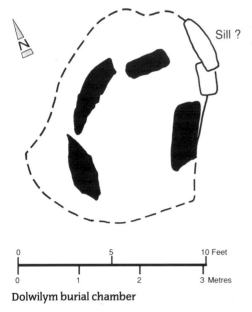
Sill ?

0 　　　5　　　　10 Feet
0　　1　　2　　3 Metres
Dolwilym burial chamber

32

Twlc y Filiast burial chamber, during excavations

This antechamber was defined by three small uprights, of which only the socket-holes remained, though another prostrate stone which lay nearby may well have been a fourth sidestone. The antechamber was separated from the main chamber by a low stone sill, and may itself have been covered by a capstone. A small pit was found dug into the floor of the antechamber, and fragments of cremated bone found within and around it may have been from a cremated burial deposited in the antechamber at the time of the construction of the monument.

The only artefacts found during the excavation of the tomb were a crudely shaped stone amulet said to represent a metal axe, and a flint scraper from the cairn material outside the chamber. The tomb is thought to belong to the portal dolmen group of chambered cairns of the Irish Sea area. The name of the site translates as 'The Den of the Greyhound'.

3

The First Metallurgists

In about 2000 BC new styles of pottery and implements began to appear in Britain which show how close by now were the ties of trade and foreign relations with the Continent. It was at this time that the first metal objects began to be manufactured, though the change from a purely stone-using economy to one using metal was very gradual. No one is sure whether new people from the Continent came to Britain, bringing with them the metal objects and new styles of pottery, or whether, as now seems more likely, these artefacts arrived by way of trade. But the popularity of the new pottery vessels, called 'beakers', soon became widespread. The fine, highly decorated beakers are found in burials over most parts of Britain and, indeed, Europe, and they seem to have had a symbolic meaning, perhaps associated with burial deposits of food and drink. The earliest metal objects, first of copper, then of bronze, are also known to us from burials, and accordingly are mostly personal items, such as axes and daggers, awls and pins.

At about the same time, a great variety of small circular monuments, used both for ritual and funerary purposes, began to be built. The emphasis within burial ritual seems now to have been on the individuality of the dead. These new funerary monuments are found on higher ground than the lower-lying land favoured in the Neolithic, suggesting the colonisation of upland areas. This expansion of settlement on to what is now marginal land may have been made possible by the rather warmer climate of the 2nd millennium.

The same lack of settlement sites that bedevils our understanding of the Welsh Neolithic continues in the earlier Bronze Age. A few round timber houses have been discovered quite fortuitously during the excavation of other more obvious sites. A circular timber house was found at Stackpole, near Pembroke while evidence for settlement has been found at Llanilar, near Aberystwyth, and Potter's Cave, Caldey. More commonly found are 'burnt mounds', piles of burnt cracked stones always near water, described variously as Bronze Age cooking places or as debris from fires lit for the production of steam for a primitive kind of 'sauna' bath.

Funerary and ritual sites, however, remain our main source of information about the early Bronze Age. Beaker pottery is occasionally found in Neolithic chambered tombs, but the main type of Beaker burial was a crouched inhumation within a cist, often covered with a round mound or cairn. Later, cremation became almost universally used, the ashes being interred in pottery urns of various types such as

Artist's impression of Early Bronze Age metalworkers at work

'cordoned urns', 'collared urns' and 'food vessels', and then covered with a circular earthen mound (or 'barrow') or a cairn of stones.

The presence of deposits of cremated bone at the many types of ritual sites known from the period suggests that there was, in the mind of the people, a close association between ceremonial and burial practices. The predominantly circular ritual sites seem to be closely related to henges which, in some areas, continued to be used. New monuments that now appear include simple stone circles of upright stones, and 'embanked stone circles' on which the stones are set in a surrounding bank. Both are rare in Dyfed. Commoner are the different types of earthen or stone rings, of which there are a great variety; some are simple 'ring cairns', or circular banks of stone, while others incorporate structures such as stone kerbs. Standing stones, single or paired, in groups or rows, or combined with rings or cairns, are common features of our landscape. What is less well known is that the stones themselves were often just part of complex ritual sites which incorporated stone platforms, wooden structures, pits containing cremated bone, pottery or charcoal and burials. Standing stones were often positioned on what is now open moorland on natural passes or routeways. This has led to the suggestion that they were erected to help the seasonal movements of pastoral communities. Some of these ritual sites may have had a calendrical purpose related to the movement of heavenly bodies, and could have been used to calculate the timing of seasonal activities or festivals. Some may have been used as ceremonial meeting places, or as shrines with a secondary funerary function, or indeed in a combination of these ways.

Society was probably by now quite settled and territorial with an agricultural system sufficiently developed and stable to support a ruling class and a class of specialist craftsmen who produced an increasingly sophisticated range of tools, weapons and jewelry. In the second half of the 2nd millennium BC, however, there seems to have been a major upheaval in the nature of society, partly due to widespread movement of populations in Europe and partly to a deterioration of the climate. The thin, unforgiving and now over-exploited soils of the uplands became unusable and the abandonment of agriculture in higher areas led in turn to further pressure on lower-lying farmland. For the first time defensive settlements were built, often situated in naturally strong positions such as on hilltops or promontories, and defended by mighty banks and ditches which frequently remain visible today. These hillforts became commoner still in the Iron Age, when the settlements of this aggressive society continued to require defence.

24
Gors Fawr, Mynachlog Ddu
Stone circle
Late 3rd–2nd millennium BC
OS 145   SN 135294   U2

1ml (1.6km) N of Efailwen on A478 at Cross Inn, take further of 2 L turns on to Mynachlog Ddu road. 1.1ml (1.8km) along road, take 1st L, then after 0.9ml (1.4km) take 1st R. 0.6ml (1km) along this road, site on LHS of road through gate

Wales is not noted for its stone circles, and those in Dyfed are generally small and unspectacular. The charming circle at Gors Fawr, however, is comparatively large and is

justly famous both for the fine preservation of the stones and for the splendour of its atmospheric setting. It is situated in the foothills of the Preselis within sight of Carn Meini to the north, the source of at least some of the famous bluestones of Stonehenge. The rough ground around it is peat-covered and often boggy and lies at the eastern end of the mysterious, wind-swept and mist-ridden Gors Fawr moor.

The circle has 16 stones, all weather-beaten boulders of igneous rock, which stand up to 1m in height. One stone on the south-west and another on the north have fallen while through the ages others have gradually become tilted. The stone setting is not quite circular, as its east–west diameter (22.5m) is somewhat greater than the north–south

Gors Fawr. Drawing by David Gunning

measurement. The sizes of the stones themselves vary according to their position in the circle which seems to be slightly graded towards the south-west. Two more tall stones, about 2m in height, stand 134m to the north-east of the circle. They were probably associated with the circle despite their apparent lack of symmetry with it. Some authorities consider these outliners to contain their own axial alignment on midsummer sunrise over the nearby Foeldrych hilltop, 1.5ml (2.4km) away to the east. The area surrounding Gors Fawr circle is littered with boulders and may conceal further stone settings or other features.

This site is one of a number of ritual monuments which cluster in this part of the foothills of the Preselis, obviously a place of great importance in the 3rd and 2nd millennium BC. Burial chambers of the early Neolithic lie not far away at Dolwilym (no. 22) and Carn Besi and there may have been another at Temple Druid, Maenclochog – these public monuments may have been superseded in the late Neolithic by the henge at Castell Garw, and later again by the stone circles here and at Meini Gwyr (no. 25) and by the numerous single and paired standing stones which are common in the area. It is possible that these monuments reflect the importance attached to the Preseli area as the source of a good raw material for the prestigious polished stone axes of the Neolithic, a stone of such renowned worth that it was chosen for use at distant Stonehenge.

25
Meini Gwyr, Efailwen

Embanked stone circle

Late 3rd/2nd millennium BC

OS 145   SN 142266   U2

1ml (1.6km) N of Efailwen on A478 at Cross Inn take nearer of 2 L turns signed Maenclochog, and park. Site behind 4th house on LHS, through gate by far side of house

Grimes 1963

Embanked stone circles, or circles of stones bordered by an external bank, are uncommon in south-west Wales and the presence of one of these rare monuments at Meini Gwyr reinforces the sense of importance that this area seems to have held in the early prehistoric periods. There is a concentration of Bronze Age sites clustered around the Meini Gwyr circle, which has led to the suggestion that it was a focus of ritual importance in the 2nd millennium BC, perhaps inheriting a significance from what is probably an earlier henge site just to the north, at Castell Garw. Visible from Meini Gwyr, and some 250m to the west, is a group of three stones, two standing and one prostrate. There are also in the vicinity a number of barrows and standing stones and a cairn circle.

Meini Gwyr circle consists of a broad, low, roughly circular bank 36.6m in diameter with a narrow entrance on the west. There is no sign of a ditch, and Professor Grimes's excavations in 1938 confirmed that there never had been one. The bank is composed of clay and turf scraped from the surface rather than excavated from a quarry ditch. On the eastern side of the ring, almost opposite the entrance, are two stones, 1m and 1.7m high respectively, and 6.5m apart. These two stones are the only survivors of what was originally a circle of 17 stones, 18.3m in diameter, which stood on the inner slope of the bank. The excavations showed that the entrance itself had also been stone-lined. In

front of the entrance, Grimes found a pit with charcoal within it; and in a hearth on the south-east side of the bank were sherds of a type of pottery known as 'food vessel'. The hearth overlay a stone-hole and therefore evidently was used after the stone circle itself had been altered. The early or mid-2nd-millennium food vessel pottery found within the hearth suggests that the main period of use of the site was some time before that date.

The areas of the interior that were excavated were found to be featureless and gave no clue as to the function of the site. It is assumed, however, as with other stone circles, that the site had a ritual rather than a domestic function. Not far away to the west of Meini Gwyr, at Letterston, was another embanked stone circle which was excavated before its destruction in the 1960s. It seems to have been similar to Meini Gwyr in date and in many of its features, including a charcoal-filled pit situated some way beyond its entrance. This circle was, however, later covered by a round barrow.

26
Cornel Bach and Ty Newydd Stones, Maenclochog

Standing stones

2nd millennium BC

OS 145   SN 082279, SN 118310   U2

From Maenclochog (N of Narberth) take B4313 N for 400m. Just beyond 30mph sign, park and walk along track on RHS (E) of road. Site on far side of 1st field on RHS. Private, but owner kindly allows access through gate

Cornel Bach stones, standing inconspicuously on one side of a pasture field, are typical of the paired standing stones commonly found in the Preselis. The stones are 40m apart and stand on ground which slopes slightly towards a stream on the north-east. The south-west stone is 1.7m high with a rectilinear base and is surrounded by a low,

Cornel Bach standing stones

round mound. The north-east stone is 2m high. The stone on the south-west has a flat top with some signs of it having been dressed while the other rises to a point, a characteristic combination of shapes on these stone pairs.

Ty Newydd stones (SN 118310) lie 3ml (4.8km) to the north-east. Continue north along the B4313 for 800m, then take the right turn toward Crymmych for three miles (4.8km). Just beyond the forest, note Gate standing stone (SN 111303) four fields further along on the left – it is nearly 3m high with a chisel-shaped top. After Glynsaithmaen Farm and immediately beyond the bridges is a junction with a track on the left of the road from which the stone pair is visible. Walk

down the track (which can be very boggy) to the stones which stand 10m apart between the track and the river in rough, boulder-strewn moorland bordering a marsh. The larger, eastern stone is 2.3m high and tapers to an uneven squared top. The western stone is slighter, with a more slender rectangular cross-section. The stones are also known as Cerrig Meibion Arthur or 'Stones of the Sons of Arthur'.

Cornel Bach and Ty Newydd paired stone settings are complemented by another fine pair which stand at SN 158313 only 2.5ml (4km) to the east. These are on private land and it is necessary to get permission to visit them.

27
Foel Eryr Cairn, Maenclochog
Round cairn
2nd millennium BC
OS 145 SN 066321 U4

From Maenclochog (N of Narberth) take B4313 N towards Fishguard to New Inn crossroads. Turn R towards Eglwyswrw on B4329, and after 1.6ml (2.5km) park in car park on RHS of road. Cross road and follow track on LHS of road to summit of hill

Foel Eryr cairn

Foel Eryr cairn stands on the summit of a small rounded hillock at 468m above sea level on open common on the south side of the Preseli range. It is a simple, drystone round cairn, 17m in diameter and 2.5m high, and was presumably erected to cover a burial. A National Park observation beacon has been built nearby to interpret the splendid views to all sides. Foel Cwm Cerwyn cairns (no. 29) may be seen on the skyline to the south beyond the forestry plantation.

28
Tafarn y Bwlch, Waun Mawn and Tre Fach Stones, Maenclochog

Tafarn y Bwlch standing stones

Standing stones
2nd millennium BC
OS 145   SN 081337   U4

From Maenclochog (N of Narberth) take B4313 N towards Fishguard to New Inn crossroads. Turn R towards Eglwyswrw on B4329 and after 2.5ml (4km) park by roadside by fork in road. Follow track on L of roads on to common for 40m to site on LHS

Dyfed has very few of the more sophisticated Bronze Age stone settings such as stone rows or circles, but pairs of standing stones are commonly found in this area of Preseli at least. The Tafarn y Bwlch stones, both about 1.3m high, are characteristic in that one stone, the one on the east, has a pointed top, while the other is more rounded. They are more unusual, however, in that they are so close together. The stones stand on slightly sloping ground, on a pass through the hills which may well have been used in prehistoric periods. The stones could have acted as markers for this track while also holding, perhaps, other funerary or ritual significance. They have come, through the ages, to rest at rather an uncomfortable angle of tilt.

Waun Mawn standing stones are 40m further along the track. The westernmost

stone stands on the right of the track and is 2.3m high, rounded in cross section, with a pointed top. To find the eastern stone, continue walking east across the common for another 40m – it is a boulder with a rough pointed top, and stands some 1.8m high. Nearby lie three prostrate stones which were probably once upright. Another stone, some 2m long, lies 10m to the east, near a small broken stone, while another 2m-long stone lies 28m to the west. It has been suggested that these stones could be the remnants of a large stone circle. A description of the site earlier this century records a fifth stone on the south which would give the circle a circumference of about 50m.

Tre Fach standing stone (SN 064351) stands at the other end of the track. The more energetic may reach it by continuing along the main track from the western Waun Mawn stone for 1.3ml (2km) – a map is advisable. Alternatively, take the car along the left hand road at the Tafarn y Bwlch fork, and then turn left, left and left again (3.2ml, 5.2km). The standing stone is in a rough pasture field a little way from the side of the road, through a gate on a footpath. It is 3m high, an elongated diamond shape with a pointed end. It may well have served to mark the other end of the mountain track. It is known locally as Garreg Hir or 'Long Stone'.

29
Foel Cwm Cerwyn, Maenclochog

Round cairns
2nd millennium BC
OS 145   SN 095315   U4

From Maenclochog take B4313 N towards Fishguard to New Inn crossroad. Turn R towards Eglwyswrw on B4329, and after 1.6ml (2.5km), park in car park on RHS of road. Walk along track up hill along ridge keeping forestry plantation to RHS. At far corner of plantation turn R, keeping forestry to R, and walk to OS beacon

This is a fine group of four hilltop round cairns. The first is 3.3m high and is surmounted by the OS beacon. It was explored by Fenton, the 19th-century antiquarian, who found within it a central cist grave containing a cremation covered by an inverted urn. The others are between 1m and 2.5m high and 10m and 17m in diameter. They are all well preserved and are covered with rough grass and reeds.

30
Crugiau Cemmaes, Nevern

Round barrows
2nd millennium BC
OS 145   SN 125416   U2

From Nevern follow B4582 NE towards Cardigan for 3ml (4.8km), past crossroads, to a National Park Viewpoint lay-by on LHS (N) of road. A track leads a few metres to an OS beacon, which stands on one of the barrows

Two burial mounds stand, one on either side of a reservoir, in an area of open land on the summit of a small hill. The northern one is 3m high and 25m in diameter and has an OS beacon on its summit. The southern mound has roughly the same dimensions but, being

crossed by a field boundary, is rather more mutilated. From the northern mound the plough-spread remains of another two barrows are visible in a field across the road to the north.

The four barrows were noted by the antiquarian Edward Lhuyd in 1695 when, apparently, one had recently been dug. Five urns, burnt bones and ashes were reported as being found and one of the urns was presented to the Ashmolean Museum in Oxford. At that time several other barrows were visible and, later on, Fenton speaks of the site as the largest barrow group in Pembrokeshire after the Dry Burrows (no. 37). Even in the 1920s, another two mounds were evident, one to the south and one to the north. The southern one was apparently in the hedge of the modern road, on the parish boundary.

31
Bedd Morris, Newport

Standing stone
2nd millennium BC
OS 145   SN 038365   U1

From Newport, take A487 W towards Fishguard for 0.5ml (0.8km), then turn L (S) down Gwaun Valley road. The standing stone is 2ml (3.2km) along road, on RHS by roadside

This well-known standing stone is situated at the junction of two ancient passes across the Preseli hills; one is now the modern road, the other a rough track leading west from this point. The function of the stone in prehistoric periods may, therefore, have been as a way marker, despite the sepulchral nature of its modern name (bedd = grave). As the inscription on the face of the stone shows, Bedd Morris has been used as marker in our own age, to show the junction between two parishes. Although it is now so prominent a landmark, it appears not to have been mentioned by antiquarian writers, which has led some authorities to doubt that it stands in

Bedd Morris standing stone

This well-preserved ring cairn consists of a low, circular bank some 20m in diameter. It is clearly visible from the road due to the slight natural eminence where it stands, though it is overlooked by higher ground to the south. The stones which make up the simple ring bank may be seen through the grass and heather cover.

Ring cairns are often found, on excavation, to be associated with burials, normally cremations, and have within them large quantities of carefully buried charcoal. Closely related to round cairns, they are generally thought to combine a funerary and ritual function. They may have architectural elaborations involving settings of boulders within or around the bank structure, but Glyn Gath seems to belong to the simplest and most common form of a plain stone ring.

33
Parc y Meirw, Llanllawer
Stone row
2nd millennium BC
OS 157   SM 999359   U1

its original position. It is over 2m in height and tapers to a pointed top. Its name refers to a traditional association with Morris, a notorious robber who lived among the rocks on the summit of the hill commanding the pass.

From Fishguard, take B4313 Gwaun Valley road to Llanychaer. Turn L opposite public house. Drive 0.5ml (0.8km) further, then turn R. Site is 0.6ml (1km) along road, in hedge on RHS, visible from road but owner kindly allows access through gate (ensure gate is left shut)

32
Glyn Gath Ring Cairn, Newport
Round cairn
2nd millennium BC
OS 145   SN 017366   U3

From Newport, drive W along A487 Fishguard road for 3ml (4.8km) to Dinas, then turn L (S) down Gwaun Valley road and drive 1.8ml (2.9km) to road junction. Site is a few metres from roadside on RHS, just short of RH turn

At Llanllawer is the only extant stone row in Dyfed. A modern hedgebank now obscures what must have been a splendid setting of large upright stones, though the bank may, of course, have helped preserve it. Four stones, 2–2.7m in height, are still standing: the eastern two act as the field gateposts, whilst two prostrate stones rest in the bank to the west. Before the enclosure of the field eight stones were visible and these are shown in a 19th-century sketch. An interesting detail is a large prostrate stone which lies at right angles to the main line, next to the three erect stones on the east. This must have been the original

Nineteenth-century drawing of Parc y Meirw stone row

position of the stone which now lies in the hedgebank as the westernmost of the group. The two other recumbent stones, shown as lying between the third and fourth standing stones, presumably lie buried in the hedge.

The stone row is orientated roughly north-east/south-west, and is some 45m long. It stands on the road which runs along what is probably an old trackway across the Preselis, and may therefore have had some significance as a marker. Its main function, however, was probably associated with ritual and, like stone circles, may have been aligned to relate to the movements of sun, moon or stars. As is often the case with megalithic sites, the traditional name of the row, Parc y Meirw ('Field of the Dead') associates the spot with death.

A conspicuous standing stone known as Ty Meini ('Stone house') stands quite near, on the roadside at Dinas.

34
Rhos y Clegyrn, St Nicholas
Standing stone
2nd millennium BC
OS 157   SM 913354   U4

2ml (3.2km) E of Mathry on A487 St Davids–Fishguard road, take minor road N towards St Nicholas for 1.3ml (2km). Turn R (E) at crossroads. After 0.3ml (0.5km), park at signed footpath on RHS. Walk down track on RHS for 0.5ml (0.8km). Site on LHS of track

Lewis 1974

The fine standing stone at Rhos y Clegyrn (or 'Moor of the Stones') is 2.7m high and tapers to a rounded tip. Nearby, on the right of the track and 15m to the south-west of the stone, is a low circular bank, 20m in diameter, difficult to make out in the gorse cover which has now overwhelmed the site. Richard Fenton, in his *A Historic Tour Through Pembrokeshire* (1811), describes the site as a large 'druidical circle' of stones where an axe-hammer had been dug up. This has led to the suggestion that this ring is in fact the remains of an embanked stone circle like Meini Gwyr (no. 25), but which has now lost all of its encircling stones. A similar but smaller ring bank lies 85m to the north-east of the standing stone, and a survey carried out in the 1960s showed that there were also low curving banks of unknown date or function to the west and south of the complex.

Excavations near the standing stone in the 1960s revealed various kinds of pits (some for the probably ritual setting-up of stone or wooden uprights), small stone rings and a stone-hole which must have held a second large standing stone on the north-east. Rhos y Clegyrn must therefore have originally been a paired stone setting. Between the two standing stones was a cobbled pavement, similar to one found at the standing stone at

Rhos y Clegyrn standing stone, during excavations

houses found below the hillfort at Clegyr Boia (no. 60), suggests that they were the summer dwellings of pastoralists, situated, as they were, near water and near the moor which may well have been suitable, then as now, for rough pasture.

Ffynnon Druidion standing stone (SM 921365) lies nearby. Drive along the minor road for a further 1.3ml (2.1km) and turn right at Ffynnon Druidion farm. The prominent standing stone is on the right of the road, 400m south of the farm. It is on private property, but is visible from the road as it stands on a low, irregular natural mound. The proximity of several other monuments in the area, a burial chamber (now destroyed), a burial mound and another standing stone, suggest that the area possessed a great significance in the 3rd and 2nd millennium BC.

Stackpole, South Pembrokeshire (see no. 38). Under the centre of the paving was a deposit of cremated bone with a quantity of pottery, including food vessels.

Below the Bronze Age cobbling and probably unrelated to it were the remains of at least seven flimsy rectangular huts, which may date to the Neolithic period. The insubstantial nature of their construction, compared with the more robust Neolithic

35
Plumstone Mountain Barrows, Hayscastle Cross
Round barrows
2nd millennium BC
OS 157   SM 917234   U3

From Haverfordwest, take B4330 Croesgoch road N for 6ml (9.6km). After a RH turn signed

Plumstone Mountain barrows, middle barrow (right) with Plumstone Rock (left)

Treffgarne, take next L, a signed bridleway, and drive up track for 500m to end. Barrows visible on moor 100m ahead, just below rock outcrop

Two of the round burial mounds of this group lie close together on heathland just below the Plumstone Rock outcrop which commands splendid views over the valley of the Western Cleddau. These two mounds are both about 1.3m high and 14m in diameter, and their irregular profile suggests that they have been disturbed in the past. A third, larger mound (2m high and 30m in diameter) lies in the corner of a field, 400m further west. None of these mounds have been excavated.

36
Upper Lodge Stones, Haroldstone
Standing stones
2nd millennium BC
OS 157   SM 861143   U1

From Haverfordwest, take B4341 to Broadhaven (6ml, 9.6km), then minor road N towards Haroldstone West. Site 0.3ml (0.5km) along road, on RHS (E), by entrance to Upper Lodge

Upper Lodge standing stones are half-hidden in the hedge bank bordering the road. The southern one stands just north of the entrance to the house and only 1.3m of its height is visible, as presumably much of the stone is embedded and concealed in the bank. The second stands a little to the north; its jagged top suggests that it has been damaged and may have stood much higher.

These two stones (and a third which is apparently embedded in the bank) were, according to a 19th-century description, originally part of a stone circle which was demolished, and the stones were then set up in the garden wall.

A third stone, called Harold's Stone, stands in the garden at St Catherine's, a bungalow on the left-hand side of the road 0.3ml (0.5km) further north. Permission is of course required to visit this stone. If the lower two stones are indeed the remains of a stone circle, Harold's Stone may have been associated with this setting, but presumably would have stood outside it.

37
Dry Burrows, Corston Beacon and Pwllcrochan, Pembroke
Round barrows
2nd millennium BC
OS 158   SR 948997   U1

From Pembroke, take B4320 W for 2.5ml (4km). Dry Burrows barrow group lies on either side of road just before Speculation Inn. Barrows visible from road

Fox and Grimes 1928

Dry Burrows must rank as one of the finest barrow groups in Dyfed. The group consists of seven barrows, five of which lie in a field to the south of the road, one in the next field to the east, and one in the field opposite on the north side of the road. A possible eighth barrow lies on the south. The barrows are in varying states of preservation, but one survives to 2.7m in height and three others are over 1m high. There is no public access into the fields, but the barrows are clearly visible from the road.

John Fenton, the son of the Pembrokeshire antiquarian, excavated several of the round barrows in October 1811. This early excavation was most unsatisfactory by modern standards, especially as we do not known which mounds were excavated, but nevertheless it showed the barrows to have contained a rich variety of complex burial forms. On the original ground level under one barrow was a covered stone cist, on the floor of which were large quantities of burnt human bones. Another barrow had burnt bones gathered into four heaps, but there was no sign of a cist. A third contained a cremation covered by an inverted urn enclosed in a small cist, while another had a similar inverted urn cremation, but with no cist.

Corston Beacon (SR 934999) is 1ml (1.5km) further west along the B4320, and, though there is no public access on to the barrow, it is visible on the left of the road. It is a single round barrow about 20m in diameter and 1m high, and is worth noting as its excavation in 1927 revealed an inhumation burial of a man set within an elaborate cist with massive side- and capstones. A fine bronze dagger, deposited with the body and now in the National Museum of Wales, is of a very early Bronze Age form, and has the handle partially preserved.

The Pwllcrochan barrow group (SM 926003) consists of four round barrows, three in one field, and one in the next field to the north. The best preserved is some 1.7m in height while the others are considerably lower. They also lie on private land but are clearly visible on the right of the Pwllcrochan road.

38
Harold's Stone, Bosherston

Standing stone

2nd millennium BC

OS 158   SR 967958   U2

From Pembroke, take B4319 towards Castlemartin for 3.5ml (5.6km). After St Petrox, at Sampson Cross crossroads, turn L down drive marked 'Stackpole Home Farm' and turn R (after track marked 'Dairy') and ask permission to visit in farmyard (owners kindly grant access on request). Turn L on to Bosherston road. 500m along, park and walk down track on LHS through gate, for 500m. Stone in hedge, in field on LHS

Standing stones are comparatively rare in the southernmost part of the country, but Harold's Stone is an impressive example,

Harold's Stone

some 2m high, with a fine, almost delicate appearance. It stands at the edge of a field on a slight mound of stones which could be an original part of the standing stone's setting but could be due entirely to field clearance or cultivation. The name of the stone may derive from a fanciful association with Earl Harold, who, we are told by Giraldus Cambrensis, set up stones to commemorate his victories over the Welsh in 1063. A number of stones have had the name attached to them, though, of course, it is improbable that they are anything to do with the famous earl.

Two other fine standing stones found nearby are known collectively (with Harold's Stone) as the 'Devil's Quoit', and are said to 'dance the hay' together to celebrate the harvest each year.

Just the other side of the Bosherston Fishponds to the east is the Stackpole Warren standing stone. This is unfortunately inaccessible, but worthy of mention as the excavations around the stone in 1977–9 showed how complex these sites can be. First to be built at Stackpole was a circular timber structure with a porch, possibly a Bronze Age domestic house. Later, the standing stone and another post setting were erected; around them was laid a large stone pavement consisting of over 3,000 stones set upright in rows, reminiscent of the cobbling around the Rhos y Clegyrn stone (no. 34). Near the stone was a crouched human burial in a pit. The entire area of Stackpole Warren contains many traces of settlement and agricultural activity from the Bronze Age to the Roman period and was evidently extremely attractive to early farmers.

39
Mynydd Llangyndeyrn, Pontyberem

Cairns, stones and burial chambers

2nd millennium BC

OS 159 SN 482132 U2

From Cross Hands, take A476 S to Tumble, then B4317 R to Pontyberem. Turn R on to B4306, and 2ml (3.2km) beyond Pontyberem, cairns are an open moor on RHS of road, at top of hill, just beyond road sign 'Crwbin'. Walk along track, and cairns are on ridge top to LHS

Ward 1976, 1983

Mynydd Llangyndeyrn, a long distinctive ridge of high ground now quarried on its north side for limestone, seems to have been a focus of activity in the Bronze Age. The sites need some searching out amongst the rock outcrops and scree, and it is probably best to begin at the OS beacon at the summit of the hill, built on top of the first site, a low, flat-topped cairn, 11m in diameter and 0.5m high. Another cairn a few paces to the south-west consists of a circle of stones with a disturbed cist in its centre. To the south-east is a ring cairn with a bank of stones 4m in diameter. The interior has been disturbed, forming a conical depression.

Two Neolithic burial chambers known as Bwrdd Arthur and Gwal y Filiast stand side by side on the north of and just under a rock outcrop to the east. They are probably sub-megalithic in type. The western chamber is the better preserved with a 2.5m long capstone still resting on surviving sidestones about 1m above ground level. The eastern chamber has collapsed completely with its uprights slumped outwards, and seems to have been smaller than the rectangular western chamber. It is impossible to say whether they were quite separate monuments or were both enclosed by the same cairn.

Mynydd Llangyndeyrn, cist grave within old field boundary

Another cairn lies 400m further east along the ridge, within a stone field boundary. Its internal cist retains only three of its four side-slabs but the capstone is still in position (see illustration). A few paces to the south is a ring cairn, 10m in diameter, which consists of a low ring of stones with an entrance on the south-west defined by a large upright stone set on either side, and possibly another entrance on the south-east. A further 400m east again are a ring cairn 8m in diameter, one round cairn and two irregular field clearance cairns.

Running east–west between the cairns are a number of low stone banks, with others crossing them at right angles. The way in which they incorporate the cairns has led to the suggestion that the field system was created at much the same time as the cairns. This would then be a rare survival of a 2nd-millennium field system, curiously uncommon in Wales outside Gwynedd.

The prominent standing stone on the west (road) side of the OS beacon was prostrate until 1976 when excavations revealed the stone-hole. Pits were found nearby, indicating the presence of some timber structure built up against the stone, and charcoal from one

of these gave a radiocarbon date of 1140 BC. A ring trench was also discovered, similar to those found around the Rhos y Clegyrn stone (no. 34). The standing stone has now been re-erected in its original position and is some 3.5m high. A second, much smaller standing stone is situated 10m to the north. This too was excavated to reveal its stone-pit. The function of the stones is, of course, uncertain, but they may have marked or served in some way the access route into this area of evident religious, funerary and perhaps agricultural importance.

40
Tair Carn Isaf and Uchaf, Llandeilo
Round cairns
2nd millennium BC
OS 159, 160   SN 683168–695175   U4

From Llandeilo, drive S on A483 0.5ml (0.8km) to Ffairfach crossroads. Turn L, then R to Trapp

Tair Carn Uchaf round cairns

(2.5ml, 4km). Cross river bridge in Trapp, and branch L at pub. Drive 2ml (3.2km) further (over crossroads and take L fork at junction, towards Brynamman) to crossroads. Turn L and park 100m along road – site on hilltop on R of road: climb straight up low hill and follow ridge top to L. Steep 1ml (1.6km) walk, can be boggy. Map advisable

These two groups of drystone cairns are in classic positions at either end of a high moorland ridge. The walk is a little steep, but the views across the valley are glorious. The western group, Tair Carn Isaf ('Lower Three Cairns'), is near an OS beacon, which helps locate the cairns which are fairly low. From south-west to north-east, they are 20m, 15m and 12m in diameter respectively, and about 1–2m high. All are mutilated to a greater or lesser extent. An outlying cairn stands a little way to the west, separated from the others by a low saddle of land.

Tair Carn Uchaf ('Upper Three Cairns') are 1km further north-east along the ridge, and are easily visible from Isaf. All three are well-preserved and intact drystone cairns, situated on a series of high points. The central cairn is the most impressive both from a distance and near-to. It is 3.2m high and 22m in diameter. The other two are smaller, about 18m in diameter and 2.5m in height.

None of these cairns have been excavated, but they were almost certainly used for burial during the Bronze Age. Burial cairns may be found singly or in lines or groups, with sometimes as many as six to eight together, and these two groups of three cairns sharing a hilltop setting are by no means uncommon. Many other cairns may be seen among the hills in this area, which suggests that it was considerably less bleak during the better climate of the 2nd millennium. The more prominent eastern group has long been used as a boundary marker, and still marks the junction of the four communities of Ffairfach, Llangadog, Quarter Bach, and Cwmamman. The cairns may be seen from far away and are easy to pick out from Carreg Cennen Castle (no. 124).

41
Carn Pen Rhiw Ddu, Bryamman
Round cairn
2nd millennium BC
OS 160   SN 728189   U4

From Brynamman, take A4069 N towards Llangadog for 4ml (2.4km). Park in car park on RHS of road opposite a disused quarry. Cross road, and walk up hill, keeping quarry and quarry road on L, to 1st summit. Walk is 450m and not steep. Rocky slope near site is visible from road

Carn Pen Rhiw Ddu (or 'Cairn on the Summit of the Black Hill') is a fine, well-preserved cairn, characteristic of the Black Mountain Bronze Age burial cairns, while being more accessible than many. It lies on the north-east tip of a broad spur of high ground, and is some 2.5m in height and 11m in diameter. The cairn is composed of a drystone heap of jagged, grey-white limestone boulders, now rather misshapen due to the attentions of walkers.

For those who would like a more strenuous walk, another well-preserved drystone cairn, known as Carn Pen y Clogau (or 'Cairn on the Head of the Crag') is 0.7ml (1.1km) further south-west along the ridge at SN 717186. It is very conspicuous, and its large size makes it clearly visible from Pen Rhiw Ddu on the next summit.

42
Bryngwyn Stone, Llandeilo
Standing stone
2nd millennium BC
OS 159   SN 671224   U1

From Llandeilo, take A483 S across bridge to Ffairfach crossroads. Take minor road L (E), cross river and fork L. After 1ml (1.6km), take 1st R and follow road for 2ml (3.2km). Site in bank on RHS of road in woodland opposite pull-in

There are a number of standing stones in this area, but unfortunately most are on private land and Bryngwyn Stone, less spectacular than others, is at least easily accessible. The standing stone is 2.5m high, and has a chisel-shaped top. Its position in a hedge bank results in its periodically becoming overgrown. It is fairly close to the magnificent hillforts of Carn Goch (no. 76) which may be conveniently visited during the same trip.

43
The Abermarlais Stone, Llangadog
Standing stone
2nd millennium BC
OS 146   SN 695294   U1

Abermarlais standing stone

From Llangadog, take A4069 Llanwrda road for 1ml (1.6km) to T-junction and turn R on to A40 toward Llanwrda. After 0.5ml (0.8km), site on LHS of road at entrance to Abermarlais Park, just past lay-by

This is a massive, blunt-headed standing stone, almost square in cross-section and some 3m in height. It is said to have been moved here in about the year 1840, from its former position a little further within the park. Tradition also states that Sir Rhys ap Thomas had had the stone placed upright to commemorate the Battle of Bosworth Field – he was of considerable assistance to Henry VII before that battle, and benefited later from the generosity of his grateful king. It is quite possible that Sir Rhys did re-erect the stone there, in the grounds of his manor, though it is most likely that it was first used as a Bronze Age standing stone.

Because of its prominence and massive size, the stone has always attracted attention and invited disturbance. It is probably the stone around which the antiquarian Fenton dug in the early 19th century to explore the

ground around its massive base. Excavations later in the same century, undertaken for the purpose of securing its foundations, showed the stone's base to be buried in over 1m of soil. The stone is often known as Garreg Fawr or 'Great Stone'.

44
Crugiau Edryd and Neighbouring Cairns, Llanybyther
Cairn groups
2nd millennium BC
OS 146   SN 535395   U1/4

From Carmarthen, take A485 Lampeter road 12.7ml (20km) N to RH turning marked Rhydcymerau. 3.4ml (5.4km) along this road is a turn to L to communication masts. Park here and walk up concrete track past masts to cairns, one of which has an OS beacon on top. Crugiau Edryd is accessible by wheelchair; the other cairns require a walk

The area around Mynydd Llanybyther and Mynydd Llanllwni is rich in Bronze Age funerary monuments. The four sizeable heather- and grass-covered cairns known as Crugiau Edryd have been built in a line running north-east/south-west, each about 35m apart from the next. They are 16m–22m in diameter and between 1m and 1.9m high. Hollows on the surface of some of the mounds suggest that they may have been disturbed in the past.

Just over a 1ml (1.6km) back down the road, the prominent Crug y Biswal cairn lies on the left, at the junction with the track to Brynllewelyn. Directly opposite it, on the other side of the road, is a fine ring cairn, 24m in diameter, surrounded by a low bank.

Two further accessible groups of cairns lie on the hillside nearby. The two cairns of Crugiau Leir (SN 502371) lie on the summit of a hill on the left of and 2ml along the next road to the left signposted to Brechfa, and the saucer-shaped Mynydd Llanfihangel cairn (SN 502355) lies on the summit of a moorland hill on a junction 1ml (1.6km) further along the same road.

Crugiau Edryd cairn group from the air

45
Trichrug Round Barrows, Cilcennin

Round barrows

2nd millennium BC

OS 146   SN 542599   U2

From Lampeter, take A482 towards Aberaeron. After 4ml (6.4km) take RH turn on to B4337 Llanrhystud road and follow through Trefilan (note motte on RHS of road at junction) for 4.3ml (6.9km) to forest on LHS. Turn L on to forestry track and leave car. Walk 400m along track, then fork R. Site a few m further in clearing

Four fine burial mounds lie in an unplanted area by the side of a forestry track, and are covered with heather and brambles. The north-west mound, that nearest to the track, is especially well preserved, being some 4m high and 33m in diameter. The next two are lower and one has an OS beacon on the top. The fourth is a ring cairn with a low enclosing bank and a level interior, 14m in diameter.

Burial cairns were often constructed in groups in the Bronze Age, either in an apparently haphazard pattern, or as in this case, in a 'linear cemetery'. The association of round cairns and a ring cairn makes this group especially noteworthy.

46
Nant y Gerwyn and Groes Fawr Cairns, Tregaron

Round cairns

2nd millennium BC

OS 147   SN 802573   U4

Trichrug round barrows, north-west mound

Groes Fawr cairns, cist grave

From Llanwrtyd Wells, take minor road to Abergwesyn (5ml, 8km). Take LH road toward Tregaron for 5ml (8km) over 3 bridges and through forest. Just beyond 4th bridge, cairns are on RHS (N) of road, past twists in road, in unenclosed grassy area skirted by forestry

Nant y Gerwyn cairns lie in a row on unenclosed moorland. The low burial cairn nearest the road is 3.5m in diameter. It contains a cist grave, the capstone from which lies dislodged to the south. To the east and north are two more cairns, both of which have hollows in the centre which might indicate the former existence of cists, now robbed out. Indeed, small stones which may have been orthostats lie to one side of the northern cairn. A fourth cairn lies to the north-east, and consists of a cairn of boulders piled up on a natural stone outcrop.

This area is rich in Bronze Age funerary monuments. Groes Fawr cairns (SN 726599) lie quite close, but have to be approached from Tregaron. The most prominent has a fine internal cist, around which the cairnstones have been piled to build a beehive-shaped drystone sheep shelter. Many others may be visited with the help of the 1:50,000 map, such as the Graig Wen Cairn (SN 685514), or the Sarn Helen cairns (643476 and 648482).

47
Hirnant Circle, Ponterwyd
Round cairns
Late 3rd–2nd millennium BC
OS 135   SN 753839   U2

At Ponterwyd, on A44 11ml (18km) E of Aberystwyth, take Nantymoch road to N. After 1.8ml (2.9km), over stream and past Hirnant

Farm, just beyond cattle grid, park at 1st gate on LHS. Site is through gate, along fence to 2nd gate

Hogg 1977; Marshall and Murphy 1991

Hirnant circle is an inconspicuous setting of 16 small stones, 6m in diameter; two further stones may have stood in the gaps on the east and south-east. The stones, irregular boulders which vary considerably in size and shape, probably originally formed the kerb of a low flat cairn used for burial and ritual functions. A high proportion of the Bronze Age cairns concentrated in the area are 'kerbed cairns' surrounded by a kerb of small upright stones.

From here, Disgwylfa Fawr cairn can be seen, about 1.5ml (2.4km) due west, across the river and on the nearest summit. Its excavation in 1937 revealed within the cairn an internal ring of slabs in the centre of which lay, one above the other, two coffins formed of oak trunks. The upper, smaller one contained cremated human bones, a flint blade and a finely decorated food vessel. Radiocarbon dates suggest that the upper burial may be a secondary cremation, inserted over the inhumation burial some 600 years later.

Nant Maesnant-fach cairn lies 0.8ml (1.3km) further north by the side of a track which forks right from the road, where the road bends to the left. It is a little way from the reservoir, 400m down the track, through a gate. Powergen kindly allows access, but warns visitors to keep off the soft edge of the reservoir. The cairn, 1.8m high and 11m in diameter, is surrounded by a kerb.

A ring cairn on the south of the reservoir was excavated in 1962 before the flooding of the area. The cairn, 13m in diameter, had a rough stone kerb surrounding the low stone bank and an entrance on the south. A number of pits and stake holes were found in the centre – three pits were covered with slabs and, in one of these, a Bronze Age urn was discovered with, enigmatically, the cremated

Aber Camddwr round cairn, during excavations

dismembered, burnt remains of a child, the head of which had apparently been removed prior to burial. This was interpreted as a sacrificial deposit by the excavator, who suggested that the site was a sacred structure incorporating the elements of a round-house – a mortuary house for the dead.

The temporary lowering of water levels in 1984 allowed the excavation of another cairn at Aber Camddwr (see illustration), which was then recreated in a small fenced enclosure on the right of the road 0.7ml (1.1km) beyond the dam at the south end of the reservoir. It is a platform cairn, with a circular kerb around a low stone platform rather than a mound. On one side was a kerbed annexe, under which was a pit filled with charcoal and burnt bone which gave a radiocarbon date of 1260 BC. In the centre of the cairn was a slab-lined grave, which probably had held an inhumation, though no trace of any body remained. Again, the upright stones and stake holes perhaps represented a round-house, the annexe possibly representing a porch. Some hundreds of years later the site was apparently reused for a more ceremonial function, as holes which had held standing stones were found around the cairn. Pollen analysis suggests that the surrounding area was grassland with oak and hazel woodland nearby. Oak seems always to have been used for cremations, probably because its high energy value made it more effective in achieving the necessary temperature.

48
Bedd Taliesin, Talybont
Round cairn
2nd millennium BC
OS 135   SN 671912   U2

From Talybont, 7.5ml (12km) N of Aberystwyth on A487, take minor road immediately N of river bridge inland. Then take 1st L, and at T-junction turn R. Pass no through road on R, and road to Gwarcwm Isaf on L, and drive through road gate (1.5ml, 2.4km from

Bedd Taliesin round cairn, detail of cist grave

Talybont bridge). Site few m further on RHS of track, just beyond fork

In the centre of this low round kerb cairn is a 2m-long cist, with two side-slabs which have now slumped inwards. The large capstone has been dislodged from the top of the cist and now lies nearby rather uncomfortably balanced upon a pile of small boulders. An upright boulder protruding through the grass on the north-east of the cairn must mark the position of the kerb of stones which would have encircled the mound.

This grave is one of the more accessible of the kerb cairns with internal cists, a type of Bronze Age tomb still fairly commonly found in upland Wales, but generally difficult to visit because of their remote locations. The grave takes its name from a fanciful association with the 6th-century Welsh poet Taliesin who is supposed to have lived at the foot of the mountain and to be buried here (bedd = grave) – the nearby village is also named after him. The story is told that a skull was found within the cist, which, of course, may well be the case.

4

The Iron Age

The adoption of iron working in about 600 BC in Britain was as gradual a technological innovation as that of bronze working before it, and heralded no great change in settlement pattern. Indeed, iron tools appear to have remained scarce and probably expensive in Wales throughout the early Iron Age. The trend, first established in the late Bronze Age, of moving settlement away from the harsher uplands on to lower-lying land, coastal areas and river valleys continued. Inevitably, there were greater demands on the available agricultural land, and, in response to the tension caused by those demands, defended settlements on hilltops were increasingly commonly constructed to serve as the headquarters of this more warlike society. Larger regionalised groupings of people began to emerge, forming the basis of the tribal areas which are known to have existed later at the time of the Roman conquest.

Some of the earliest hillforts so far recognised are in the Welsh Marches, but the relatively late date of the hillforts of Dyfed may suggest that this area suffered particularly from the effect of climatic deterioration, and there may even have been a hiatus in settlement. An exception to this was the low-lying coastal south-west where, perhaps, the mild conditions and fertile soils permitted the continuation of settlement. Excavations at the promontory fort at Dale (no. 68) for instance, suggest that this was one such site, occupied in the late Bronze Age, earlier than any hillfort yet discovered in Dyfed.

When settlement recovered, the characteristic type of site found in inland south-western Dyfed was the smaller defended settlement, many hundreds of which still survive as familiar earthworks in the landscape. Most are small, often circular, defended enclosures, under 1.2ha in extent, bounded by a single bank and ditch, and often located in weaker positions on hillslopes. They can only have housed limited numbers of people, perhaps extended family units. Positioned amongst these farms are larger fortified sites of apparently higher status. These hillforts, defensively sited and defended with strong banks and ditches, may have exerted some control over the smaller surrounding farmsteads based on long-standing systems of patronage and tribal allegiance. Later in the Iron Age, the number of small enclosures in these inland areas proliferated, while, for some reason, the accompanying hillforts were abandoned. This trend continued into the Romano-British period when settlements were often undefended, or had much

Reconstruction drawing of an Iron Age hillfort interior

slighter fortifications, and were situated on lower-lying ground.

The Iron Age settlements of the upland areas of north and east Dyfed are slightly different. Here there were a number of larger hillforts, while the small defended farm hardly appears. Unlike the pattern further south and west, these hillforts apparently continued to be occupied in the later Iron Age and Romano-British period as well. Excavations on some of them, such as Pen Dinas near Aberystwyth (no. 79) and Caer Cadwgan near Lampeter (see Appendix), suggest that it was quite normal for these sites to have their origins early in the Iron Age and to have been occupied for a long period up to or even into Roman times. Hilltop settlements such as Foel Trigarn (no. 49) in the Preseli hills became densely occupied fortified villages inhabited well into the Roman period. Whether their defences continued to be functional at this later time or whether they survived merely as relics is uncertain.

Defensive settlements can differ from one another considerably, as the builders altered their techniques to exploit the topography and available materials to best effect. Hillforts usually lie on the summits of hills, with their defences constructed to follow the contours of the high ground. Others (called 'promontory forts') were built on promontories, either on the coast, where the sea protected two sides of the headland, or inland, where steep slopes gave a natural defence on two sides of a ridge – thus the man-made defences only needed to cut off a short length of level approach. These fortified settlements are frequently found to have been constructed, altered and repaired over long periods, and many types of ramparts were built. These include earthen banks revetted with timber or with stone, timber-laced ramparts, simple stone walls; and simple earthen dump ramparts. Excavation often shows the banks to have been surmounted by a timber rampart walk with a defensive parapet.

The different areas of Dyfed inevitably supported different types of agricultural economies. The upland areas of the north and east must have relied heavily on a pastoral economy based on sheep farming. The inland area must also have been primarily pastoral, though its rather better soils may have allowed limited agriculture and certainly better grass for the herds and flocks. The small, fertile coastal south-west zone, however, was very suitable for agriculture. Here, unique in Dyfed in the later 1st millennium BC, arable field systems are found adjacent to settlements, and the island of Skomer (no. 67) has fine examples of these small square or rectangular fields bounded by stone walls. In striking contrast to the earlier Bronze Age, burials dating to the Iron Age are very rarely discovered. The few that have been discovered are probably ritual in character, and consequently we do not know whether the main burial tradition was that of cremation or inhumation. But the disposal of the remains was evidently much less concerned with providing a lasting memorial.

Excavations on settlements suggest that in comparison with the south and east of Britain, life during the Iron Age in south-west Wales was generally rather poor. This remained the same in the later years of the millennium, when the Roman expansion had reached Britain's doorstep. Close trading links were established with the Continent and luxury goods, finewares, metalwork and Mediterranean agricultural produce were imported. Coinage began to be used, and there is a suggestion that writing was adopted. Little of this contact and intense political activity is evidenced on Welsh sites. The descriptions of Britain written by the incoming Romans are uninformative when it comes to the life of the people of remote south-west Wales – though Caesar describes the importance of the Druids in Anglesey, a powerful, priestly caste who revered sacred groves and springs. We do at least know that this is the area where the tribe of the Demetae lived at the time of the Roman conquest, but even after that momentous event, south-west Wales remained little affected by outside contact.

49
Foel Trigarn, Crymmych
Later prehistoric hillfort
*1st millennium BC–early 1st
millennium AD*
OS 145   SN 158336   U4

*From Crymmych on A478, take minor road on
S of village W towards Mynachlog Ddu for
0.8ml (1.3km). At road fork, keep L, then park
at signed footpath on RHS of road. Follow path
on to moor, straight up hill to summit*

Baring Gould 1900

The hillfort, crowning the eastern summit of
the main Preseli range at 363m above sea
level, is enclosed in places by drystone walls
and elsewhere by earthen banks with a stone
revetment. These have now collapsed to form
a rocky heap in which a few stretches of stone
facework are still visible. There is no sign that
there were ever any ditches surrounding the
fort.

The fort has three defended enclosures: the
main, inner, and probably earliest enclosure,
1.2ha in area, with a rampart on all sides save
the south where short stretches of walling
only were required to join the natural
outcrops; a second 0.8ha enclosure on the
north and east, the bank of which follows the
main wall concentrically, about 37m away
from it; a third of roughly similar area and
probably the latest in date, is a rectangular
annexe added to the east. The rampart
around the main enclosure is the mightiest,
and stands up to 3.5m high externally, while
that around the annexe is the slightest.

Some of the simple gaps through the
defences of the fort must be original
entrances. Those through the wall of the inner
enclosure on east and west, those on the
south-west and north of the second enclosure
and that on the west of the annexe look
particularly convincing candidates.

Foel Trigarn is interesting for its well-
preserved internal features, especially the
levelled platforms for houses. The main
enclosure, where 77 platforms have

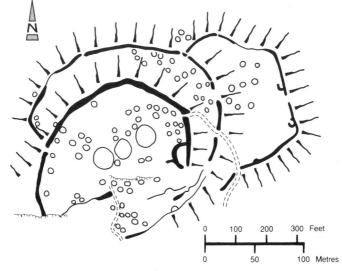

Foel Trigarn hillfort, the three defended enclosures

apparently been counted, and the middle enclosure, with some 63, were evidently densely occupied, and there are other platforms both in the annexe, and unenclosed on the hillside around the fort. A total of 220 platforms were apparent in 1899 when some of these buildings were excavated. Iron Age and Roman spindle whorls, pottery and stone vessels, glass beads and jet rings were found, most of which are now in Tenby Museum. Building so massive a fort would have involved a tremendous input of resources and the site evidently continued in occupation over a long period of time – it is, therefore, unlikely that all these huts would have been occupied simultaneously. Even so, the remains do suggest quite a busy settlement.

Within Foel Trigarn are three massive cairns, up to 3m in height. These probably Bronze Age burial monuments are very prominent on the summit, and indeed are the features from which the site gets its modern name (translated as 'Hill of the Three Cairns'). It is always interesting to speculate upon the attitude of the Iron Age fort builders to these pre-existing, massive structures in the interior of their stronghold. Was the tradition of their sanctity enough to safeguard them from dismantling? Or were they put to good use as look-out stations, or, if we are wrong in attributing a Bronze Age date to the structures, even built for that purpose?

50
Carn Alw, Crymmych
Iron Age hillfort
Late 1st millennium BC
OS 145   SN 139338   U4

As for Foel Trigarn (no. 49). Climb to Foel Trigarn (or skirt it on N), then walk westwards along ridge for 1ml (1.6km) to rocky outcrop on N edge (RHS) of ridge of high ground

Drewett 1987; Mytum and Webster 1989

Carn Alw hillfort stands at 255m above sea level, amidst a rock-strewn sloping hillside

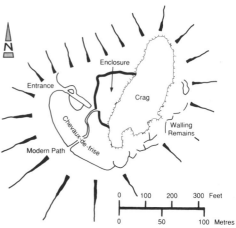

Carn Alw hillfort

adjacent to the outcrop of the same name. The oval hillfort measures some 30m by 65m and is defended by a simple drystone rampart which incorporates naturally outcropping rock within its circuit. Much of the wall stone has collapsed into the surrounding scree, but in better preserved sections the original drystone facework of the wall can still be seen. There is no apparent external ditch.

The defences are most impressive on the west, where the well-preserved stretch of rampart is strengthened by a *cheveaux de frise*, a defensive device consisting of large numbers of small upright stones set into the ground as an extra obstacle against attack on a weak side or entrance. In this case many thousands of small stones up to 1m in height have been placed in an arc around the simple gap entrance, and a fine stone-lined pathway leads through it to the entrance on the north-west. Three bands of stones can be distinguished within the *cheveaux de frise*: an outer, densely-packed band, a inner more sparsely covered zone and the innermost zone where the stones are again densely packed and incorporate numbers of natural boulders which have rolled from the crag above. *Cheveaux de frise* are by no means commonly found, and this is a good example.

Carn Alw is very different from the nearby Carn Ingli (no. 52) and Foel Trigarn (no. 49) in that it has no signs of habitation within its walls. This has led to the suggestion that it was not a fortified village, but rather a summer upland grazing base or a refuge at time of threat. Thus, contact with the permanent settled lowlands to the north would have been a priority, and hence the provision of the good roadway from the entrance down the hill to the north.

Surrounding Carn Alw hillfort are traces of many more enclosures, houses and fields with clearance cairns. Dating such ancient sites is very difficult, but a recent survey of the area suggests that the hillfort may possibly have been preceded by a late Bronze Age unenclosed agricultural settlement just to the south, and may have been succeeded, in the late Iron Age or Romano-British period, by a larger defended enclosure on the north. The low stone banks that delimit the fields can be seen better in winter and spring than summer, when they are buried in the bracken. The small enclosures on either side of the entrance-way to the hillfort are probably medieval or later, as they appear to have been constructed from boulders removed from the fort wall.

Due south of Carn Alw is Carn Meini, showing rocky and jagged on the skyline. It is probably the source of some of the blue dolerite stone, much prized as a material for polished stone axes in the Neolithic, and, in its most celebrated form, as the bluestones in the inner stone setting at Stonehenge.

51
Castell Henllys, Newport
Iron Age inland promontory fort
Late 1st millennium BC–early 1st millennium AD
OS 145   SN 117391   R2
Pembrokeshire Coast National Park

From Newport on A487, travel 4ml (6.4km) E towards Cardigan. Site is signposted from A487. Take rough track on L (N) to signposted car park. Walk 100m to site. Entrance fee; opening hours: April–October, 9.30–17.00 (tel: 023 979 319 in season)

Mytum 1989

The inland promontory fort of Castell Henllys is a particularly interesting site to visit, as, following the excavation of the interior, reconstructions of Iron Age houses have been built on the foundations of the prehistoric timber dwellings. This recreated Iron Age settlement gives a vivid illustration of the living and working conditions of the original inhabitants.

The fort lies on a small spur overlooking the River Gwaun and is one of a number of inland promontory forts in the area. The main defensive earthworks lie on the northern, gentler approach and consist of a large inner bank, a ditch and a smaller outer bank. The defences curve around to the natural scarp on the east, but on the west stop short at the site of the original entrance, still used as the modern entry point. The entrance was partly built of stone and would have made a dramatic impact on anyone approaching the fort. A double ditch system originally ran outside the entrance as an additional defence.

The main, northern defences had three phases of development. The outer bank and the first phase inner bank were of simple dump construction, and the outer bank had a palisade on its summit. Subsequently, the inner bank was given a pebble-paved wall-walk and a substantial palisade for at least part of its circuit. Finally the bank was raised to its final height. On the severely sloping south-west and south-east, a slight bank was raised and the slope below was terraced to create the appearance of a massive defensive work. Palisades gave additional strength to the bank for at least part of its circuit.

In the interior of the fort, gullies and postholes associated with a number of round-houses have been discovered, and so far three houses have been reconstructed. Five settings of four postholes, usually interpreted as granaries raised off the ground to protect the grain from pests, have been found as well

Castell Henllys, the reconstruction of a round-house in progress

as evidence for iron working and other agricultural activities. We cannot know for certain how the buildings looked nor even how many would have been inhabited at the same time. But the reconstructed houses, with their wattle-and-daub walls, reed-thatched conical roofs, and central open hearths give a feeling of scale which is difficult to appreciate from plans alone. Other reconstructions include a pottery kiln, an iron smelting furnace, and a short section of timber fencing on the top of the outer rampart.

Outside the fort on the north is a rectangular annexe which was found on excavation to be a quite separate settlement, built in the Romano-British period when the fort had been abandoned; it was positioned on lower-lying ground with less regard for defence. Below the annexe enclosure bank was found a most interesting feature belonging to the earlier Iron Age defences. Irregular rows of upright shale slabs had been set into the ground to stand about 0.4m high, forming a *cheveaux de frise*, designed to slow down any attack on the northern side of the fort.

The excavations at Castell Henllys suggest that the Iron Age settlement housed a community of several families with a population of perhaps 100 or more people. The grand scale of the defences suggests that contemporary society was by no means settled and peaceable. Perhaps the site may have held some territorial sway over the adjacent countryside. Excavations are taking place on a number of nearby sites, such as that at Henllys Top Field slightly to the north, to try to throw light on this relationship between the dominant defensive site and the smaller, probably subordinate surrounding farmsteads.

52
Carn Ingli, Newport
Prehistoric hillfort
Late 1st millennium BC
OS 145   SN 063373   U4

From W side of Newport on A487, take Gwaun Valley road. After 1ml (1.6km), park and walk to rock outcrop on skyline on LHS (E) of road. Follow track to next visible outcrop; Carn Ingli visible at far point of ridge. Short, steeper route is via footpath E of Newport (map essential)

Hogg 1973

The spectacular hillfort of Carn Ingli lies on the eastern end of a high moorland ridge and commands extensive views over the north coast and river valleys to the east and south. The 4ha fort is a long triangle in shape, about 400m by 100m, and is situated on two rough peaks separated by a saddle of lower ground. The slopes of the hill are strewn with a chaotic mass of tumbled rock, and the south side is so steep that no further defences were necessary. Elsewhere a stone wall bounds the fort, linking the prominent rock outcrops. Two further ramparts curve around the rocky slope on the east, and there are traces of a perhaps unfinished outer bank on the short north side.

The stone defences are now very collapsed though a few sections of the original drystone facework still survive and it has been calculated that the wall may originally have been about 3m high. The fort interior is subdivided by cross-walls into four sections, which may represent successive periods of expansion of the site. The first enclosure may have been quite small, just around the summit. The large annexe on the north and the two on the south may have been added subsequently, and the two sections of walling further down the slope on the east themselves form separate enclosures which may have been added later still towards the end of the life of the fort. Carn Ingli may have been first enclosed in the Neolithic and adapted later for use in the Iron Age. Another

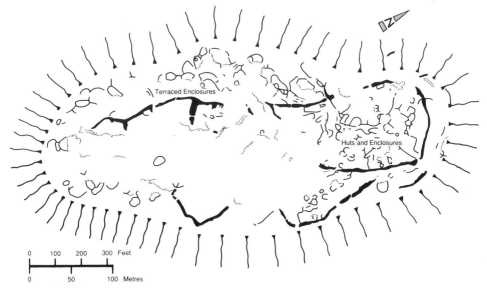

Carn Ingli hillfort

theory suggests that it was first built in the Iron Age, but altered through long occupation lasting even, perhaps, into the medieval period.

Later alterations to the fort may account for the extraordinary number of entrances which would presumably have weakened an enclosure with any serious military purpose. There are nine simple entrances through the main bank and one through each of the three cross-walls; some still retain traces of the passage walling.

The hillfort seems to have acted as a fortified village, and about 25 circular or quadrangular houses have been noted which could have held a population of about 150. The expansion of the fort may have been due to the pressure of an increasing population. However, the end of occupation at the fort was apparently sudden and enforced as there are signs that the defences were deliberately slighted. It is tempting to associate this destruction with the coming of the Romans, though, of course, it may have been much later, during, perhaps, the largely undocumented turbulence of the early medieval period.

Outside the south and west sides of the main fort, and within the fort on the north and east are a number of terraced, soil-filled enclosures surrounded by drystone walls with simple entrances. These may have been cultivation plots used by the Iron Age farmers for arable, or for the enclosure of animals. On the slopes to the north-east and south-west are a number of drystone round-houses which may be contemporary with the occupation of the hillfort. Easiest to find are a group just to the south of the prominent Bronze Age cairn of Carn Briw to the south-west. Whether these small houses and attached enclosures represent separate farms sheltering below the hillfort to which they owed allegiance and from which they obtained protection, or, alternatively, represent extramural settlement attached to the hillfort in some way, we will probably never know.

The hillfort's name is translated as 'Rock of the Angels' and derives from a tradition that it was here that St Brynach met and talked with angels.

53
Carn Ffoi, Newport
Iron Age hillfort
Late 1st millennium BC
OS 145   SN 049379   U2

From W side of Newport on A487, take Gwaun Valley road, 0.8ml (1.3km) down this road, opposite track on RHS, park and walk 200m to outcrop on LHS of road. Site can also be reached by walking 1ml (1.6km) NW across ridge from Carn Ingli (no. 52)

The small oval hillfort of Carn Ffoi lies on a slight, rocky summit on the west of the Carn Ingli section of the Preseli range. Its single, drystone rampart, now very spread through collapse, incorporates three natural rock outcrops. It is badly disturbed on the east but survives to a height of about 3m on the other sides where it incorporates some large upright stones. There is now no sign of a ditch outside the stone rampart, and it is most likely that sufficient stone existed in the natural scree to provide material for the rampart without a quarry ditch needing to be painfully hewn out from the rock.

There are now two gaps in the rampart, one each on the west and south, which are probably the sites of original entrances. The southern one is approached by a stone-lined trackway, which may be an original feature. A number of drystone hut circles may be seen along the line of the rampart. The domed interior of the enclosure is overlooked by higher ground to the east which must have created a weakness in defence. It would be interesting to understand the relationship between this site and Carn Ingli (no. 52), its much larger neighbour nearby to the east.

Aerial view of Carn Ffoi hillfort

54
Tregynon Fort, Newport
Inland promontory fort
Late 1st millennium BC
OS 145   SN 053345   U2

From Newport on A487, turn S uphill at crossroads in centre of village. At T-junction turn L towards Cilgwyn and Gwm Gwaun. After 2.5ml (4km), turn L at T-junction toward Maenclochog then almost immediately fork R up steep hill. After 2ml (3.2km) turn 1st R, and follow signs to Tregynon Restaurant. Park by restaurant and walk over stile, between ponds, and follow path to R to site

The diminutive promontory fort of Tregynon lies on a wooded ridge overlooking the steeply sloping valley of a small stream near its confluence with the Gwaun river. The semicircular defences are well preserved, and the single bank stands some 4m high above

Tregynon Fort

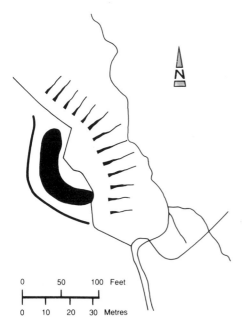

0   50   100 Feet

0   10   20   30 Metres

the bottom of the boggy, encircling ditch. The fort is divided by a modern hedge bank, but a stile provides access between the two halves. On this bank has been placed a panel giving information about the site and the historic landscape around it.

The oval-shaped interior of the enclosure measures about 30m by 20m, and has been mutilated in the past by quarrying and by the erosion caused by a stream which, until recently, ran through the centre of the site. This has now been diverted to flow away from the fort in a small waterfall over the steep, eastern slope. The man-made defences are found only on the gentler western side, as the natural slope on the east is severe enough to make further strengthening unnecessary.

55
Pen Castell and Castell Treruffydd, Moylegrove
Coastal promontory forts
Late 1st millennium BC
OS 145   SN 111459   U2

From Nevern, drive on B4582 E towards Cardigan for 3ml (4.8km) and take LH turn to Moylegrove. In Moylegrove, turn L, then immediately R towards Ceibwr Bay (0.8ml, 1.3km). Park at Bay, then walk along coastal footpath to R (N) for 500m to Pen Castell

Pen Castell lies on an irregular, rocky headland, and the single bank and ditch curve around the eastern, landward side to defend a small, triangular interior. The bank is about 2.5m high externally, and is broken on the south-east where there is a simple gap entrance. The coastal path skirts the site to the east, and there is a modern wall on the outer lip of the ditch.

The promontory fort of Castell Treruffydd (SN 100449) is situated 1ml (1.6km) further south along the coastal path. Return to Ceibwr Bay and continue along the path around the bay to the next irregular inlet at

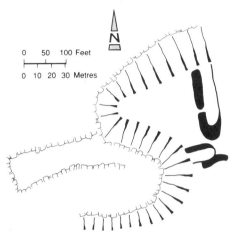

0 50 100 Feet

0 10 20 30 Metres

N

Pen Castell promontory fort

This spectacular hillfort lies on a ridge of high ground south of the rocky coastline at Strumble Head, and dominates the surrounding landscape for miles. Most of the formidable encircling defences are of similar drystone construction to the other north Pembrokeshire hillforts, such as Foel Trigarn and Carn Ingli (nos 49 and 52). At first sight they are quite difficult to make out, as the hillside is strewn with natural rock scree, and also some of the ancient walls have been incorporated into modern field walls. The main plan, however, is not complex.

The inner rampart is well preserved and incorporates four natural rock outcrops in its circuit, which encloses a roughly rectangular, flat area, 0.7ha in extent, now covered with bracken and grass. The wall survives to a height of 1–2m and there is no trace of any ditch. There are, in addition, two outer ramparts on the gentler, east side, which end in crags, and the entrances through the middle of all three walls are inturned for extra protection. Another outer wall on the west forms a triangular annexe to the main hillfort, and short stretches of walling run between outcrops on the precipitous north and south to link the outer defences on the west and east. Finally, the outermost wall on the east is reinforced by a substantial 4m-high bank with an external stone revetment, an outer ditch and a low counterscarp bank. The southern end of this bank seems to have been levelled at some time and a relatively modern well-chamber has been built on top. The innermost wall on the south and west, and the outer western wall have been partly rebuilt as modern field walls. It seems likely that the fort defences were constructed over a period of time, increasing the size and strength of the fort in response, presumably, to an increasing need for space and security.

The level platform for one circular house has been found within the interior of the fort, but a number of rectangular huts lie against the south and west walls. Some of these buildings were noted and sketched by the antiquarian Edward Lhuyd as early as the end of the 17th century. The rectangular huts are

the mouth of the Ffynnon Alwm. The path crosses the interior of the site at the cliff edge. The cliff sides here are especially prone to erosion and a fair amount of the internal area of this fort has slipped into the sea – consequently, the whole site is rather irregular and confused. It has a single curving bank and ditch, with possibly a small section of an outer bank on the south. The entrance is positioned in the centre of the defences.

56
Garn Fawr and Garn Fechan, Llanwnda

Iron Age hillforts

Late 1st millennium BC

OS 157   SM 896388   U3

From Fishguard, take A40 N to Goodwick then turn L towards Llanwnda and Strumble Head. After 3ml (4.8km) turn R opposite Trehillin Farm towards Strumble Head. Fort 0.5ml (0.8km) on LHS. Car park (from which fort is visible); track to fort

Hogg 1974

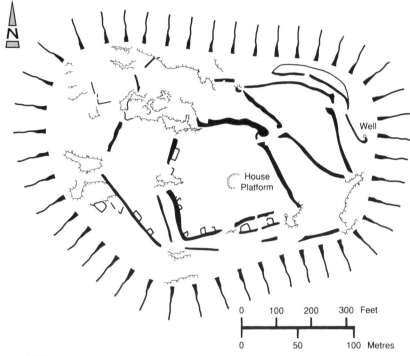

N

Well

House
Platform

| 0 | 100 | 200 | 300 Feet |

| 0 | 50 | 100 Metres |

Garn Fawr hillfort

of inferior construction and are certainly later than the fort wall – it has been suggested that they are medieval. A modern lookout station has been built on one part of the site and an OS beacon stands on another.

Across the road, 300m to the east, is the smaller hillfort of Garn Fechan. This is sited on a secondary knoll on the ridge, and is separated from Garn Fawr by a saddle of lower ground. This smaller enclosure is defended by a 2.6m-high drystone wall, now very collapsed, which incorporates two large outcrops in its circuit. The entrance may be at the existing gap on the north-east side, near which are the remains of a round-house.

West of Garn Fawr at a distance of 450m is the promontory fort of Dinas Mawr (also accessible on coast footpath, near Youth Hostel). The proximity of these three forts suggests that they were connected in some

way, though of course there is no certainty that they were exactly contemporary.

57
Caerau Promontory Forts, St Davids
Iron Age promontory forts
Late 1st millennium BC
OS 157   SM 788308   U4

From St Davids, take A487 towards Fishguard. Fork L on to B4583, then R on to minor road towards Abereiddy. After 4ml (6.4km) take L turn to road marked Caerhys and Llanvirn. 0.7ml (1km) down this road, park in beach car park. Walk back up road to stile and R (W) along signed coastal path 900m to site which lies on path

Caerau forts form an interesting complex, situated along an irregular series of jutting coastal promontories. The two forts are linked together by a bank and ditch and were therefore probably occupied together for at least part of their history. The fort on the east is the simpler, with a single bank and wide outer ditch cutting off the rounded promontory. A slighter bank and ditch links this with the larger, more complex, western fort, which has an impressive system of three banks and ditches. The original entrance is on the south-west, where the banks turn in to provide a defended and twisting passage into the interior. It is most probable that this complex defence system belongs to at least two periods of construction. The modern coastal footpath bisects the entire complex, which assists in access to the site, as the interior tends to be very overgrown.

For those with time to spare, 0.7ml (1km) further west along the coastal path (SM 775303) is Castell Coch, another Iron Age promontory fort. This somewhat eroded promontory is defended by a stout inner bank, a ditch and a slight outer bank. There is a simple gap entrance in the centre of the defences, which are weaker to the north, where the natural slope towards the cliff edge becomes steeper. The partly rock-cut track which leads to the entrance is probably a modern feature, perhaps connected with slate quarrying on the cliffs below.

These promontory forts are characteristic of a number of similar sites which lie on the suitably fractured and rocky coastline from St Dogmaels west to St Davids Head. They are conventionally dated as Iron Age, though few have been excavated. There is no real reason why some sites should not have been occupied in the Romano-British or even the medieval period.

Aerial view of Caerau promontory fort

58
St Davids Head, St Davids
Iron Age coastal promontory fort
Late 1st millennium BC
OS 157   SM 722279   U4   NT

From St Davids, take B4583 (or any signed road) NW to Whitesands Bay and park in beach car park (fee in summer). Take signed coastal footpath R (N) and follow coastline for 1ml (1.6km) to St Davids Head

Baring Gould 1899

The fine coastal fort on the rugged, rocky promontory of St Davids Head is defended by a well-preserved system of one large, now spread, drystone rampart about 100m long, with two lesser stone walls outside, perhaps with shallow ditches between. The main, inner rampart stands about 3m high above the bottom of the outer ditch. The original

stone facing of the rampart may be seen surviving in one or two places. There is now a causeway through the defensive system on the south, which is almost certainly the site of the original entrance. The difference in style between the main, inner and the slighter, outer banks has led to the suggestion that the defences were constructed at different periods. The defences run north–south to cut off the promontory, which is bounded on the north-west and south by high sea cliffs. This naturally strong position is further strengthened by the fact that the headland is partly separated from the mainland by deep natural clefts, which must have made the task of building the necessary additional man-made defences easier still.

The interior of the fort is 3ha in area, but much of the far end of the promontory is now bare rock outcrop. Nearer the defences the footings of six circular stone-walled houses may be seen quite clearly. Four houses lie on the south and, as they are contiguous,

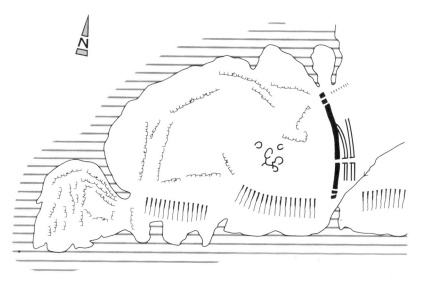

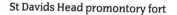
St Davids Head promontory fort

probably acted as a single unit; one of these is a more complex building than the others, and has an annexe on its southern side. The other two houses are free standing, each about 2.4m away from the central group. The buildings are roughly circular, 4.5–6m in diameter, with walls about 1m thick. They each have one simple gap entrance.

Small-scale excavations at the fort in 1898 opened some of the houses and uncovered their entrances and central hearths. Glass beads, flints, spindle whorls and pottery were found and may now be seen in Tenby Museum.

In the moorland to the east of the fort is a fine series of field systems and enclosures bounded by low stone walls which start and finish in the rock outcrops on each side of the valley. The fields may well be contemporary with the use of the fort, and indeed contemporary with the even more extensive series of fields on Skomer Island (no. 67). The fields are not easy to see, as the bracken tends to obscure them in summer – the best view is from the summit of Garn Llidi on the south, on a fine day in early spring.

59
Castell Heinif, St Davids
Iron Age coastal promontory fort
Late 1st millennium BC
OS 157   SM 724247   U2   NT

From St Davids take minor road W to St Justinians and park in car park. Walk down to coastal footpath and follow it L (S) for 0.3ml (0.5km) to site

The small promontory fort of Castell Heinif has been much eroded by the sea, but the single bank and the ditch which curve around the eastern landward side are still impressive. On the particularly gentle southern approach a supplementary defence has been created by a second, outer bank being interposed between the inner bank and ditch in a manner characteristic of the promontory forts of this

area. The interior is about 0.3ha in area, and slopes gently towards the sea; both the interior and the defences must originally have been far greater in extent before their severe coastal erosion. There are gaps through the defences on the north and south, which could be the site of entrances; the southern gap looks the most convincing, but of course the position of the original entrance could have been lost to the sea.

60
Clegyr Boia, St Davids
Neolithic and Iron Age site
4th and late 1st millennium BC
OS 157   SM 737251   U2

From St Davids, take minor road W towards St Justinians. Fork L on to Porthclais road and after 0.5ml (0.8km) turn R at crossroads. Site is on rocky outcrop by track on RHS of road leading to Clegyr Boia Farm, 1.5ml (2.4km) from St Davids

Williams 1952

The small rocky hillock of Clegyr Boia stands prominent in the bleak landscape west of St Davids. This naturally defensible site has been further strengthened by a rampart which incorporates a number of outcrops in its circuit. On the north-east a second, outer rampart adds to the defence of the gentler approach. The level rectangular enclosure measures 85m by 28m, and occupies rather more than half of the southern side of the summit.

Excavations here in 1902 and 1943 showed that the hill had originally been occupied in the Neolithic period. Round and rectangular huts of timber and daub, some with wall footings of stone, were found, one under the later rampart, and a Neolithic midden or rubbish heap lay on the west. The excavators discovered many sherds of a hard round-bottomed pottery found also at burial chambers such as Carreg Coetan (no. 5), along

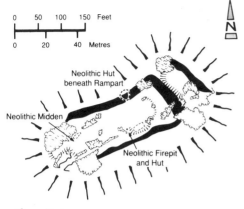

0   50   100   150 Feet

0   20   40 Metres

Neolithic Hut beneath Rampart

Neolithic Midden

Neolithic Firepit and Hut

Clegyr Boia

century AD rather than Iron Age. Another
exciting possibility is that the defences are
contemporary with the later of the Neolithic
houses. Neolithic defended hilltop sites have
recently been discovered elsewhere in Britain,
though they are as yet a rarely recognised
type of monument.

61
Caerfai and Porth y Rhaw Forts, St Davids

Iron Age coastal promontory forts
Late 1st millennium BC
OS 157   SM 763240   U4   NT

*From E outskirts of St Davids on A487 take 1st
R towards Caerfai Bay. Follow road to Caerfai
Bay, and park in Bay car park. Walk on to
signed coastal path and follow path to L 500m
to site*

with polished stone axes and flint scrapers.
The discovery of a Neolithic settlement, one of
the first to be found in Wales, was of foremost
importance, and few other examples have
been found to date.

Some time after this initial settlement, the
hill was reoccupied. The later settlers built
their defensive rampart over the site of one or
more of the earlier huts. The earthen rampart
had an inner and outer stone revetment and
on the south-west was a complex inturned
entrance, with a stone revetment, double
timber gates and a roofed guardroom.

The excavations uncovered no houses
which were demonstrably contemporary with
the rampart, nor were any distinctive Iron Age
artefacts discovered. The defended
settlement was thought to be Iron Age
because of the appearance of the small round
stone-built 'guard chambers' within the gate
structure of the rampart; however, the
paucity of artefacts meant that the date of the
fort was never proved. The name Clegyr Boia
('Stronghold of Boia') associates the site with
the 6th-century Irishman Boia who challenged
the removal of St David's religious house to its
present position, and who was killed and his
stronghold taken and destroyed by his
countryman Lisci in AD 520. There remains
the possibility that the fort is indeed 6th-

The irregular, rocky promontory of Caerfai
has been impressively defended by a series of
four massive banks and ditches, and the
sheer extent of these defences makes this site
striking and unusual. The small size of the
interior seems out of proportion with the
scale of the defences, but doubtless much of
the promontory has fallen into the sea. The
banks and ditches lie on the north, landward
side, and the entrance is on the east.
Immediately south of this, the neck of the
promontory narrows dramatically over a
natural arch over the sea, but the interior then
opens out to a gently sloping rectangular
area. Three hut circles have been noted in the
interior.

Porth y Rhaw promontory fort (SN 786242)
is another 1.5ml (2.4km) eastward along the
coastal path. This, too, has been eroded by
the sea, but the defences and gate system of
the fort are more impressive. A large outer
ditch defends and connects three small
promontories, the eastern two of which are
also defended by a triple bank and ditch
system. The entrance on the east, which

forces the incomer to turn a series of S-bends before entering the fort, is especially impressive and would have been a formidable defensive feature. The complex form of the earthworks is almost certainly the end result of several phases of construction. The easternmost promontory contains what is probably the remains of a round-house, 9m in diameter.

62
Solva Head, Solva
Iron Age promontory fort
Late 1st millennium BC
OS 157   SM 802239   U2   NT

From St Davids, drive on A487 Haverfordwest road E for 3ml (4.8km) to Solva and park in harbour car park. Walk across footbridge over stream and take coastal footpath R on to promontory overlooking sea

The craggy, triangular promontory of Solva Head stands at the end of a high, narrow coastal ridge overlooking the harbour. The headland has been enclosed by a single bank and ditch which encircle the entire site. On the landward, north-east side, the bank is enlarged to form a massive defensive structure up to 3.6m high, with an external ditch. A second, outer bank and ditch system provide an additional defence on this gentler approach.

The site is crossed by the coastal footpath, but the interior and defences become very overgrown with wildflowers. There are apparently the traces of house platforms in the interior, but these tend to be obscured by the growth. The views of the village and harbour of Solva and the adjacent coastline are very splendid, and this fact, coupled with the easy accessibility of the site and the proximity of Solva's excellent tea places, makes this site a pleasant spot for a family afternoon out.

63
Treffgarne Rocks Fort, Wolf's Castle
Iron Age hillfort
Late 1st millennium BC
OS 157   SM 956250   U2

From Wolf's Castle, S of Fishguard on A40, drive S for 0.6ml (1km) and park in lay-by on RHS by Nant y Coy Mill. Walk up road marked Public Footpath just beyond lay-by, then take path on LHS on to open moorland. Fork L to follow path to site on rock outcrop on LHS

The oval interior of this spectacular sited fort, 0.25ha in area, is defended by a single bank and ditch on the west, north-east and south sides, with an additional outer bank on the gentler western approach. On the east the Treffgarne rocks are themselves incorporated within the defensive bank, though the slope is precipitous on this side. The inner rampart stands up to 4m in height on the west and the outer bank is 1.8m high. The ditches are also well preserved. The entrance was probably on the south, where the banks turn in on either side of a break.

The setting of the hillfort is made especially dramatic by the extraordinarily shaped rock outcrop which overlooks it on the west, and which is visible for miles around. Between this outcrop and the fort are a number of round-houses which may well be contemporary with the hillfort. They do tend to become very overgrown in summer and are consequently difficult to find.

The hillfort is noteworthy as it forms an apparent focus for a number of smaller, circular defended enclosures situated along the sloping valley sides to the north and east. They may well be contemporary and may have had some subordinate relationship with the hillfort, perhaps producing agricultural goods for the dominant family in the hillfort in return for the protection afforded by this territorial organisation. This grouping of sites may well have been common throughout

Treffgarne Rocks hillfort from the air

Dyfed in the Iron Age, but in most areas the vulnerable smaller sites have been destroyed. Here we have a hint of how the countryside in the 1st millennium BC may have been organised. One of these smaller sites can be seen from the hillfort to the north-west on the skyline beyond the small wooded valley and the track beyond.

Four of the smaller farmsteads lie in the woodland across the main road, and two may be visited as they lie along a public footpath. Take the left turn to Spittal, to the south, and park near the railway bridge. Walk down the signed track to the left for 400m and, at the house, follow the signed path to the left, to a pair of gates. Take the signed path left into the wood, follow it for 400m, across a stile and through the conifers for 400m, and the site is

bisected by the track (at SM 961245), half in the forest, half in the adjacent field. The sloping enclosure is surrounded by a single bank and ditch. The northern site (at SM 961248) is a little further along the track in a clearing on the right of the path. It is a simple, circular enclosure, 30m in diameter, with a single bank 1m in height. Both sites are good examples of the unspectacular hillslope enclosures which are so common a site type in south-west Dyfed. Another of them (at SM 959233) is visible from the A40 at a point 500m north of the Spittal turn, in woodland on the western roadside. It is a small circular enclosure (40m in diameter), which has a single bank and ditch, and an embanked entrance-way leading into the site from the south-west.

64
Crundale Rath, Haverfordwest

Iron Age defended farmstead
Late 1st millennium BC
OS 157   SM 985189   U2

*On N outskirts of Haverfordwest on A40
Fishguard road, fork R on to B4329. After 1ml
(1.6km), fork R towards Clarbeston Road. After
1.3ml (2km), park opposite Little Rathe farm
and walk through gate on to public footpath
(unsigned) on RHS of road. Walk up slope
keeping to path by hedge, to site on summit on
RHS in adjacent field*

This circular hilltop enclosure – characteristic
of many in south-west Dyfed, often termed
'raths' after somewhat similar sites in Ireland

– is known variously as Crundale Rath,
Rudbaxton Rath or simply 'The Rath'. It lies on
the summit of a small hill and is defended by a
double bank-and-ditch system. On the north,
where the slope is naturally steeper, the outer
bank peters out, though it has been further
reduced by cultivation. On all other sides the
two banks and the ditch between them are
well preserved and impressive, though there
is now no trace of the outer ditch.

The original, simple entrance was probably
on the north side; the gap on the south-east is
modern. Just visible within the interior is a
low, semicircular bank which encloses a small
area on the south-west. This may be the result
of a refurbishment of the hillfort in the
medieval period – hence the fresher, more
acute angle of the probably reconstituted
bank and recut ditch, and hence also the
inner division, which formed, perhaps, the
inner stronghold of the castle. Two iron rings

Crundale Rath

(torcs?) and an iron model of a hand, probably votive, were found here in about 1865, and are now in the British Museum.

The medieval St Leonard's chapel lay on the slope of the north-eastern bank, but nothing now remains save its St Leonard's Well, restored in the early years of this century. The chapel was granted to the Knights of St John, Commandery of Slebech.

65
Mill Haven and Howney Stone Forts, Talbenny
Iron Age coastal promontory forts
Late 1st millennium BC
OS 157   SM 817125–SN 820128   U2

From Haverfordwest, take B4327 towards Dale. After 7ml (11km), at Hasguard Cross, take minor road R to Talbenny (1ml, 1.6km) and at crossroads travel straight on along track for 1ml (1.6km). Park by farmhouses on L and continue along track, past Lower Broadmoor Farm to coastal footpath (signed). Turn R on to path; short walk to Mill Haven fort

Mill Haven Fort (the southernmost of the pair) is characteristic of the simpler coastal promontory forts of this area. It has only a single bank and ditch which form a semicircular defence on the south-eastern, landward side. A simple gap in the centre of the system is the site of the entrance, which leads into the long, gently sloping interior. It has been suggested that the level area against the rampart just inside the entrance might indicate the site of one or two houses.

Howney Stone Fort (SN 820128), which is reached by continuing northwards along the coastal footpath for another 300m, is a rather more sophisticated affair. The promontory is cut off by one high inner bank and a ditch, and has an entrance in the centre. However, south of the entrance, a second, outer bank and ditch curve around to add to the defence of the gateway, and force a oblique and narrow route to the interior. The ditches seem to be at least partly rock-cut. The interior is about 0.5ha in area.

66
Deer Park Fort, Marloes
Iron Age coastal promontory fort
Late 1st millennium BC
OS 157   SM 755090   U2   NT

From Haverfordwest, take B4327 SW towards Dale. After 10ml (16km), take minor road R to

Deer Park fort

76

Marloes, drive through village and continue 2ml (3.2km) to road's end in Martinshaven. Car park just by site

The 20ha promontory of Deer Park is defended along the eastern neck by a single bank, and the natural slope outside has then been scarped to increase the defence and give the impression of a much higher bank. Towards its southern end, where the slope flattens out, an external ditch has been added and the bank increases in height as it approaches the entrance. The entrance is on the south, and has a supplementary defence in the form of a second L-shaped inner bank which forms a sinuous entrance passage into the interior. A second entrance, 75m to the north, is slightly inturned and is probably original. A few flint flakes have apparently been found in the huge fort interior.

The promontory takes its name from the deer park which was planned here as an enhancement of the Edwardes' estate. There is no evidence that deer were, in the event, ever introduced. More in evidence are the red-beaked choughs, a rare member of the crow family, which nest here.

The smaller promontory fort of Watery Bay lies 0.7ml further south-east (left) along the footpath. It has a fine triple bank and ditch system defending the rocky promontory on the landward north-east side. The defences inturn to protect the entrance which is on the east.

67
Skomer Island, Marloes
Iron Age settlement and field system
Late 1st millennium BC
OS 157   SM 715090   U2   CCW/
Dyfed Wildlife Trust

From Haverfordwest, take B4327 Dale road for 10ml (16km). Turn R to Marloes, follow road 2ml (3.2km) to Martinshaven. Boats to Skomer from Martinshaven harbour, most days,

10.30am, May to Sept (tel. National Park: 0437 764591 ext. 5135 for details)

Evans 1986 and Guidebook

The island of Skomer is an archaeological paradise because of the extraordinary survival of its many prehistoric remains. It has in recent centuries been used primarily for grazing, which has helped in this preservation. The 19th-century fields are confined to the centre of the island; elsewhere the field banks, houses and enclosures are all ancient.

The rectilinear prehistoric fields have low boundaries formed by lines of stones or earth and stone banks, which originally would, of course, have been considerably higher. Other fields on sloping ground are demarcated by lynchets, or 'steps', formed when soil, loosened by cultivation, creeps downhill to pile up against a field boundary. These field systems can be seen all around the island, while the settlement sites are concentrated in cohesive groups on the south-west, south, east and north. The settlements are remarkably well preserved, composed of groups of the footings of small stone-built round-houses, field-clearance cairns and small irregular plots. The houses, often built in pairs, may have had thatched roofs supported by a single central post at the apex and by the house walls at the base.

An archaeological trail has been established around the island. First, near the landing point on the east, is Haroldstone, a Bronze Age standing stone visible on the skyline from the sea. Prehistoric field boundaries may be seen nearby. The trail continues west, then north (right) to pass a concentration of field boundaries and three groups of linked round-houses, two of which have been laid out for display. A rectangular stone-walled enclosure 120m to the north-west may have been used for some specialised work with animals such as sheep shearing. A group of nine small burial cairns lies further north on the trail, not far from the northern cliffs.

Field boundaries and cairn groups may be

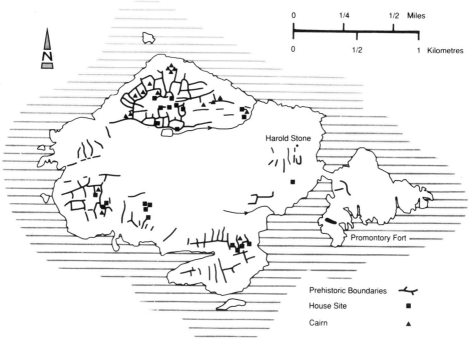

Skomer Island

seen on the trail on the south-west and all along the south of the island. Some longer rectangular fields on the centre of the south coast are especially well preserved. Another group of houses, this time all separate dwellings but still clearly associated with field boundaries, lie on the south side of the valley of the Wick stream.

South of the Neck, (normally inaccessible, reserved for birds) is South Castle promontory fort, defended by a single bank and ditch broken by a simple entrance which has an additional outer bank to its west. The lack of field systems on the Neck is noteworthy, perhaps reflecting the military character of this section of the island which may have been a refuge in time of danger. Not all the houses on Skomer were necessarily inhabited at the same time, and some may be earlier or later than the fort. The prehistoric settlement of the island, with perhaps 100–200 people,

may have been quite short-lived – there are comparatively few houses, and the field systems seem to remain as first laid out with none of the subdivisions or alterations which might suggest a longer occupation.

68
Dale and Great Castle Head Forts, Dale
Iron Age promontory forts
1st millennium BC
OS 157 SM 822052 U2

From Haverfordwest, take B4327 SW to Dale (12ml, 19km). After passing harbour, take minor road L to Dale Fort. 0.7ml (1km) down this road, there is just room to park before Field Study Centre gate, where signed footpath joins road on RHS. Follow path into field and on to Dale fort

Benson and Williams 1987

The promontory fort at Dale Point must have been a large and important settlement. Its extent is now less easy to appreciate because the seaward end of the promontory has been built on by one of the mid-19th-century Milford Haven forts, which has, in turn, been converted into a Field Studies Centre. A single straight bank and ditch and a slighter, outer bank cuts off the promontory across the narrow neck. The simple gap entrance lies in the centre of the defences.

Excavations at the fort show that there had been occupation on the headland well before the Iron Age. The discovery of beaker pottery and a few traces of early pre-fort structures suggest that there was probably some sort of settlement here in the early Bronze Age. The fort itself was shown to have had a long and complex occupation, and there were several distinct phases in the defences. Firstly, a series of timber palisades, and a bank with a stone revetment were built to defend the headland in the Late Bronze Age. These were later replaced by an Iron Age defensive bank strengthened with internal stonework. A series of radiocarbon dates, centering around 790 BC, were taken from an occupation

surface which lay between these two phases of defences and are the earliest dates yet taken from a Dyfed hillfort. Perhaps the equable climate of this area, and its suitability for arable cultivation, helped the population to resist, or recover from, social or climatic crises in the later Bronze Age.

The gate of the Iron Age fort was evidently a formidable structure; the excavations revealed massive sockets dug for the gate timbers. The stone revetment on the front of the Iron Age defensive bank was also uncovered and some of this stonework remains open for display. Outside the bank was a deep ditch, still partially visible.

Castle Head promontory fort (SM 798057) lies on the opposite, west side of the Dale peninsula. Return to Dale harbour and follow the one-way system to the church. Turn left on to the minor road opposite the church, and 500m down this road, park by the signed access path to the coastal path. Walk down to the coast path and turn left. The site is 20m along the path, on the next promontory.

The promontory fort consists of a roughly level, triangular-shaped nose of land which has been defended on the eastern, landward side by a double system of banks and ditches. A slighter third bank has been interposed in places on the north. The geological faulting in the bedrock, which has resulted in an abrupt change in level, makes the promontory stronger still. A simple gap entrance lies in the centre of the banks and ditches. The interior is small in comparison with the impressive defences, and has presumably suffered considerably from coastal erosion. Two worked flints from the site are in Tenby Museum.

69
Priory Rath, Milford Haven
Iron Age defended farmstead
Late 1st millennium BC
OS 157   SM 905071   U1

Dale promontory fort, stone revetment on defensive bank

From Milford Haven (7ml, 11km SW of Haverfordwest), follow A4076 towards

Priory Rath from the air

70
Bosherston and Flimston Forts, Bosherston
Iron Age promontory forts
Late 1st millennium BC
OS 158   SR 971948   U2   NT

From Pembroke, take B4319 Castlemartin road S for 2.7ml (6km), then take minor road on L to Bosherston (1.3ml, 2km). Park in National Park car park and follow signposted circular Fishponds walk clockwise (to L). Bosherston fort lies over first bridge on promontory above lakeside walk

Haverfordwest for 0.3ml (0.5km). At Steynton crossroads, opposite pub, take LH turn (W) towards Thornton. After 1.3ml (2km), turn L into Howarth Close. Follow estate road round to L, and park at top of hill. Site just by road

Not all Iron Age defended settlements are on hilltops or on promontories. Some are on the sides of hills and are called 'hillslope enclosures'. Dyfed has a fair number of these, but few are accessible to the public. This large but not tremendously attractive site, visible from the road, must suffice as an example.

The circular, sloping interior is surrounded by a bank, 3.3m high, an external ditch and a slight counterscarp bank which together provide a wide and formidable defence system. The defences on the south and east are impressive but peter out on the west and north where the natural slope alone sufficed and was merely scarped to enhance its strength. The defences on these sides have suffered considerably from plough erosion, but are still visible as low undulations in the field. There was only one entrance into the enclosure, and it lies on the south.

Bosherston promontory fort is situated on a roughly triangular promontory of high ground between two steep valleys, probably originally coastal creeks. The point of the headland is cut off and defended by a 180m-long double bank and ditch system on the landward north-west side. A third bank with no ditch lies 30m inside the promontory, with smaller lateral banks attaching it to the main defences. A separate internal enclosure is thus formed, used, perhaps, for the herding in of livestock. Further in again are the remains of another slighter bank and ditch which may have belonged to an earlier defensive system. A simple entrance is sited towards the southern end of the ramparts and leads straight through the outer three defences, but not apparently through the inner; this supports the idea that this inner defence is earlier in date.

The interior tends to be very overgrown, and the entire site can be difficult to enter, but a programme of selective clearance is being carried out by the National Trust to make access easier. When the growth is not excessive, the terraced positions of round timber houses can be traced within the fort. Excavations in the 1920s uncovered a midden, or rubbish heap, in the main ditch, in which an Iron Age ring-headed pin was found.

To visit Flimston Fort (SR 926945), drive further down the road to St Govan's Head and

Bosherston promontory fort

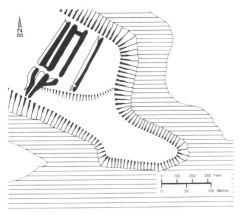

Aerial view of Flimston promontory fort

park in the car park at the end of the road. This is a restricted road through the army range and access along the road is forbidden when the red flag is flying to show that firing is in progress. Walk along the coastal footpath to the right (west). After 1ml (1.6km), the promontory fort known as Buckspool Down Camp at Castle Head may be seen. A curving series of three banks and ditches defend a triangular promontory, but the fort has been rather disturbed in the past by quarrying.

Another 1½ml (2.4km) walk reaches Crockysdam Fort, a rather feeble promontory fort where a single semicircular bank and ditch cuts off a sloping rocky headland. Flimston Fort is another 0.5ml (0.8km) away.

A superb series of three banks and ditches cuts off an irregular promontory which has suffered evident erosion from the sea, and is almost certainly much reduced in size since the Iron Age. The external bank is 30m from the two smaller inner banks, and this arrangement of defences, so widely spaced as to form what is almost an outer annexe, is reminiscent of Bosherston.

71
Greenala Fort, Lamphey
Iron Age coastal promontory fort
Late 1st millennium BC
OS 158   SS 007966   U4

From Pembroke, take A4139 E to Lamphey, then turn R along B4584 to Freshwater East (1.7ml, 2.7km). Turn R on to Stackpole road and 0.5ml (0.8km) along road, park in Freshwater East car park (charge). Walk over bridge and join coastal footpath (signed) to R. Walk for 1.3ml (2km) to site on Greenala Point

The irregular, rocky headland at Greenala Point has been impressively cut off from the mainland by a massive series of four banks and ditches. The defences encircle the main promontory on the northern, landward side, and the three outer earthworks are extended westwards, to enclose another, smaller area, which has the effect of adding to the defence of the entrance. The outer entrance is positioned in the centre of the northern defences, but from here a long, narrow and sinuous passage leads to the inner gate which is on the west. This is defined by the innermost bank which, at its western end, runs south to protect the inner enclosure. This bank is inturned at the centrally-positioned inner gate, as an extra defence. The defences may well have been altered and extended in more than one period of construction.

The interior of the fort, 0.5ha in area, is small in comparison with the magnificence of the defences and undoubtedly much of it been lost to the sea. Numbers of round-houses have been noted in the interior, but these are obscured and difficult to see on the ground. On the cliff side, the remains of a kitchen midden and a skeleton were found in the last century.

72
Park Rath, Carew
Iron Age defended farmstead
Late 1st millennium BC
OS 158   SN 063048   U2

From Pembroke, travel NW on A4075 St Clears road for 2ml (3.2km), then turn R on to A477. After 1.5ml (2.4km), turn L on to A4075 Haverfordwest road, past Carew Castle, for 1.6ml (2.5km). At crossroads, turn R, follow road for 300m and park at track on RHS. Walk down track to Park Farm. Site is on RHS of house. Access kindly allowed down private drive by owners of Park Farm; public footpath passes between house and site which is easily visible from footpath

Park Rath

The small enclosure at Park is another of the so-called 'raths' of South Pembrokeshire (see no. 64), which are simple defended farmsteads, usually circular in shape, built probably for an extended family group rather than a larger unit of people. Although these comparatively inconspicuous sites are vulnerable to damage from cultivation, many do survive and are especially characteristic of the Iron Age in south-west Dyfed. Park Rath is a rather charming example hidden away among the fields north-east of Carew Castle (no. 113).

The enclosure has a circular, slightly dished interior, and enclosing it are a single bank and ditch with, in places, an outer counterscarp bank now incorporated into a modern hedge bank. There are gaps in the defences on the north and south; the southern one is almost certainly the original entrance, while the northern one is probably a modern break.

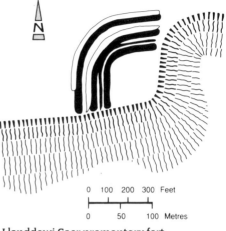

Llanddewi Gaer promontory fort

73
Llanddewi Gaer, Llanddewi Velfrey
Iron Age inland promontory fort
Late 1st millennium BC
OS 158   SN 145161   U4

From St Clears, take A40 W toward Haverfordwest for 8.5ml (13.6km) to Llanddewi Velfrey. Take 1st L just past Preseli Filling Station and, after 300m, turn R at crossroads. Follow road another 600m to public footpath sign near Penbanc. Park and cross stile on LHS. Walk along field, past OS beacon on LHS. Obliquely opposite beacon, cross another stile and walk down long narrow field. Another stile at the bottom leads on to outer ditch of site. Very overgrown by bracken in summer

This is a fine inland promontory fort of massive proportions. The natural slopes on the south and east down into the valley were almost sufficient defence and were only strengthened by a slight scarping. On the flat north and west, however, a fine series of three banks and ditches curve around to cut off the nose of high land. The formidable defences are about 52m wide overall, and berms of flat ground of between 4.5m and 6m in width divide the inside face of each bank from the outer lip of the next ditch. The fact that the central bank is not quite concentric with the inner and outer banks, and indeed at one point actually clips the innermost ditch, suggests that the fort originally had only two widely spaced defences; this would have provided an outer enclosure some 24m wide. Later the middle bank and ditch were inserted to meet, perhaps, an increased need for defence which outweighed the desirability of retaining the outer enclosure.

It is unfortunate that the site is so obscured with scrub both in the flat interior and on the defences which, however, remain most impressive. The entrance is on the eastern end of the northern defences, and the natural slope on the east forms one side of the entrance passage which is 52m long. A striking feature of the fort is the small size of the interior compared with the massive defences, which have an overall area three times greater than the 61m-square interior.

74
Gilman Point Fort, Pendine
Iron Age coastal promontory fort
Late 1st millennium BC
OS 158   SN 228076   U4

From St Clears, take A4066 via Laugharne 8ml (12.8km) to Pendine and park (crowded in season). Climb coastal footpath on W end of

bay *(near Cliff Snack Bar), and follow for 800m to site on highest point of first headland*

The large promontory fort at Gilman Point lies on high moorland 90m above sea level. It is naturally defended on the east, south and west, and the landward northern and north-western sides have been defended by a massive curving bank and ditch. The rock-cut ditch is 1.5m deep, and the bank stands some 3.3m above it. A second, slighter bank and ditch lie a considerable distance inside the enclosure, and effectively divide the interior into two. This may be an earlier defence abandoned when the site was extended, or a contemporary or later subdivision of the interior.

Just to the north of the outer defences is a circular enclosure about 45m in diameter, with walls of stone blocks and an inturned entrance. The fact that the ditch of the promontory fort clips the enclosure suggests that this circle is earlier.

There are reports of there being traces of round-houses in the interior both of the fort and of the northern enclosure, but they are usually obscured by bracken and grass and are virtually impossible to find. Also there are traces of possibly contemporary field walls on the slopes on the west, again rather obscured by the dense vegetation.

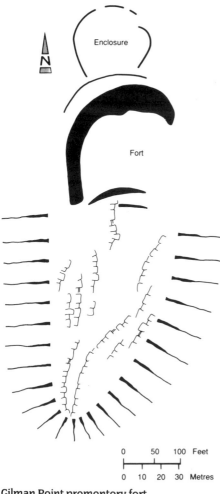

0   50   100 Feet

0   10   20   30 Metres

Gilman Point promontory fort

75
Allt Goch and Goetre Forts, Lampeter
Iron Age defended enclosures
Late 1st millennium BC
OS 146   SN 593501, 603510   U4

From S side of Lampeter, take minor road L (E) before river bridge towards Llanfair Clydogau, for 1.5ml, and park on road. Walk up long track to Bwlchgwynt farm on LHS of road. At farm, follow track to L and across 2 fields to site on RHS, skirted by woodland. Map advisable

Castell Allt Goch is an oval hilltop enclosure consisting of a single bank and ditch defending a sloping interior, with a supplementary system of two banks and ditches on the gentler eastern slope. It seems that the enclosure was originally smaller, and was confined to the northern half of the present site, as a bank, now rather eroded by cultivation but still quite visible, bisects the interior from east to west, and probably formed the earlier enclosure defence. The bank of the main enclosure is in good condition, but the external ditch has disappeared save for a stretch alongside the eastern defences and a slight dip outside the bank on the west. The entrance was probably on the west, and may have served the original enclosure in its south-west corner, as well as the later, enlarged site. The outer defences on the east have been eroded by cultivation but survive up to 1m in height.

The larger enclosure of Castell Goetre lies to the east. Follow the footpath alongside the woodland, keeping the wood to the left, through seven fields, through gates and stiles. Then turn left, to follow the footpath which skirts Castell Goetre on the west,

allowing a reasonable view of the fort. The interior of the enclosure has been divided into five fields, making the entirety of the site difficult to appreciate, but the main circuit of the defences remains reasonably clear, despite some drastic clearance and cultivation in places. The defences consist of a single bank and ditch and an external counterscarp bank which encircle the site, though they are now virtually invisible on the north. A small stretch of defences on the wooded north-eastern side is well preserved and gives an indication of the appearance of this site before erosion by ploughing.

76
Garn Goch Forts, Llandeilo
Iron Age hillforts
Late 1st millennium BC
OS 159, 160   SN 690243   U3
Brecon Beacons National Park

From Llandeilo, travel S along A483 to Ffairfach crossroads. Turn L (E), and keep L to follow river for 3.4ml (5.4km). Turn R, follow road for 1.2ml (1.9km) (past RH turn to Trapp) to rough track on R (signed) on to common. Park at end of track (from which fort can be seen) and walk up path

Hogg 1974

The western end of the rocky ridge of Garn Goch is the site of two well-preserved hillforts. The larger of the two, known as Gaer Fawr (or 'Great Fort') lies on the eastern summit. The 11ha oval interior is surrounded by a single massive stone-built wall with an additional outer rampart on the north-west. The main wall incorporates a number of natural outcrops and varies in strength from the massive western section, where it is 6.5m high and some 25m wide, down to the far slighter wall on the two steep long sides. It is now very ruinous, but there are a few places where its facework survives, especially on the better-preserved sections on the west. The

Allt Goch hillfort

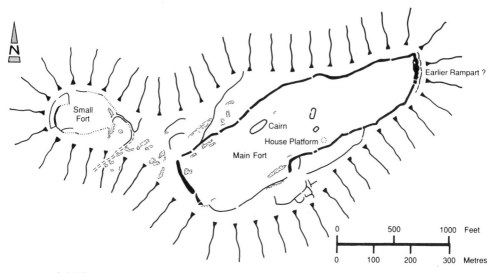

Garn Goch hillforts

outer stone wall on the north runs at some distance from the main rampart to form an annexe, which, however, is unenclosed on the east; perhaps it was never completed. It is almost certainly secondary and adds another 4ha to the enclosed area.

There are eight openings through the rampart, all lined with upright slabs and probably all original gates. The wide gap on the north-east may be the main entrance, while the broad gateway on the south-west was obviously also important. There are six further small 'posterns', four on the north-west and two on the south-east. The hillfort may have been preceded by an earlier, slightly larger fort: outside the eastern and south-eastern rampart are two stretches of an earth-and-rubble bank, incorporating two gateways which could be the remnants of an earlier defence system. It is only visible on the east, and may have been destroyed by, or lie beneath, the later walls elsewhere.

The interior of the fort is very overgrown with bracken, which tends to obscure the traces of the single round-house on the south. Prominent within the interior, however, is a

large drystone cairn, which is probably a Neolithic or Bronze Age burial mound. There are also two irregular stone structures which may be later sheep folds, but could possibly be Iron Age.

Gaer Fach (or 'Small Fort') lies 183m to the west. This is a smaller, roughly circular site, 1.5ha in area, defended by a single weak drystone rampart. On the west a second wall has been added, built of laid slabs of stone, different in style from the outer, earlier wall. It was probably never finished, as it stops abruptly on the south after only 100m. The entrance to the fort is on the east, where two out-turned ramparts form a narrow passageway for 60m down the slope into the saddle of lower ground between the two forts, though at the bottom it turns away from the larger fort and does not seem to pass directly to it. This, coupled with the fact that the main entrances of Gaer Fawr apparently lead away from, rather than towards, the smaller fort, does suggest that the two forts were not occupied at the same time. In Gaer Fach, also, a single round-house has been discovered.

77
Pen Dinas Lochtyn, Llangranog
Iron Age hillfort
Late 1st millennium BC
OS 145   SN 315548   U2   NT

From A487, 12ml (19km) SW of Aberaeron, 10ml (16km) NE of Cardigan, take either B4334 or B4321 W to Llangranog and park on beach car park. Climb steps of coastal footpath on RHS (N) and follow path up slope to stile on RHS. Cross stile and follow path through field to stile at small quarry at junction of two tracks to LHS. Take RH track and cross stile by gate. Follow road up slope, keeping L at next junction, through gate to site

This prominent coastal hillfort is well sited on a high, rocky hillock overlooking the sea, and commands extensive views on all sides over the Cardigan Bay coastline. So strong are the natural defences that the height of the man-made banks on the inside of the fort is negligible. The outer slopes of the oval hilltop have been scarped on the west, south and east to form a high defensive bank up to 2.5m high externally, and traces of an external ditch remain. The defences are strongest on the landward east side, and weakest on the strongly sloping sea-facing west and north. Traces of an internal ditch, probably used as a quarry for material for the defences, may be seen along the west side. The original entrance was on the east and is now used by the modern road. The interior of the fort is about 1.5ha. Excavations in the interior have uncovered traces of round-houses and other domestic buildings of the inhabitants.

With the same appreciation of the strategic strength of the site as the Iron Age fort builders, the Ministry of Defence maintains a small station on the fort for tracking the flight paths of missiles. Apart from the station building, however, the fort enjoys open access and visits are quite safe.

78
Castell Bach Fort, Newquay
Iron Age coastal promontory fort
Late 1st millennium BC
OS 145   SN 360581   U2   NT

From Aberaeron, take A487 SW towards Cardigan. After 7ml (11.2km), turn R on to A486 Newquay road. After 2ml (3.2km), at Cross Inn turn L toward Llwyndafydd, and at 1st crossroads (1.5ml, 2.4km) turn R toward Cwmtydu. Drive 2ml (3.2km) to sea and park at beach car park. Take coastal footpath R (N) past Heritage Trail panel along National Trust land for 0.5ml (0.8km). Site on coast below path

This is a rather unusual promontory fort. The headland on which it stands is broad and flat and is overlooked by higher land to the south, which must presumably have been a weakness in the security of the inhabitants. There are two components to the fort's defence, a single outer bank and ditch and two inner banks and ditches. The outer defences form about a quarter of a circle and run from the cliff to the slope on the south. Widely separated from them are the semicircular inner banks which are about 2m in height; the ditch between them is well preserved, though the outer ditch is only visible as a slight dip. They run concentrically to the outer defences, about 107m away.

Castell Bach promontory fort

Whether both inner and outer defences are contemporary cannot be ascertained without excavation, but the outer enclosure may have been used for enclosing livestock for security at night, while the inner defence protected the inhabitants. The interior of the fort is tiny and much has doubtless been eroded by the sea. The position of the entrance is now not clear, and that too may have been lost.

79
Pen Dinas, Aberystwyth
Iron Age hillfort
Late 1st millennium BC
OS 135   SN 584804   U2

From Aberystwyth, take A487 S across river bridge and through Trefechan. Just beyond Trefechan, take RH turn marked No Through Road. Follow road 0.5ml (0.8km) and park in pull-in just beyond gate on LHS signed public footpath. Walk up track up to monument on summit

Forde 1963

This prominent, well-known coastal hillfort is sited on two dramatic knolls of a short ridge, which gives the fort an outlook over the coast and the flat valleys of the Rheidol and Ystwyth rivers to the east and south-west.

Excavations on the site in 1933–7 suggested the following phases of development. Firstly the northern knoll, 1.6ha in area, was defended by a bank with a timber revetment and a V-shaped ditch. The entrance, protected by inturning banks, was on the south side. Later, the southern enclosure was added, enclosed by a bank revetted with stone and a 3m-wide ditch. This later enclosure had two entrances, one each on the north and south sides. Excavation showed that the gates had four posts in a square formation. Later again, the southern fort defences were remodelled to their present form with a single bank and ditch on the precipitous west side, and three strong

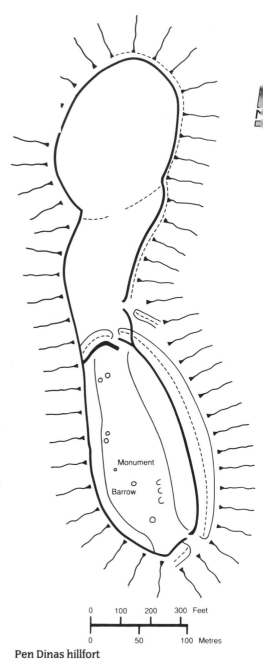

Monument

Barrow

| 0 | 100 | 200 | 300 Feet |

| 0 | 50 | 100 Metres |

Pen Dinas hillfort

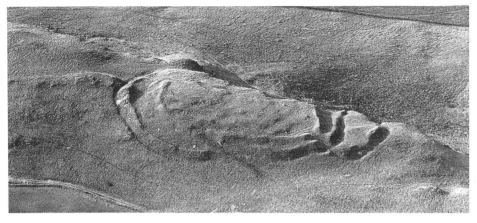

Pen y Ffrwd Llwyd hillfort from the air

banks and ditches on the gentler east. Finally, the defended area was extended by the addition of a stone wall and ditch around the saddle of lower ground between the two forts, and this was continued as an extra defence around the northern enclosure. This intermediate enclosure had a gate on the east, which, after various modifications, eventually conformed to the standard four-post structure found on the others. The total area of the defended area was then 3.8ha.

The southern enclosure is open rough ground, and within the interior some eight house platforms, level areas cut into the sloping ground, can still be seen. Most of the buildings were circular, though one of the two excavated in the 1930s was roughly D-shaped. This house had had upright timber supports for the roof, though nothing remained to show of what the roof had been built. The decorated Iron Age pottery and a 4th-century Roman coin found in the fort are in the National Museum of Wales. The excavations also uncovered spindle whorls, loom weights, one glass and one stone bead, as well as 100 uniformly sized pebbles which could have been stored for use as sling shot.

The Wellington Monument was raised in 1852 as a celebration of Wellington's victory at the Battle of Waterloo in 1815. There is also a Bronze Age round barrow in the interior of the southern enclosure which is the accessible part of the hillfort in local authority ownership. The northern enclosure is farmed privately and is not open to visitors, though it can be viewed from the southern summit and from the footpath which descends the slopes on the east of the hill.

80
Pen y Ffrwd Llwyd Fort, Ystrad Meurig
Iron Age inland promontory fort
Late 1st millennium BC
OS 135   SN 709688   U4

From Aberystwyth, take A487 S towards Aberaeron. After 3ml (4.6km) at Llanfarian, take A485 Tregaron road L to Lledrod (6ml, 9.6km). Turn L and follow signs to Ystrad Meurig (4.5ml, 7.2km). In village, turn L and drive 0.5ml (0.8km). Park near track to L opposite Pen y Graig Farm. Walk up track, and fork L, following track past quarry to site

(800m). Site and track on private property, but owners allow access

This moorland fort stands at 350m above sea level, and is defended naturally on the west by a rocky outcrop from which there is a precipitous drop on to the marshy land below. No man-made defences were necessary on this side. On the other sides a semicircular system of two banks and ditches curve around to protect a sizeable, gently-sloping interior of 0.5ha. The two banks are insignificant internally but about 3m in height externally. The defence of the gentler approach on the north-east has been strengthened by a short stretch of an additional bank. On the south the outer bank incorporates some massive rock outcrops within its circuit. There is an entrance on the north-east and another on the south-east where an oblique path runs into the interior.

Within the interior of the fort may be seen the low footings of at least one round-house, with possibly the remains of two or three others.

81
Coed Ty'n y Cwm Forts, Trawscoed
Iron Age inland promontory forts
Late 1st millennium BC
OS 135   SN 687740, 687736   U4

From Aberystwyth, take A487 (Aberaeron road) S for 1ml (1.6km), then turn L on to B4340 Trawscoed road and drive 6.5ml (10km) to Abermagwr. Turn L and after 1ml (1.6km) park near LH turn to Llanfihangel y Creuddyn. Walk down RH track opposite, past Cwmnewidion Isaf. Follow track, forking R to cross stream, go into field opposite and follow field to L, keeping wood to LHS. Go through far gate, then walk R up slope through 2 fields to stile on RH fence marked Footpath. Go over stile and northern fort is straight ahead on hilltop, skirted by forestry

Aerial view of Coed Ty'n y Cwm forts

These two small but well-preserved promontory forts are close to one another, separated only by a saddle of lower ground and a stream. The northern fort is subrectangular and is now skirted by forestry on the sloping ground to the west. The single bank is up to 2.5m high internally on the east and south while on the north it gradually reduces in strength to become merely a scarping of the steep natural slope. On the precipitous west side there appear to be no man-made defences. The entrance, which is marked by a slight inturning of the banks, is on the north-east, though there is a gap through the defences on the south-east which might also have been an entrance.

The second, smaller, promontory fort lies 300m to the south (inaccessible, but visible from the northern site). It is situated at the end of a spur of high ground and has no man-made defences on the precipitous western side. The fort is roughly rectangular in shape and its defensive bank, less splendid than that of the northern fort, has been formed by the scarping of the natural slope.

5
The Roman Period

The invasion of Britain by the Emperor Claudius in AD 43 was the first step in the Romans' gradual conquest of England and Wales and their assimilation of these countries into the Roman Empire. By AD 78, the conquest of Wales was complete, and in the early 2nd century, armed forces were relocated on a new frontier – Hadrian's Wall in the north. Nevertheless, central and northern Wales remained under direct military control until the end of Roman rule in the early 5th century.

We know the names of five tribes whom the Romans found living in Wales: the Ordovices of the north-west, the Deceangli and Cornovii of the north and east, the Silures of the south-east and the Demetae of the south-west. The conquest of the Demetae by the Roman army seems to have been efficient. The enormous size and remote situation of the forts at Y Pigwn and Arosfa Garreg (no. 83), temporary camps thrown up as a defence for the army on the march, show how the large forces of several thousand soldiers advanced quickly across the country from the east to establish control of routeways.

After the first campaigns, the mighty legionary fortresses of Caerleon and Chester were of primary strategic importance. A network of auxiliary forts was then built at important positions along major routeways with permanent garrisons which could act as a more direct, local defence. The sites of many of them are known, and the history of some has been revealed by excavation. Stretches of the roads built to connect these forts also survive, but no certain Roman fort or road has been found west of Carmarthen, and strong military action seems to have been unnecessary in the far south-west. The poverty and remoteness of the area, a lack of social cohesion or, perhaps, a benign attitude towards Roman rule on the part of the native population, meant that there was no real reason to keep a tight military hold here. Further east and north, however, a string of forts defended a main north–south route in west Wales. Roads connected Roman Carmarthen south to Loughor, east to Llandovery, and north to Pumpsaint, Llanio, Trawscoed and ultimately to north Wales and Caernarfon. The withdrawal of troops early in the 2nd century meant that many forts were reduced in size and some were abandoned altogether.

The impact of Roman civilisation elsewhere in Britain brought about the building of new road systems, and placed a new emphasis on urban life. Evidence for intensive Romanisation is rare in Dyfed, remote from the main areas of Roman

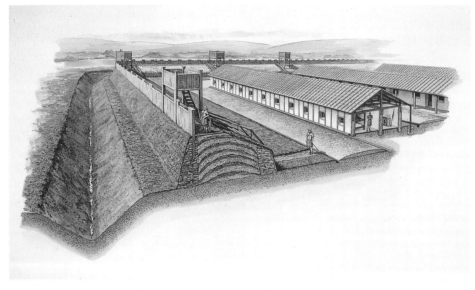

Reconstruction drawing of Roman fort defences and barracks

interest. Nevertheless the impact of Roman rule must have been felt even here. A few sophisticated Roman buildings have been found, which may have been the houses of provincial Roman officials. No splendid Roman villas have been discovered, but a small number of less wealthy, but still Romanised, farms have been excavated. Roman artefacts, such as the finely decorated hard-fired red samian pottery, and Roman coarse pottery and coinage, have been discovered on small circular defended farmsteads which, on field evidence alone, would have been described as Iron Age. For there is little doubt that the majority of the population continued to live in their isolated farms, paying their taxes to different masters, and perhaps aware of the Roman army, especially in the early years, as more mouths to consume their agricultural produce, but with no startling revolution in their life style. Alongside the continuing occupation of small defended farms and some hillforts, there appears to have been a tendency for some new farming settlements to be built in undefended positions, as the *'pax Romana'* lessened the need for defence in the middle years of Roman rule.

Alongside the auxiliary forts grew up civil settlements (or *'vici'*) which were often planned as part of the initial layout of the site. These settlements presumably acted as service centres, providing for the consumer needs of the military. Only one of these civil settlements in the south-west outlived its associated military fort and became an urban centre in its own right. Moridunum (no. 82), later to become Carmarthen, was initially a *'vicus'* for the fort, but was developed under Roman rule to serve as the tribal administrative centre or *'civitas* capital' of the Demetae. Roman provincial administrators would encourage the growth of urban life in Moridunum to ensure smooth administration by a council of local aristocracy, the town then acting as a centre for markets, trade and communication. The market in the town was presumably the main medium of exchange by which the local inhabitants of the neighbouring farms obtained the few imported articles which (as excavation has proved) they had in their possession.

The gradual disintegration of Roman imperial control in Britain throughout the 3rd and 4th centuries AD is difficult to detect in the sparse archaeological evidence found on sites in south-west Wales – indeed, affluent living certainly continued at Moridunum until well into the 4th century. But by the early 5th century, after a series of political upheavals and the increasing depredations of invading groups of Scots, Picts and Irish, official Roman government was withdrawn, and the period of Roman rule in Britain came to an end.

82
Moridunum, Carmarthen
Roman town, fort and amphitheatre
1st–4th century AD
OS 159   SN 410202   U1

Carmarthen town centre, various car parks.
Amphitheatre to E of St Peter's car park on A40

Little 1971; James, H 1978, 1982; James, T 1980

The modern town of Carmarthen is built on the site of Moridunum, the only Roman town known in west Wales, which probably developed from the '*vicus*' or civil settlement outside the Roman fort. It grew to become the '*civitas* capital' (or headquarters) of the former tribal area of the Demetae. Little now remains of the defences above ground, but as the modern street pattern still respects their line, they may be followed on foot. On the north of the town the defensive bank ran east–west along what is now the rear of Richmond Terrace, along the back gardens, and this line may now be followed by walking along that road from the access lane on the far (northern) end of St Peter's car park. Access to part of the rear of the defences may

be gained either from Richmond Terrace itself via a small lane between nos 15 and 16, or from the small (signposted) car park on the northern side of Priory Street.

The defences then turned south, and the eastern town boundary ran inside the line of Old Oak Lane and the footpath Llwybr yr Ardd, south-east from no. 25, Priory Street. Along this path, the slope of the ground to the east shows the former existence of the bank most convincingly. The defences then turned south-west and at this point, the south-east corner of the town (where the footpath emerges on to the Esplanade), the slope to the south and east shows the defensive nature of the position. The southern line runs along the Esplanade and the Parade. The bank turned to the north-west at what is now the southern end of Parade Road, and the western line runs along Parade Road and Little Water Street, back to the north-west corner at Francis Terrace. Thus an area of some 13.2ha was enclosed.

The town defences have been shown by excavation to have been solidly built with two distinct phases of construction. The first phase, dating to about AD 200, consisted of a clay bank fronted by two massive V-shaped ditches. In about AD 275–300, the defences were radically remodelled. The outer ditch was filled with a large stone wall, and a wide bank was built behind it over the old bank and the first ditch. A ditch was then dug as an extra defence outside the bank and stone wall. What events prompted the initial construction of the defences and their subsequent remodelling, we do not know.

Most Roman towns had carefully planned interiors with the streets laid out on a regular grid pattern. Part of the main east–west road of Moridunum almost certainly lies beneath the modern main road, Priory Street, though the construction of St Peter's church, which may predate the Norman Conquest, must

have caused Priory Street to deflect southwards from its Roman line. Excavations around Priory Street and in the northern half of the Roman town, have located a substantial east–west aligned street north of, and roughly parallel to Priory Street; a second street at right angles to it connected the two east–west roads, so it is fairly certain that Moridunum conformed to the norm. The north-eastern corner of Moridunum was evidently a busy 'artisan' quarter for some 250 years. During this time, there were many changes in the style and size of the houses, though the street plan remained the same, with the roads being efficiently resurfaced

Aerial view of Carmarthen, showing the line of Roman defences of Moridunum, 'fossilised' in the modern street pattern

and maintained. Excavations have revealed traces of closely-packed rectangular timber buildings, end-on to the north side of the northern street front, while better-quality buildings seem to have been restricted to the south. In the 3rd century, a splendid house stood on a corner plot, with a large granary, among the ruins of which was found a considerable quantity of charred spelt wheat. The house, probably two-storied, was interpreted by the excavators as a corn merchant's or maltster's house with, perhaps, a shop attached. By the later 4th century this quarter was rather run down, but a substantial 4th-century building in the north-west of the town was found to have had the 'hypocaust' underfloor central heating for which the Romans are famed.

The large public buildings must have stood in the centre of Moridunum. No excavations have taken place here, though a bath-house was uncovered during building work by the Victorians in the south of the town and a temple is known to have stood in the north-east quarter of the town. The amphitheatre has also been located and partially excavated. It was sited outside the eastern boundary of the town and is now laid out as a public park on the north side of Priory Street. It was cut out of the natural hillslope on the north, and the spoil was used for the bank for the southern seating. There were entrances at either end. The theatre could have seated 4,500–5,000 people, almost certainly exceeding the population of the town, and probably would have provided parades and shows and acted as a meeting place for the native population from the surrounding countryside as well. A small section of the timber seating has been reconstructed to give an impression of how the theatre may have looked. The main area of the elliptical arena floor, originally some 30m by 50m in extent, is visible, but the west and southern banks of seating still remain covered by the gardens of the adjacent houses.

The Roman fort, the earliest Roman foundation here, was sited to the west of the later Roman town. Nothing of the fort remains above ground and its exact position is not known, but it undoubtedly lies below the densely built-up Spilman and King Streets. It was located there so that it could control the river crossing which was probably sited at the present-day bridging point.

Civilised life continued at Moridunum well into the 4th century, at a time when some towns in Roman Britain were in decline. But by the 5th century, Roman administration in the province of Britain had fallen apart, and Moridunum can at this date no longer be classed as a Roman town. We know very little about what remained of the town after the end of Roman rule, until it re-emerged as a medieval town some 700 years later.

83
Y Pigwn and Arosfa Garreg Forts, Llandovery
Roman marching camps
1st century AD
OS 160   SN 828313   U2

From Llandovery, take A40 Sennybridge road for 8.5ml (13.6km) to Trecastle and take 1st R. After 0.4ml (0.6km), take RH turn and drive to gate across road. Park and walk along track for 1.4ml (2.2km). Earthworks of Y Pigwn camps immediately to R of track, just before track slopes downhill

Jones 1966, 1968

Marching camps are thought to have been temporary forts put up by the Roman army when it was on campaign. When the place for the overnight stop was marked out, the soldiers would themselves use their iron entrenching tools (a sort of spade), to dig the encampment ditch. With the earth, they raised a defensive bank, on the top of which they would put the palisade stakes which were part of each soldier's pack. The camps would have housed the army for short stays, with the soldiers probably sleeping in their leather tents rather than in built accommodation. At Y Pigwn, on what is now open moor, there are two marching camps superimposed one upon another, and there is another larger one close by at Arosfa Garreg. They probably date from the conquest period, about AD 75. The earlier camp at Y Pigwn and Arosfa Garreg could be contemporary, used in a single campaign to crush resistance in this difficult hilly country.

The camps at Y Pigwn are situated on the summit of the Mynydd Bach Trecastell, just to the north of the Roman road. Despite disturbance by lead quarrying on the south-eastern side, they display the characteristic 'playing card' shape of the Roman fort, which may best be appreciated from the aerial photograph. The 15ha camp is overlain by a smaller one, 10ha in size. The ramparts survive as low, grassy banks and the outer ditches are also quite visible. The fact that the smaller camp is the later of the two is clearly demonstrated at the south corner where the bank of the earlier, larger camp is broken by the later one. The photograph shows well how the entrances are protected by '*claviculae*', curving banks raised to defend the entrance in the main defensive bank. With the help of the photograph these can be seen on the ground; the one on the north-west side of the inner camp is especially well preserved.

Y Pigwn Roman forts from the air

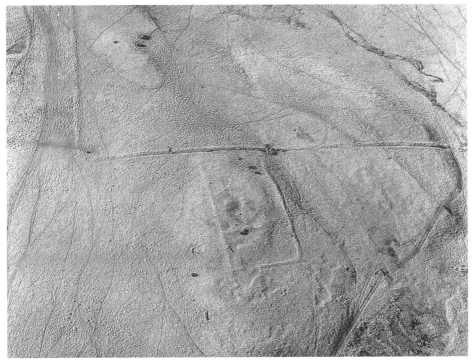

Aerial view of Arosfa Garreg Roman fort, detail of fort defences and annexe

It seems strange that a later force needed to build a second camp on the same site, but this may be to do with the fact that the second utilisation of the site was evidently by a smaller number of soldiers – reusing the original camp would have meant that stretches of rampart could not have been sufficiently well guarded with the reduced number of military personnel.

Another rather more enigmatic earthwork lies on the hillside 540m west of Y Pigwn at SN 820310. Continue along the track until it becomes fenced on the right-hand side. A little further, there is a low groove in the hillside on the left of the track, just to the left of a small stream valley. Walk up this groove to a rock outcrop and just to the left is the highest point of the site. This is a much smaller earthwork, about 29m square,

defined by low banks with a mound in the north corner, and an entrance on the north-east, fronting the road. The geometric appearance of the site, the rounded corners of the banks and the spectacular views that it commands over the Roman road where it zig-zags downhill from Y Pigwn, all suggest that it could have been a Roman fortlet or signal station. However, the mound in one corner is unusual in Roman camps, and gives the site the appearance of a medieval motte-and-bailey castle. It could, of course, have been a Roman site later adapted to suit Norman military needs.

To proceed to Arosfa Garreg camp (SN 802264) drive back east towards Trecastle along the Roman road (this is the road which ran from Llandovery (Roman *Alabum*) to Brecon, and demonstrates the legendary straightness of Roman roads). At the T-junction with the minor road, turn right, and travel along this road for 1.4ml (2.2km). Turn left over the river bridge, follow the road to the left and 0.3ml (0.5km) later, turn right. After 3.5ml (9km), Arosfa Garreg is on the left of the road. The road actually cuts the north-western corner of the camp, but the earth-works of this site are very low, and the site is rather difficult to find. Park by some sheep tracks on the left of the road, 0.6ml (1km) east of the gate and cattle grid. There is a marshy area associated with a stream nearby. Climb up the slope on the sheep track, forking right where the track divides. The track approaches the camp bank at a part where it is reasonably well preserved and more visible than most sections. The bank may be followed from this point to the camp corner where it curves around to the right. The annexe on the east is also visible from here.

The massive, remote marching camp at Arosfa Garreg is 2ml (3.2km) south of Y Pigwn. It encloses 18ha and has an annexe to protect dead ground on its eastern side. This is sufficient a size to hold virtually an entire legion, or at least a sizeable '*vexillatio*', or battle detachment of both legionaries and auxiliary troops. For comparison, fort sizes in west Wales range from 2.5ha (Llandovery) to 1.2ha (Llanio). With patience it is possible to trace on the ground not only the entire circuit of the banks and annexe, but also two of the entrances with their defensive '*claviculae*' which survive on the east and south sides. A section was excavated in 1964 across the eastern rampart and it was noted that there was no external ditch. The bank was constructed of earth and stones with an external turf revetment.

A permanent fort (as opposed to a marching camp) was built at Llandovery early on in the Roman conquest. The site is around St Mary's church on the north of the town. But very little is traceable, though the break in the slope on the west, over the road from the church, shows the position of the western rampart and the north-west corner of the fort. Much of the rest of the area has been

developed, as unfortunately is often the case with auxiliary fort sites. Small-scale excavations in the 1960s showed four principal building phases, the final phase being the reduction of the fort to a fortlet in the early 2nd century AD.

84
Dolaucothi Gold Mines and Fort, Pumpsaint
Roman gold mines and fort
Roman, medieval and modern
OS 146   SN 665403   R3   NT

Pumpsaint is on A482, 7ml (11.2km) SE of Lampeter. Fort underlies part of village and is bisected by road. Gold mines signposted from southern end of village. Car park; entrance fee during season, though much of site and footpaths accessible at all times of year free of charge

Jones and Little 1973, 1974; Burnham and Burnham 1986, 1989; Annels and Burnham 1986

The Romans were skilled in finding out about sources of metal-bearing rocks in their new provinces and in organising their exploitation. The gold at Dolaucothi may, of course, have already been discovered and worked in prehistoric times, and we may be sure that the Romans mined the precious ores. In one of the deep stopes discovered during modern mining, part of a Roman man-powered timber drainage wheel was found, and Roman pottery and gold artefacts have been found on or near the mines. However, intermittent mining has continued at Dolaucothi through the centuries and it is far from certain that any of the now-accessible mine workings date back to the Roman period.

Although the Romans possessed the technology to treat gold trapped within other minerals, at Dolaucothi they were primarily interested in the available 'free gold', which could be liberated by grinding alone. It was

Dolaucothi gold mines, entrance to Upper Roman Adit

nevertheless quite difficult to extract this free gold which was finely disseminated among the 'host rocks' of the local black shales and siltstones, and there was, inevitably, a prodigious amount of waste. Water was crucial to the whole process of prospecting, exploitation and processing and a system of leats was constructed to gather water for a distance of 6.6ml (11km) up the Cothi valley, and 3.6ml (6km) up the parallel valley of the Annell. The water was collected in a series of tanks on the hillside, then released in sudden bursts on to the working area. This is the 'hushing' technique which we know that the Romans used in their mines in Spain, although unfortunately the date of the

present extensive system of leats at Dolaucothi remains uncertain. The water was used at the prospection stage to remove overburden, and during open-cast mining to clear away discarded debris from the exposed gold-bearing rocks. It could also be used in firesetting and quenching to crack the rocks and in washing the ores.

Initial prospecting would be done by driving sloping tunnels, or 'adits', into the hillside. When deposits were found, large open-cast areas would be dug, and deeper tunnels or stopes cut down to well below the river level. The adits could then be reused as access, ventilation or haulage tunnels. Although we cannot be certain of their date, two adits at

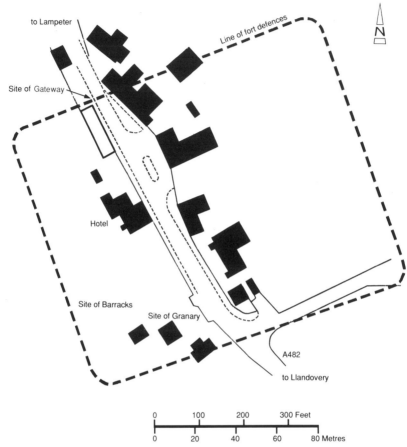

to Lampeter

Line of fort defences

Site of Gateway

Hotel

Site of Barracks

Site of Granary

A482

to Llandovery

N

0	100	200	300 Feet
0	20	40	60	80 Metres

Pumpsaint Roman fort

Dolaucothi have been called the 'Upper and Lower Roman Adits', as their trapezoidal section is reminiscent of those found at Roman mines elsewhere. Pick-marks on their walls and roofs show that their excavation must at least predate the first regular use of blasting techniques in the later 17th century. When the high-grade material had been separated by hand, it was then crushed and ground to a fine mix using large pestles and mortars and rotating grinding stones. Then the gold would be separated from the waste by sieving, followed by panning, or by recovery in a settling tank.

Initially, Dolaucothi gold was probably sent to the imperial mints in Trier or Lyons, but in the 2nd century its importance to the state apparently declined. It is probable that the mine was let out to private contractors and some gold smithying may have taken place on site, producing, perhaps, the gold artefacts found at Dolaucothi. How long this civilian concern operated is unknown, though 3rd- and 4th-century material from the area implies a degree of continuity.

Despite the uncertainty of the Roman date of the various workings, a visit to Dolaucothi is very worthwhile, especially in the summer when accompanied tours underground to see the later, deep mines are arranged. The footpaths are supplied with information panels, and mining equipment from another mine at Halkyn has been erected here, which gives a much more vivid impression of how the works must have looked in the 1930s. A visitor centre with video film explains the history of the mining processes.

The Roman fort at Pumpsaint may have been sited here to protect and control the mining of the precious gold. The A482 bisects the fort, most of which lies in the fields on the east of the road, while the smaller section lies on the west around the Dolaucothi Arms. The steep slopes down to the river on the west give some appreciation of the defensive nature of the site. The first fort was 1.9ha in area and was established probably in the mid-70s AD. In the first half of the 2nd century AD, when the initial conquest and pacification of the area had safely been achieved, the fort was reduced in size to a fortlet and the eastern half of the original fort was demolished. Excavation in the hotel car park revealed two phases of barrack blocks associated with the fort, but which were replaced by workshops when the fortlet was built. Stone footings of a massive granary belonging to the original fort were also found; this granary was evidently later demolished to make way for the new defences and road of the smaller fortlet.

The fort was defended by a turf-and-timber rampart with multiple outer ditches. The later fortlet had a remodelled rampart with a stone revetment, and a single outer ditch. The modern road runs over the northern gateway and excavations have revealed one of the wooden gate towers of the earlier fort gateway, later replaced by a masonry tower when the stone defences of the fortlet were constructed. The gate is noticeably off-centre, and perhaps was originally one of two entrances on this side. Just to the south lay the stone-lined well of the fort, later replaced by a cistern, and to the south again was a large subterranean timber-walled structure, interpreted as the cellar of a larger building, and used, perhaps, for cold storage.

A bath-house, built of brick and tile, was found in the 19th century, situated outside the fort to the south-west to avoid the risk of fire, but no traces of this building are now visible. The fort was connected by road to the fort at Llanio (the Latin name of which was *Bremia*), and the line of this road is now followed by the road to Ffarmers.

6

The Early Medieval Period

By the early 5th century, Roman rule had come to an end, and the former political stability was in turmoil. In 383, Magnus Maximus, an army officer from Britain, rebelled against central authority and claimed the Roman imperial throne in the Western Empire. Although he was defeated, his uprising became legendary and he was renowned in later years either as a political wrecker who allowed the Scots, Picts and Irish to gain a hold in the country, or as a hero with a Welsh wife to whom many of the Welsh princes traced their ancestry. During the 5th century devastating raids on the coasts of Britain were commonplace. An Irish dynasty almost certainly came to power in west Wales at this time, possibly encouraged by the native people to settle here to help guard the country against attack from other savage groups of raiders. The inscribed stones tell us a few of the names of the rulers of this time. One stone now in Carmarthen Museum in Abergwili (see Appendix) commemorates a 6th-century ruler, Voteporix, called the 'tyrant of the Demetae' by Gildas, a chronicler who wrote about the overthrow of Roman rule.

During these years, Wales became a distinct political entity with Celtic rulers who claimed respectable ancestry going back to Roman times, were Christian by faith and spoke an early form of Welsh. The country was quite separate in every way from England, where the pagan Anglo-Saxon invaders ruled over their new territories. The newly emerging Celtic kingdoms were not left in peace for long. Between the 9th and 11th centuries the Vikings, sailing from their bases in Ireland and the Isle of Man, raided, with legendary ferocity, settlement and monastery alike. They left very little positive trace of their presence, though place-names such as Fishguard ('the place of fish') and the influence of their fine interlace art on crosses such as that at Carew (no. 94) bear witness to their activities in Dyfed. The Celtic monastery at St Davids (no. 91) was frequently and heavily raided by the Vikings and while the threat from the sea tended to lessen contacts with Ireland, it hastened political ties with England in a search for common defence and perhaps also helped bring the Celtic church out of its isolation.

A few great rulers emerged in this period to defend Welsh lands. Rhodri Fawr ('the Great'), a ruler in north Wales, had built up a sizeable kingdom which included parts of modern Dyfed, but was still fighting the Vikings at his death in 878. His grandson Hywel Dda ('the Good') is thought to be the founder of the kingdom of Deheubarth, a compact area which covered the whole of south-west Wales from the Dyfi to the Tawe. Hywel recognised the overlordship of the English kings of Wessex, but within Wales achieved supremacy over the whole country save the south-east. He was evidently a very able man who did much to bring his kingdom into the sphere of the wider world. He is the first Welsh ruler known to have issued his own coinage and is also credited with drawing up a Welsh law code, valid for all Wales, which formed the basis of the later Welsh legal system. The effect of this remarkable achievement was in fact far longer lasting than the precarious political unity that he had built up, as upon Hywel's death in 950, the separate kingdoms once again reverted to their individual identities.

The 700 years between the collapse of Roman rule and the conquest of the Normans are difficult years to study. The few excavated settlement sites in Wales which have yielded evidence of occupation during this period differ hardly at all from earlier Iron Age or Romano-British settlements. Hillforts, promontory forts and circular enclosed farmsteads seem to have been built or reoccupied as in the preceding 2,000 years. Only on three sites in Dyfed – Coygan near Carmarthen, Longbury near Tenby, and Gateholm (no. 93) – do we have certain evidence for settlement, though it seems likely from documentary sources that Dinefwr (no. 123) was an important seat of government. We also know virtually nothing about the artefacts produced and used by early medieval people in Wales, apart from the fine imported pottery and ornate metalwork occasionally found on important, richer sites.

Written sources, such as the law code of Hywel Dda copied some 300 years after that king's death, give us some clues about the nature of society in early medieval Wales. At the top of the broad-based pyramid was the ruler, then came the various degrees of noblemen and freemen who owed him services and who themselves held rights in the grazing and arable land. At the base of the pyramid were the majority, the bondsmen, who were closely attached to the soil. Many were huddled into bond hamlets clustered around the lord's '*llys*' or seat. Here they raised his crops and guarded his flocks and laboured to construct or repair his buildings.

Early Christian stones are the only artefacts from this period to survive in reasonable numbers. Christianity had been introduced into Wales during the late Roman period but was not widely practised until the 5th or 6th centuries, the 'Age of the Saints', when the country was evangelised by missionary monks from Ireland and the Continent who reinforced the lingering Christian tradition and established monasteries and churches throughout the land. Some of the earliest of the stones are roughly dressed slabs with Latin and/or Ogam inscriptions, used in the 5th and 6th centuries primarily to mark the positions of the graves of the aristocracy. The Ogam script was an Irish form of writing developed for inscription on wood or stone. The Ogam alphabet comprised 20 letters arranged in sets of five, represented by groups of notches which would be incised along the edge of the

Artist's impression of an imaginary visit by a nobleman to his father's memorial stone, in the 5th century AD

stone. A clumsy form of writing, only allowing short inscriptions, Ogams had ceased to be used on monuments in Wales by 600 AD, being replaced by Latin. From the 7th to the 11th centuries, stones with decorated incised crosses and more elaborate sculptured crosses appear, often in association with early monasteries or churches, and these may have been used to mark church property.

The church in early medieval Wales was based upon the *clas* or religious community which served as school and mission centre for the clergy. Beyond these centres other churches were built for local people. These early buildings, probably normally of timber, and now often built over by later churches, rarely survive and inscribed or sculptured stones are often the only tangible link that we have with them. A circular churchyard may also be a clue to an ancient foundation, as a number of early sites were surrounded by circular enclosures. Early medieval cemeteries are rarely discovered, though at a few sites in Dyfed, including Bayvil, near Nevern, and Llanychlwydog near Fishguard, groups of cist graves, all aligned east–west, have been excavated.

Before the Norman Conquest changed the course of events so radically, one last powerful Welsh ruler, Gruffudd ap Llywelyn, prince of Gwynedd, achieved by painstaking conquest a political unity in Wales that had not been seen since the days of Hywel Dda. During the last eight years of his life (1055–63) he was the effective ruler of the whole country. His ambitions led him into conflict with King Edward, and a double-pronged campaign led by Earl Harold and his brother Tostig was sent to overthrow him. The Welsh ruler was driven into hiding, and in his extremity, his Welsh allies deserted him. As a result of a plot, in August 1063, this 'head and shield and defender of the Britons' met his end.

Key to Transcriptions

This chapter uses the following conventions in the transcriptions of early Christian gravestone inscriptions:

The inscriptions are written in capital letters. Editorial insertions within the inscriptions (also in capital letters), and the translations of the inscriptions themselves, appear in italics.

Square brackets indicate letters which are assumed, but indecipherable in the inscription.

Round brackets indicate letters or words which are inserted for comprehension or translation, but which are not present in the original inscription.

An oblique line indicates the beginning of a new line in the inscription (quite frequently in the middle of a word).

85
Clydai Inscribed Stones, Boncath
Early Christian stones
5th–6th and 7th–12th century AD
OS 145   SN 251355   U1

From crossroads at Boncath (off A478 Tenby– Cardigan road, 4ml, 6.4km S of Cardigan) carry straight on to Bwlch y Groes, past 2 R and 2 L turns. Go straight over Bwlch y Groes crossroads to Star. Turn L on to Cwm Cych road. Clydai church 0.5ml (0.8km) further, on RHS. Key at Hendre Farm further along road

Nash-Williams 1950, nos 306–8

Inside Clydai church are three inscribed stones, on one of which has been added a later ring-cross. This latter stone, the shortest of the three, has Ogams on the left (originally the right) angle of the face reading: D[O]V[A]TUCEAS, or: (*The stone*) *of Dovatucis*. The partly defaced Latin inscription reads vertically: DOB[I]TVC / FILIVS EVOLENG[I], or: (*The stone*) *of Dobitucus, son of Evolengus* and is datable to the 5th or early 6th century. Some time after the first inscription, the stone was reused; it was set head down in the ground, and an outline ring-cross with a detached double stem incised partly through the inscription.

The second stone has an Ogam inscription on the left angle reading upwards and the

right reading downwards, and must originally have continued across the top: ETTERN[*I* / *MAQI* / *VIC*]TOR, or: (*The stone*) *of Etternus, son of Victor*. The Latin inscription is: ETTERN-FILI VICTOR(*is*). The last stone, slightly damaged, has a Latin inscription in two lines reading vertically downward: SOLINI / FILIVS / VENDONI (the D is reversed), or: (*The stone*) *of Solinus, son of Vendonius*. These two inscriptions date to the 5th or early 6th century. The inscriptions on all three stones are well preserved and easy to read.

86
Bridell Ogam Stone, Cardigan
Early Christian inscribed pillar-stone
5th–6th and 9th century AD
OS 145   SN 177421   U1

From Cardigan, take A487 Fishguard road. Branch L on to A478 Tenby road. After 2.3ml

Clydai stone, with Ogam and Latin inscriptions

Bridell Ogam stone

(3.7km) take minor road on RHS with church immediately on R. Stone in churchyard, S of church

Nash-Williams 1950, no. 300

This tall, pointed pillar-stone is interesting as it has an Ogam inscription, and also a later incised cross dating from an evident reuse of the stone. The Ogam inscription is inscribed along the left angle of the north face, reading upwards: NETTASAGRU MAQI MUCOI BRECI, or: (*The stone*) *of Nettasagrus, son of the descendant of Brecos.* The inscription probably dates from the 5th–6th century. On the same face is incised a circle enclosing an outline cross with square arms, possibly as late as the 9th century in date.

87
Nevern Cross, Nevern

Early Christian cross and inscribed stones

5th–6th and late 10th–early 11th century AD

OS 145   SN 083400   U1

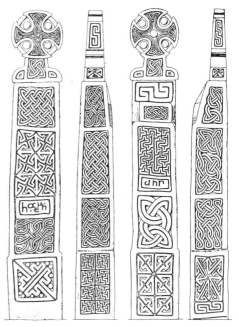

Nevern Cross. Left to right: front, right, back and left sides

From Newport, take A487 E towards Cardigan for 1.5ml (2.4km). Turn L on to B4582 to Nevern. Cross in churchyard, on LHS of road

Nash-Williams 1950, nos 360, 354, 353, 359

The large, impressive cross in Nevern churchyard is closely related in style to the cross at Carew (no. 94), and is of a similar late 10th- or early 11th-century date. Like Carew Cross, it is inscribed on the shaft, – on the front, the Latin inscription reads: H/AN./.EH, and on the back: DNS. The meaning of the first is uncertain, but DNS is probably an abbreviated form of *Dominus* (Lord).

   The cross, fashioned in the local hard dolerite, comprises two separate pieces – the upper wheel-head and shouldered neck are joined by a mortise-and-tenon joint to the

shaft, which terminates in a slightly stepped base. From the side it may be seen how the shaft is reduced in thickness towards the top by means of a chamfered offset. The wheel-head has the same curving arms to the cross as are seen on Carew Cross, a feature that characterises the 'Anglian' type. The front (east) of the cross-head has the arms filled by double-beaded two-cord knots linked by two twists, and the neck below has a square panel of interlinked oval rings. The front of the shaft carries, from top to bottom, panels of: an eight-cord plait, a swastika key-pattern, the inscription panel, a loop-pattern and, at the base, a diaper key-pattern with pellets. On the back, the arms of the wheel-head are filled with double-beaded knots linked around a central boss, and below is the same oval ring pattern as on the front. On the back of the shaft, from top to bottom, are: a band of plain square fret, a shorter panel of four-cord plait, a panel of swastika T-frets, the inscription panel, a large double knot and, at the base, a diaper key-pattern.

The sides of both wheel-head and shaft are also filled with decoration. The wheel-head has fret patterns on the sides, and the same quadruple triangular knot occurs on each shoulder. The shaft has, on the right at the top, a panel of irregular six-cord knotwork, a six-cord plait below, then an eight-cord plait, and swastika T-frets at the base. The left side of the shaft has, from top to bottom: a panel of four-cord knotwork, a six-cord knotwork, another six-cord knotwork merging below into vertical twists, a diaper key-pattern and a short band of square fret at the base.

Another early Christian stone stands in the churchyard near the high cross. It is much smaller and has a Latin inscription of the 5th or early 6th century: VITALIANI / EMERETO, or: (*The stone*) of *Vitalianus Emereto*. Vitalianus and Emeritus were common names of this period. Along the left angle of the face is an Ogam inscription: VITALIAN(*o*). Inside the church, built into the sills of the south transept windows, are two further stones. One has a Latin inscription reading vertically down: MAGLOCVN(*i*) FILI CLVTOR-, or: (*The stone*) of *Maglocunus, son of Clutorius*. The Ogam form of the inscription on the left angle of the face reads upwards: MAGLICUNAS MAQI CLUTAR|]. It is 5th- or early 6th-century in date. The other stone is decorated with an interlaced Latin cross carved in low relief, a characteristic Irish form of cross which probably dates to the 10th century. Both stones were discovered in 1906, built into the wall of the 'priest's chamber', a small room over the transeptal chapel. The church itself is of great interest, and there is a guidebook available. The dedication is to St Brynach, an Irish saint of the 6th century.

The Pilgrim's Cross – a wayside cross cut into the solid rock, with a kneeling recess with a small incised cross cut below – is a little way to the west. Walk down the road signed Nevern Castle, and, at a sharp bend to the

right, there is a path on the left. The cross, which needs to be sought out, is 30m down this path on the right-hand side, carved into an exposed vertical piece of rock face.

88
Llandilo Inscribed Stones, Maenclochog
Early Christian stones
5th–6th and 7th–9th century AD
OS 145   SN 083274   R1

Maenclochog is on B4313 Narberth–Fishguard road, 10ml (16km) SE of Fishguard. Church in village centre and often locked. Vicar's warden has key – enquire at village shop for access

Nash-Williams 1950, nos 313, 314, 345

These two inscribed stones from St Teilo's chapel (no. 139), have been moved here for safekeeping. The taller of the two has an Ogam inscription on the left angle of the face reading upwards: [A]NDAGELLI MACU CAV[ETI(?)], or: (*The stone*) of *Andagellus, son of Cavetus*. The Latin inscription is in two lines reading downwards: [A]NDAGELL- IACIT / FILI CAVET-, or: (*The stone*) of *Andagellus, son of Cavetus. He lies (here)*. Above the Latin inscription, which is 5th- or early 6th-century in date, is a coarsely incised linear Latin cross with trifid terminals which was probably added in the 7th or 9th century.

The second stone has a Latin inscription in three lines reading downwards: COIMAGNI / FILI / CAVETI, or: (*The stone*) of *Coimagnus, son of Cavetus*. The two stones thus would appear to commemorate two brothers, with the lettering on the second stone being the later in style. A third stone, which may well have originated from St Teilo's, but which stood, in the 18th century, just to the west at Temple Druid farm, was placed in Cenarth churchyard in 1896 where it remains to this day. Its inscription reads: CVRCAGN- / FILI ANDAGELL-, or: (*The stone*) of *Curcagnus, son*

Llandilo inscribed stones, Latin inscriptions

89
Llanllawer and Llanychaer Crosses, Fishguard
Early Christian stones
7th–9th century AD
OS 157   SM 987360, 992345
U1/3

From Fishguard on A487, take B4313 SE towards Narberth and Gwaun Valley. 2ml (3.2km) later, in Llanychaer, turn L opposite pub. Crosses in St David's churchyard 0.5ml (0.8km) further on, on LHS

Nash-Williams 1950, nos 323–4, 336–7, Lewis 1976

Built into the gateway of St David's church, Llanllawer, are two rough stones dating to the 7th–9th century with outline Latin crosses picked on to their faces. One cross has rounded terminals, while the other has dots in the interspaces and curved bar terminals to the limbs. A third stone, with a ring-cross and a six-armed cross incised upon it, has been trimmed and now serves as the lintel of the vestry door on the north of the church. Another, with an incised ring-cross with dots in the interspaces, is built into the outside of the south wall of the nave. A vaulted holy well (no. 134) stands near to the church in an adjacent field.

In Llanychaer churchyard (back on to the B4313, and follow the road left for 0.5ml (0.8km) to signposted track) is a fenced area within which a remarkable stone has been placed for protection. On the front is a Crucifixion score. Christ is shown as a bearded figure stretched full length, wearing a tunic; there is a circular ring-cross below. On the back is an outline Latin ring-cross with splayed arms and stem and deep central dot, with a small ring-cross at the foot of the stem. On the two sides are Latin crosses with their stems similarly terminating in ring-crosses, though one of the sides is so damaged that the top of the cross is not apparent. All the figures are worn and are rather difficult to see.

of Andagellus. If this is the same Andagellus, which seems quite likely, we have here a most unusual group of stones naming three generations of the same family.

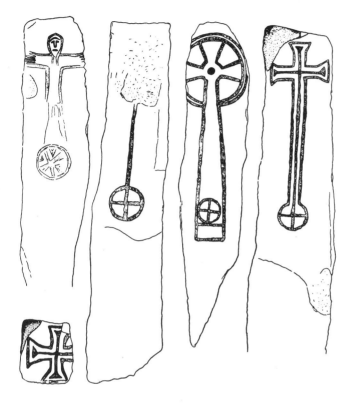

Llanychaer Cross. Left to right: front, top, right, back and left sides

The stone is 7th–9th-century in date. The presence in the area of so many early Christian stones decorated with the outline cross, a form with limited distribution elsewhere, suggests that there may have been several ecclesiastical sites founded around here in the 7th–9th century.

90
Mesur y Dorth and Mathry Stones, St Davids
Early Christian stones
7th–9th century AD
OS 157   SM 838307, 378319   U1

From St Davids, take A487 E towards Fishguard for 6.3ml (10.1km). Just past

Croesgoch, Mesur y Dorth stone is set into wall on RHS of road, by Maes y Garreg house

Nash-Williams 1950, nos 325, 346–8; Lewis 1976

Mesur y Dorth stone has an outline Latin ring-cross and stem incised on the face and probably dates to the 7th–9th century. It may have been associated with some slab-lined cist graves, perhaps from an early Christian cemetery, discovered accidentally many years ago near the Croesgoch crossroads.

Continue along the A487 for another 2.5ml (4km), and turn left into Mathry. Set into the western exterior face of the churchyard wall are two early Christian stones, each with a 7th–9th-century incised linear ring-cross. One has an additional, outer, but incomplete ring around the cross. This stone came from

91
St Davids and St Nons Crosses, St Davids

Early Christian stones
7th–11th century AD
OS 157   SM 751254   R1

St Davids is on A487, 16ml (25.6km) NW of Haverfordwest. Most crosses are in cathedral (cathedral opening hours apply); one at St Non's Chapel (see no. 136)

Nash-Williams 1950, nos 372–83; Evans and Worsley 1981

Mathry stones. Left: the slab in the church porch; right: the stone from Rhoslanog

Rhoslanog, west of Mathry, where there is a tradition of an early burial ground. However, Mathry itself is evidently an ancient site (though the church has been substantially rebuilt in modern times), and in 1720, 'stone coffins' were reported as being found in the churchyard, which suggests that there may have been an early burial ground here also. Inside the church porch is an inscribed slab dating to the 5th or early 6th century. The Latin inscription, now damaged, but fortunately noted by the antiquarian Edward Lhuyd in 1698, reads horizontally: [*MAC*] / CVDICCL / FILIVS/ CATIC / VVS, or: *Maccudiccl, son (of) Caticuus, (lies here)*. On the back is an Ogam inscription of uncertain reading, with part of an incised double-outline circle. The fact that the two inscriptions are on different faces is unusual and suggests that they are not contemporary.

The *clas* or ecclesiastical community established at St Davids in the 6th century quickly grew to become a place of great religious significance due to the reputation of its founder saint. All traces of the *clas* seem to have been swept away by the 11th century, and we know very little about the appearance of these first buildings at St Davids, nor even their exact position. However, a large number of early Christian stones do survive from this period, and provide the visitor with a tantalising glimpse into the history of the early religious community.

Several crosses, soon to be rehoused in a lapidarium outside the cathedral, stand at present at the western end of the nave. One is a 7th–9th-century stone with an incised Latin cross with forked terminals. A smaller stone has a lightly carved ring-cross with a knot design within the head and encircled by a border of fret, of a type local to St Davids, and datable to the 9–10th century. A second, similar ring-cross, but with an angular key pattern within the head, also dates to the 9th–10th century. A fourth stone, which has been used as a gatepost in the past, has on the front a large outline wheel-cross of Irish type within a border of straight fret, and the inscription: A 7 (= *et*) ω I[*H*]S XPS / GURMARC, or: (*The cross of*) *Alpha and Omega, Jesus Christ. Gurmarc (? set it up)*. On the back is a

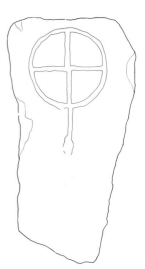

St Davids and St Nons crosses. Left to right: cross slab with seraph, the Gurmarc stone, the St Nons stone

plain outline wheel-cross. The stone is dated to the 9th–10th century. With these stones is a fragment of a large 10th- or 11th-century wheel-head cross with raised central ring and boss, cable-moulding surrounding the cross, and interlace pattern on both sides.

In the south transept, built into the east wall, is a damaged portion of a gravestone. It bears an ornamental wheel-cross in relief, with a small Latin cross above, and the remains of a second wheel-cross below. On the top left is a Latin inscription: + PONTIFICIS / ABRAHAM / FILII HIC.HED / 7 (= *et*) ISAC. QUIES/CUNT, or: *The sons of Bishop Abraham, Hed and Isa(a)c, rest here.* Abraham was bishop of St Davids from 1078 until his death in a Viking raid in 1080, so the stone is unusually closely datable. Near this slab is a broken piece of a cross-slab with a knotwork pattern and a seraph with three decorative wings.

Built into the altar front of Holy Trinity Chapel are two decorated cross-slabs. One has a wheel-cross in relief, and on the other, an incomplete slab, is inscribed: MATHEVS MARCVS LVC[*AS*] [*I*]OHAN(*n*)ES, the Latin form of the four Evangelists' names. It probably dates to around 1140.

Within St Nons Chapel, to the south of St Davids (SN 752243) is an early Christian stone

The Abraham Stone, St Davids

with an incised linear ring-cross probably 7th- or 9th-century in date.

92
Brawdy Inscribed Stones, Brawdy

Early Christian inscribed stones
5th–6th century AD
OS 157   SM 858240   U1

Brawdy is off A487 St Davids–Haverfordwest road, 8.5ml (13.6km) NW of Haverfordwest. At Penycwm, turn R (N) from main road towards Mathry (not RAF Brawdy) and 1ml (1.6km) later at crossroads, turn R. Church just before Brawdy Farm

Nash-Williams 1950, nos 296, 298–9

At the church at Brawdy are four fine inscribed stones, three of them lying in the porch. The largest, which bears the scars of former use as a gatepost, is a rough pillar-stone with an Ogam inscription on one angle of the face reading downwards: [MA]Q[I] QAGTE, or: (*The stone of*) [?] *the son of Quagte*. It apparently was found 'within an old rath' at Cas Wilia, a defended promontory a little way east to the church. Excavations have been undertaken in the fort, but as yet there is no proof of there having been any occupation contemporary with the 5th- or 6th-century stone.

The other two smaller stones are similar and are also 6th-century in date. One has a Latin and Ogam inscription, the former, now very damaged, reading: VENDAGNI / FILI V[ ]NI, or: (*The stone*) *of Vendagnus, son of V. . .nus*. The Ogam inscription reads upwards: VEN[D]OGNI. The third stone has a partly obliterated Latin inscription reading vertically down: BRIAC[I] FIL- /, with uncertain letters in the second line, or: (*The stone*) *of Briacus, son of . . .* A fourth stone, a roughly shaped slab on the floor inside the church, is inscribed MACCATR[ENI] / FILI / CATOMAG[LI]. The first name also occurs on an inscribed stone in Cilgerran churchyard (SN 191431).

93
Gateholm, Marloes

Early medieval settlement
3rd–13th century AD
OS 157   SM 770073   R4

From Haverfordwest, take B4327 Dale road for 10ml (16km). Take minor road R to Marloes, drive through village and follow road to car park (2ml, 3.2km). Park and follow coastal footpath L along coast for 1ml (1.6km) to Gateholm, a tidal island accessible only at low tide. Keep note of tide to avoid being cut off

Lethbridge and David 1930; Davies 1971

Gateholm is a small tidal island situated on the western extremity of Marloes Bay. During the medieval period it may have been a promontory which has only subsequently become cut off from the mainland. A stone bank, now turf-covered, survives in sections along the landward edge of the island and on the north-west. The interior is covered with an extensive series of footings of rectangular buildings, laid out in rows on either side of a trackway that runs down the centre of the island.

The buildings are arranged in two different ways. On the east, those on the north of the track follow the track in a simple linear arrangement, while those on the south appear to be arranged around yards. On the west, the buildings are also set around three or four yards. Estimating the number of buildings is hindered by the thick, tussocky grass that has overwhelmed the island, but it is safe to say that there are over 100.

A few of the buildings have been excavated and were found to have had walls of turf, probably derived from the stripping of the interior floor area. One building had walls faced internally by drystone walling. A larger building had two opposed doorways with jambs formed by upright slabs, two shallow pits interpreted as having supported posts for a ridge-pole, and a central hearth. A wide range of artefacts was discovered

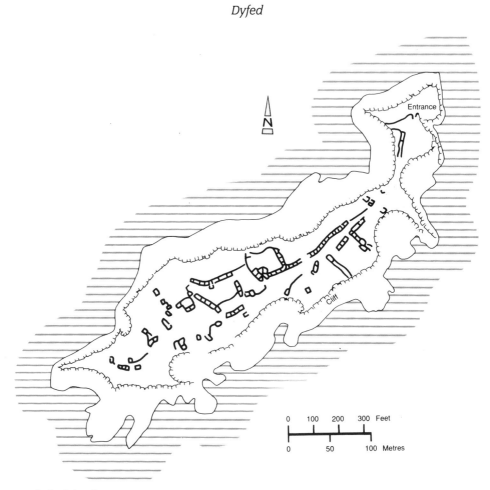

Gateholm Island

during the excavations, including 3rd- or 4th-century Roman pottery and coins. Presumably, therefore, some of the settlement dates to the later Roman period. However, one of the huts produced from its occupation surface a bronze ringed pin of 6th–9th-century style, along with a shale bracelet and a whetstone. As this hut was thought to be one of the earliest of the structures on that part of the site, it is generally accepted that much of the settlement at Gateholm dates from the early medieval period which makes it unique in

Dyfed. Whether it was, as some have suggested, a monastic site, or whether it was a secular settlement is uncertain. The excavations further uncovered high-quality ceramics imported from France, dating from the 11th to the 13th century, which suggests that there was another phase of activity on Gateholm in the later medieval period.

A little way north-west, on the footpath back to the car park, is Watery Bay promontory fort, (SM 768079) which has a fine series of triple banks and ditches defending the landward side.

94
Carew Cross, Carew
Early Christian wheel-head cross
1033–1035 AD
OS 158   SN 047037   U1   Cadw

Carew is on A477 Pembroke–St Clears road, 4ml (6.4km) E of Pembroke. Turn N on to A4075 Haverfordwest road, and after 0.5ml

(0.8km), car parks are on either side of road. Cross by side of road, near castle entrance

Cadw Guidebook

This magnificent sculptured cross is a royal memorial to Maredudd, who, in 1033, with his brother Hywel, became joint ruler of the early medieval kingdom of Deheubarth, now south-west Wales. Two years later, Maredudd was killed and thus we are able to date this stone

Carew Cross. Left to right: front, right, back and left sides

with unusual precision. On the front of the stone (away from the road), on the left hand of the two rectangular panels, can be seen the Latin inscription: MARGIT/EUT RE/X. ETG(*uin*). FILIUS, or: *(The cross of) Margiteut (or Maredudd) son of Etguin (or Edwin).*

The cross has a wheel-head and shouldered neck of sandstone joined by a tenon to a separate shaft and stepped base, made of a harder stone. The wheel-head carries the curved arms of the form known as 'Anglian', a type commonly found in Wales, northern England and Cornwall. Both head and shaft have carved decoration in low relief on all sides. On the front of the head, the knotwork pattern on the softer stone has suffered much from flaking, and has now largely disappeared. The decoration on the neck and shaft is in rectilinear panels. On the neck, there are two squares of swastika T-frets, then below, three squares of a key-pattern. On the shaft is a panel filled with a plaitwork pattern, then an irregular key-pattern, below which are two small panels, one enclosing the inscription, the other, on the right, being blank; below these is a panel of a different form of plaitwork. The bottom panel is patterned with T-frets.

The two sides of the head are plain, but the shaft sides have long narrow panels of plait. On the back of the wheel-head is a combined outline and linear cross, below which, in the neck, is a panel filled with a triangular pattern, then a band of opposed triangles. The upper panel on the shaft has a double row of three squares of swastika T-frets, below which is a row of three linked oval rings. The two lowest panels are filled with different forms of plaitwork.

The stone's original position is uncertain. It was moved to its present setting this century, slightly back from its 19th-century position on an outcrop which projected into the road.

Carew and Nevern (no. 87) are together two of the largest and most elaborate early Christian monuments in Wales. They have been compared unfavourably with contemporary English and Irish work because of a certain clumsiness in the carving and the lack of proportion between head and shaft, but none the less they remain an impressive reminder of the skill of the early medieval mason.

95
Penally Crosses, Penally
Early Christian wheel-head cross
9th–10th century AD
OS 158   SS 117992   U1

Penally is on A4139 Tenby–Pembroke road, 2ml (3.2km) SW of Tenby. Turn off main road into village, church on N of road, in village centre. Crosses in S transept of church

Nash-Williams 1950, nos. 364, 363, 366

The fine slab-cross at Penally is unlike those from Carew and Nevern in that it is sculpted from a single massive stone. But, like them, it has a wheel-head of the Anglian type, with its characteristic widely splayed, curving arms, and a slender, slightly splayed shaft with a stepped base. Both head and shaft are edged with cable-mouldings at the angles. The head is patterned in the same way on the back and front and has a pronounced central boss decorated with a four-lobed knot, and six-cord ring-twists on the arms.

The front of the shaft is a continuous band with, at the top, a single vine-scroll of Northumbrian type with three-lobed leaves, four- and five-stemmed grape-bunches, and decorative knots. Below this is a six-cord plaitwork, and at the base cruciform angular knotwork. The back of the shaft is filled with four vertical bands of triple-beaded knotwork (the upper two) and plaits (the lower two). The sides of the shaft have a continuous band of twists at the top intertwined with a lower four-cord knotwork, now eroded and defaced. The graceful monument is a happy combination of Celtic and Northumbrian styles. It probably dates to the first half of the 10th century.

Standing alongside the slab-cross in the south transept is part of another cross, its

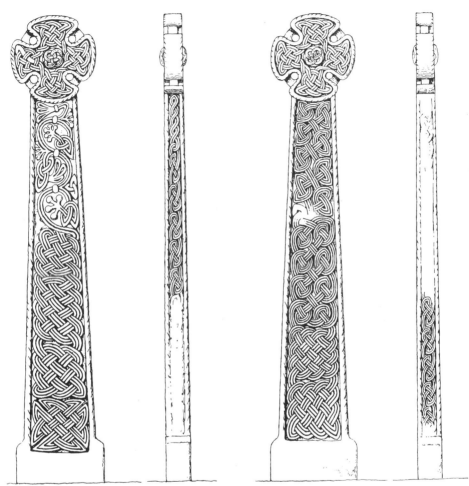

Penally slab-cross. Left to right: front, right, back and left sides

splayed shaft with cable-mouldings on the angles and carved decoration in low relief on all sides. On the front, between a key-pattern and a conventionalised vine-scroll, is a pair of confronted animals with forelegs interlaced, forward-lapping ears, back-turned heads and long tails interlacing. The animals have in their mouths parts of two other animals, who, in turn, devour the opposite ends of a vine tendril above. The motif is borrowed from contemporary Northumbrian art.

On the back of this shaft are, from top to bottom: a plait design; a triskele of Irish type; and a ribbon-animal of Scandinavian form with a long inward-curving head apparently biting the neck of a serpent, and an elaborate tail interlaced around the body. The sides of the shaft are decorated with vine-scroll and knotwork patterns on the right and two key-patterns on the left.

This cross presents a remarkable blending of Celtic Irish motifs (interlacing, spirals, key-

Penally cross shaft. Left to right: front, right, back and left sides

pattern) and those of the late Ango-Saxon art of northern Britain (twin beasts and vine-scrolls) and Scandinavian Jellinge style. It suggests the re-establishment of artistic links between these areas, ending the apparent cultural isolation of Wales since the Roman period. It probably dates to the early 10th century.

There is also a small fragment of another splayed shaft with knotwork and key-pattern designs in low relief, which probably dates to the early 10th century. It is housed in the vestry for safekeeping. Outside the church, built into the north transept east wall, is a plain incised cross.

96
Llanddowror Crosses, St Clears
Early Christian stones
9th–10th century AD
OS 158   SN 256145   U3

From St Clears, take A477 Pembroke road 1.8ml (2.9km) to Llanddowror. Park by church on RHS (N) of road. Walk down track on N side of church, into playing field beyond church on LHS of track; stones on far side

Nash-Williams 1950, nos 151–2

These two small, rough slabs are situated in what might be described as a peculiarly Welsh situation, just off the touchline of the village rugby pitch! The larger of the two has on the front a combined outline and linear cross in an irregular sunken panel. On the back is a weathered incised linear cross. The smaller stone has an outline cross in a square sunken panel. Both stones are probably 9th- or 10th-century in date, or later.

97
Laugharne Sculptured Cross, Laugharne
Early Christian cross
9th–early 10th century AD
OS 159   SN 301115   U1

Laugharne is on A4066 St Clears–Pendine road, 3.5ml (5.6km) S of St Clears. Church on LHS of road, on N side of town

Nash-Williams 1950, no. 145

This small disk-headed slab-cross, thought to date back to the 9th or early 10th century, has been recently moved from the churchyard into the church for safekeeping. On the front is a carved Latin cross with central boss, plain splayed arms and interlaced three-cord stem. There are small triquetra knots in the four interspaces, and the cross is enclosed in a border of cable decoration. The type of plait on the stem is thought to show Viking influence.

98
Llanfihangel ar Arth Stones, Llandyssul
Early Christian stones
5th–9th century AD
OS 146   SN 456399   R1

From Llandyssul, 7ml (11.2km) E of Newcastle Emlyn on A486 Carmarthen–Newquay road, take B4336 SE to Llanfihangel. At crossroads, turn L on to B4459. Church 0.5ml (0.8km) further, on LHS of road; key in nearby pub

Nash-Williams 1950, nos 157–8

Set into the church floor against the east wall of the south aisle are two early Christian stones. The larger of the two has an incised linear Latin cross with the top arm-end

crossleted. The stem is also transected centrally by a short crossleted bar, and by a longer plain bar below. There are further crosslets in the interspaces. The stone is 7th–9th century in date.

The smaller stone is a rough pillar-stone with a Latin inscription in three lines reading downwards: HIC IACIT / VLCAGNUS FI(li)VS / SENOMAGL-, or: *Here lies Ulcagnus, son of Senomaglus*. The style of the lettering dates the inscription to the 5th or early 6th century.

Llanfihangel ar Arth inscribed stone, before its removal into the church

99
Llandeilo Crosses, Llandeilo
Early Christian crosses
9th–early 10th century AD
OS 159   SN 629223   R1

In Llandeilo church (often locked) on S side of town

Nash-Williams 1950, nos 155–6

Llandeilo was the seat of the Celtic monastery or *clas* of St Teilo. It was an important house, though all that remains from that period of past greatness are two fine early Christian crosses. These now lie in the window recesses of the north aisle, which is entered separately through a wooden screen. One has a small, square 'disk'-head, perhaps from a slab-cross, and may be a local variant of the normal Celtic wheel-head. It is in the form of a quadrate cross with a plain square 'wheel' decorated with small raised bosses in the interspaces on one face, plain on the other. The cross is decorated with carved patterns within moulded borders. The five square panels on the front and back are filled with plaitwork and the strands run along the connecting arms. The sides are each decorated with three panels, one of plait on the arm-ends, and two of angular fret. The present position of the cross prevents proper examination of the bossed front face.

The second, damaged, slab has a quadrate square wheel-cross, similar to the first stone

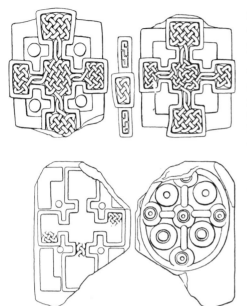

Llandeilo crosses. (Left to right) top: front, sides and back of square 'disk'-head; bottom: front and back of square wheel-cross

Silian (0.8ml, 1.3km). Church up small road on RHS

Nash-Williams 1950, nos 128–9

The tiny hamlet of Silian boasts two early Christian stones. One, a shaped stone, is built into the external face of the south wall of the church, near the west end. A Latin inscription in one line reading along the face dates to the 5th or early 6th century: [*SIL*]BANDVS IACIT (*Silbandus lies (here)*), or possibly FILI BANDVS IACIT, (. . . *son of Bandus lies (here)*). Scored through part of the inscription is a later incised linear cross with the upper terminals slightly expanded. Though obviously later, it cannot be more narrowly dated than to the 7th–11th century.

Inside the church, housed within the vestry, is a rectangular slab. Both faces of this stone have panels of carved ornament in low relief. The panel on one face is filled with a triple knotwork pattern seen also on no. 103, while on the back is a panel of square fret. This stone probably dates to the 9th or 10th century.

and decorated with plait. On the back in relief is a cross in a circular border with raised rings at the centre and arm ends, and with rings and ringed bosses in the upper and lower interspaces respectively. The irregular shape of the stone has led to its being positioned on its side. Both stones date to the 9th or early 10th century.

100
Inscribed and Decorated Stones, Silian
Early Christian stones
5th–early 6th and 8th–9th century AD
OS 146   SN 572513   U1

From Lampeter, take A485 Aberystwyth road N for 1.5ml (2.4km), then take LH turn into

Silian, decorated stone inside church

101
Inscribed Stones, Llanddewi Brefi

Early Christian stones
6th–9th century AD
OS 146   SN 663553   U1

Llanddewi Brefi is on B4343, 3ml (4.8km) S of Tregaron, 8ml (12.8km) NE of Lampeter. Park in village square outside church

Nash-Williams 1950, nos. 115–20

The date of the foundation of the church at Llanddewi Brefi is unknown but a tradition states that it was here that a synod was held in the early 6th century to combat the heresy of Pelagianism, at which St David himself spoke. It must therefore have been an important Celtic *clas*, and we know that in 1287 Bishop Bek, bishop of St Davids, replaced the Welsh married brethren here with a Latin-style college of secular canons. All that survives from the early medieval *clas* are six early Christian stones, five of which are now set in the floor of the church beneath the vaulted, central tower.

The tallest stone has a linear Latin crossleted cross and, below, an inscription which reads vertically downwards: CENLISINI BT (= *benedicat ?*) DS, or: (*The cross) of Cenlisinus. May God bless him.* The second stone has a linear Latin cross with a curved bifid foot and trifid arm-ends. The third, damaged at the top, has a linear cross with the top limb crossleted. These three stones are 7th–9th-century in date.

The fourth stone has also been damaged at the top and has a Latin inscription in two lines reading vertically downwards: DALLVS / DVMELVS, or: *Dallus Dumelus (lies here).* Dumelus is an Irish name. The inscription is datable to the 6th century. The fifth is a rough pillar-stone which has been badly damaged on the right side. On the face is a rough linear cross with a deep central hole, but the right arm has been lost through damage. It probably dates to the 7th–9th century.

Llanddewi Brefi
inscribed stones

Built into the external face of the north-west corner of the church (above the boiler house) are two fragments of a pillar-stone which has a Latin inscription now in two lines reading vertically, but originally in three lines. The original inscription reads: + HIC IACET IDNERT FILIVS IACOBI / QVI OCCISVS FVIT PROPTER PREDAM / SANCTI DAVID, or: *Here lies Idnert, son of Jacob, who was killed because of the despoiling of St David . . .* This reading was made by Edward Lhuyd in 1699, before the stone was, unbelievably, broken up for use for building after 1812. The inscription hints at the violence of the area during this turbulent period, and is important for its apparent early reference to St David. The lettering indicates a date in the 7th century for the inscription, which is thus no more than a century after the death of St David.

102
Llanwnnws Slab, Ystrad Meurig

Early Christian stone
9th century AD
OS 135   SN 685696   U1

From Tregaron, take B4343, N to Pontrhydfendigaid, then fork L on to B4340 and drive to Tynygraig (4ml, 6.4km). Turn L on to Swyddffynnon road, and after 0.4ml (0.6km) turn R up minor road to Llanwnnws church, 0.5ml (0.8km) up road on LHS

Nash-Williams 1950, no. 125

In the porch of the church stands a rough slab with a Latin ring-cross lightly carved on one face. The cross is formed of double ribbon-bands with knots at the terminals and ring-bosses in the interspaces of the cross. Above the cross on the right are the letters XPS, the Greek contraction for *Christus*. Originally there may have been a IHS (*Jesus*) on the left, but this part of the stone has been broken off. This would have given a reading: '*(The cross) of Jesus Christ*'. Below the cross is a Latin inscription in 12 lines, reading: Q(*u*)ICUNQ(*ue*) / EXPLI/CAU(*er*)IT / H(*oc*) NO(*men*) / DET B/ENE/DIXIONE/M PRO ANI/MA HIROID/IL FILIUS / CARO/TINN, or: *Whoever explains this name, let him give a blessing for the soul of Hiroidil, son of Carotinn*. The formula in the inscription can be found on other monuments datable to about AD 800 or earlier.

103
Cribyn Decorated Stone, Llanilar

Early Christian stone
8th–9th century AD
OS 135   SN 624751   U1

Llanilar is on A485 Aberystwyth–Tregaron road, 5ml (9km) SE of Aberystwyth. Church on LHS (N) of road, on sharp bend in middle of village

Nash-Williams, 1950, no. 107

The stone now in the porch of Llanilar church was, until recently, in a field in Castle Hill House, Llanilar and was moved here to prevent further weathering. It is said to have come from an earthwork at Cribyn, some 25ml (40km) to the south. It is a quadrangular pillar-stone with a roughly pointed butt. On the face is a rectangular panel filled with triple knotwork carved in shallow relief (as on no. 100). It is datable to the 9th or 10th century.

Left to right: LLanwnnws inscribed slab and Cribyn decorated stone

104
Sculptured Crosses, Llanbadarn Fawr

Early Christian sculptured crosses
9th–11th century AD
OS 135   SN 599810   U1

Llanbadarn Fawr is on eastern outskirts of Aberystwyth on junction of A44 (Rhayader road) and A4120 (to Devil's Bridge). Church on N side of main road

Nash-Williams 1950, nos 111–12

Llanbadarn Fawr was an important early Celtic monastery or *clas* perhaps of the 6th century, dedicated to St Padarn. In about 1116, it was made a Benedictine house, a cell of Gloucester, but for a time became a secular college with a lay head. In the south transept of the church is an exhibition which relates the history of the early church here and its later development. Incorporated within this well-designed and informative exhibition are two early Christian sculptured crosses which originally stood within the churchyard.

The impressive, tall, slender cross is fashioned from a single stone, and comprises a cross-head, formed by notching the shaft, and a shaft which is round in section at the base, changing to a square section above. The cross is decorated with carved low-relief ornament on all four faces now rather eroded by past weathering.

On the front, the cross-head has a key-pattern around a central ring and boss. The shaft has six panels of decoration. At the top is a key-pattern with a cross above; then are two back-to-back animals with their back-turned heads to the top and bottom respectively; then an irregular knot-pattern above an oval (a face?). Below that is a fine carved, probably seated, male figure, perhaps of a saint or ecclesiastic with ringleted hair. The spiral-shaped fold of drapery over his arm resembles that seen in drawings of Evangelists in Irish manuscripts of the period. It is tempting to identify the figure as St Padarn himself, to whom the church is dedicated. Below the figure is a panel of square key-pattern, and at the base, two figures probably representing Jacob wrestling with the angel as seen on Irish, Scottish and northern English crosses. The worn base has a now indistinguishable pattern.

The back of the head is decorated with a plaitwork pattern around the central ring and boss; the strands of this plaitwork continue into the plaitwork and knotwork of the uppermost panel of the shaft. Below this are two panels of plaitwork, and then one of a plait with a tail-biting animal head. Next is a diaper key-pattern and at the base, a whorl motif. The sides of the head have plain vertical ribbings, while the shaft sides have a key-pattern on the right, and a knotwork on the left. The stone is dated to the late 10th century.

The second sculptured stone is a roughly shaped cruciform block of sandstone. On the front, a roughly moulded border outlines the arms of the cross. The splayed shaft has a roughly incised panel and three dots, one in the centre, and one on each side at the top. The stone is apparently an attempt at sculpture by an unskilled craftsman or was unfinished, and as such is difficult to date stylistically. It is probably 9th–11th century.

Llanbadarn Fawr Cross. Left to right: front, right, back and left sides

7

The Age of the Castle

The victory over Gruffudd ap Llywelyn succeeded in removing the threat to English supremacy and re-established the overlordship of the English crown over the Welsh princes. It was by no means a conquest of the land or its people, who continued to live for a few more years in relative independence. However, the Norman Conquest of England in 1066 brought about a completely different situation for the Welsh to face. The task of subduing Welsh opposition was initially entrusted by William the Conqueror to his Norman followers. From his firm stronghold at Hereford, William fitz Osbern, a cousin of the Conqueror himself, lost no time in attacking the Welsh border and soon the whole region of Gwent had fallen into his hands. To defend his conquests, he built a series of castles on the lands of the border or 'Marches'. These castles, built to defend a single nobleman with his followers, were a quite different concept of fortification from the communal hillforts and enclosures of old, and though most were only of earth and timber, they must have looked awesome indeed to Welsh eyes.

During the first years after the Norman Conquest, the south Welsh prince Rhys ap Tewdwr seems to have succeeded in maintaining his rule in Deheubarth (the medieval principality of south-west Wales). In return for recognition by the Normans, he paid a tribute to William the Conqueror who marched through south Wales in 1081, obstensibly as a pilgrim to St Davids, but in reality to establish his overlordship in the area. After Rhys's death in 1093, the Normans made a renewed effort to take control of the accessible southern part of south-west Wales. A series of lordships were established so that the Norman Marches in Wales eventually spread in an arc from Chester to Chepstow in the east to Pembroke in the south-west. Each Norman lord built a castle at a key strategic point in his lordship to establish his supremacy and to act as the seat of his government, and, from here, he ruled in what amounted to virtual independence, subject only to the overlordship of the distant English crown. The English king himself played only a minor role in this phase of the Welsh conquest, though a few castles at important strategic positions such as Carmarthen (no. 120) and Cardigan soon came into the hands of the crown. Early in the 12th century the first Welsh castles were built in what was known as 'pura Wallia' (pure' or non-Norman Wales), which retained its separate identity for 200 years until the reign of Edward I.

Apart from a few masonry structures constructed at important Norman strong-

Reconstruction drawing of a motte-and-bailey castle

holds such as Chepstow in south-east Wales, the castles which played so important a part in the Norman Conquest were earth-and-timber fortifications which could be cheaply and quickly erected where and when the need arose. Two types of these early castles are known: 'mottes' and 'ringworks'. Mottes were massive conical mounds of earth often 10m in height, surmounted by a wooden keep or tower. The mounds were surrounded by a ditch and palisade, and a drawbridge over the ditch controlled access to the keep. This was a brilliant plan for strength and ease of construction, but the living quarters were very cramped and uncomfortable. An additional fortified area known as a 'bailey' was often added in order to increase the space available for buildings such as the kitchens and bake-houses, barns and stables, essential for the daily life of the Norman lords. The ringwork was a variation of the motte and bailey where the domestic buildings were simply protected by a circular earthern bank and ditch, usually strengthened by a timber palisade, and a strong wooden gate to protect the entrance. In Dyfed some 68 mottes and 30 ringworks survive, most of which lie in the more fertile areas of Norman settlement. The castles which proved to be best sited, at the place where

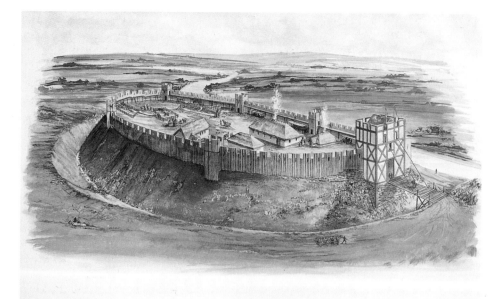

Reconstruction drawing of a castle ringwork

the '*caput*', or capital, of the lordship grew up, were rebuilt in stone and gradually developed in sophistication and size. The earthwork castles that remain to our day as simple mounds are the sites that were abandoned as no longer necessary.

Around the *caput* of the lordship, communities of traders and craftsmen would settle to serve the needs and interests of the lord and his castle. Gradually these communities were given rights and privileges in trade and some limited self-government. These rights were formalised with charters awarding them borough status, and thus towns such as Haverfordwest (no. 110) and Pembroke (no. 112) were born. Carmarthen may still have had some sort of continuing population from its days of importance under the Romans. It received its charter early on, and quickly became established as the administrative centre of the south-west. The recipients of these rights of trade in the towns of the Norman Marches at first at least, had to be non-Welsh, but the concept of urban life caught on among the Welsh also, and in 'pura Wallia', towns such as Dryslwyn (no. 122) and Dinefwr (no. 123) grew up around the castles of the Welsh princes. This growth of urban life was perhaps the most far-reaching social effect of the Norman Conquest, as, with the growth of trade and markets and the consequent wider circulation of money, the old constricted social structure gradually began to weaken, and a greater social mobility began to emerge. Later Edward I established fortified English towns around his castles to help consolidate his conquests, and the foundation of the walled town at Aberystwyth (no. 126) dates from this period. Indeed, the later 13th century was a time when many new towns were founded in Wales to serve as centres of trade, and when many existing towns increased dramatically in size. Town defences became stronger and more sophisticated, and at Tenby (no. 115) and, to a lesser extent, Pembroke and Kidwelly (no. 119), the survival of the defences and street pattern give us a flavour of how these medieval towns must have looked.

The large majority of the population, both in the Marches and in native Wales, continued, none the less, to be dependent on the soil. Under the Norman lordships, the most fertile land would be awarded by the lord to his followers or 'vassals' in return for their services. The Welsh, on the other hand, were relegated to 'Welshries', mainly in the uplands, where they were able to preserve their traditional pastoral way of life and settle their disputes by Welsh law, subject only to what tribute their alien overlords might impose. While many of the castles, Norman and Welsh alike, survive to illustrate the lifestyle of the aristocracy, little now remains of the manors and farmhouses of the Norman farmers and the dwellings of their dependants. Dyfed is poor in the earthworks of 'moated sites', or farms of men wealthy enough to surround their homes with defensive ditches. There are but few Welsh remnants, also, of the medieval 'open fields' cultivated in strips. The Hugden strip fields at Laugharne are therefore a particularly precious illustration of these early agricultural practices. The grass-covered footings of simple rectangular long-houses, built both in Welsh towns and in upland areas, survive occasionally where a settlement was later abandoned, as at Dryslwyn where the outlines of small town houses can be traced outside the castle. From the later medieval period there remain a few stone-vaulted farmhouses of a type built by wealthier farmers, such as those at Carswell (no. 129). The ruins of the finer stone houses of the aristocracy may be seen at Eastington (see Appendix) and Lydstep, while the vaulted basements of medieval urban houses still stand in a few towns in south-west Wales. Haverfordwest (no. 110) has many such medieval vaults, though the upper storeys of the houses have been completely rebuilt. But of the houses of the lower orders of society, built probably of clay and wattle and thatched with straw or reeds, hardly a trace remains.

By the reign of Henry II (1154–89), an uneasy peace was gradually emerging as agreements were negotiated with the Welsh princes by which they were left to rule over their remaining lands subject to the overlordship of the English crown. Pre-eminent among the Welsh princes of this era was Rhys ap Gruffudd, 'the Lord Rhys' as he was known, who commanded considerable power in Deheubarth and earned the benevolent respect of Henry II. He rebuilt Cardigan Castle (see Appendix) in stone, is responsible for the earliest masonry at Nevern, and Dinefwr may be his work also. By this time, the Normans were building rectangular towers in stone to replace the timber keeps which had a tendency to rot or catch fire.

Manorbier (no. 114) and Haverfordwest (no. 110) probably had such towers. A little later, in the early 13th century, a new improvement in castle design was introduced in the form of free-standing circular towers with arrowslits. These did not have the disadvantages of vulnerable corners and indefensible 'blind spots' suffered by rectangular keeps. Fine examples may be seen at Pembroke (no. 112), built by the Norman Marshal family, and at Dinefwr (no. 123), built by the Welsh.

The growth in the power of the north Welsh princes of Gwynedd in the late 12th and early 13th centuries was understandably seen as a threat by the English crown. The ambitious Llywelyn ab Iorwerth 'the Great' extended his influence over all of Welsh Wales and in 1215 even campaigned in the south Wales Marches. His grandson Llywelyn ap Gruffudd 'the Last' continued the work of reforging Welsh nationalism and gained the support of almost all the native Welsh princes. The English king, Henry III, was forced to accept his proud title of Prince of Wales. But in 1272, Edward I came to the throne and Llywelyn then faced a very different adversary, one quite determined to curb the growing power of the Welsh prince. War eventually broke out in 1276 and the year-long campaign resulted in new royal castles being built at Aberystwyth (no. 126), Builth, Flint and Rhuddlan. A short-lived peace ended on Palm Sunday, 1282 with a Welsh attack on Hawarden

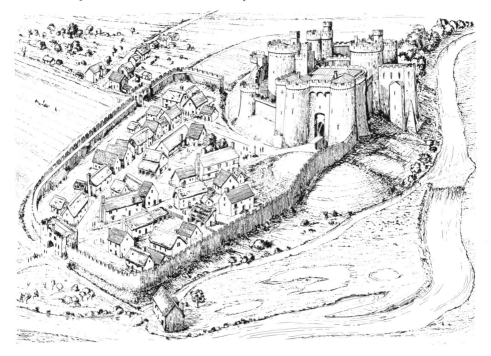

Reconstruction drawing of Kidwelly Castle and town in the 15th century

Castle. The response was quick and decisive: by the end of that year, Llywelyn was dead and the English crown pre-eminent.

During the 13th century, castle defences continued to increase in sophistication, reflecting the continuing political turmoil of the time. Attention turned for the first time away from the keep and on to the surrounding 'curtain' wall. Castles were refortified with strong stone walls with a wall-walk and parapet, and round towers were added at intervals to provide extra defence. Pembroke and Cilgerran (no. 105) provide good illustrations of this new form of fortification. Also the gatehouse became more important – to secure the defence of the entrance, always a potential weak point, a variety of devices such as the portcullis and 'murder holes' were introduced, adding further support to the battlements and arrowslits of gates and gate towers.

In response to the growing power of Llywelyn, the English introduced another quite new concept in castle building, that of the 'concentric castle'. Kidwelly (no. 119), rebuilt by the Norman Pain de Chaworth in the mid-13th century, is an excellent example: the castle has two lines of defence, one within the other, and the concentric walls are defended by towers at intervals, and by strong gatehouses at the entrances. The royal castle at Aberystwyth, in its final form at least, also followed a concentric design, and, characteristic of Edwardian castles, was sited on the sea-shore to allow for reinforcement and supply by sea in case of siege.

After the Edwardian conquest, peace and security under English rule resulted in a reduced role for the castle. But in 1400 Owain Glyndŵr led a Welsh uprising and, having captured a large number of castles including Aberystwyth, became for a short period the effective ruler of a considerable area of Wales. The rebellion petered out, however, and English authority was reasserted, their castles requiring costly repair. The lengthy Wars of the Roses between the Lancastrian and Yorkist families affected Wales as well as England and some castles, such as Carreg Cennen (no. 124) for instance, were used as important bases. With the accession of Henry Tudor after his defeat of Richard III at Bosworth in 1485, a peaceful and more orderly society was established and the need for castles virtually disappeared. Some, like Laugharne (no. 117) and Carew (no. 113), were altered drastically by the new Tudor aristocracy to modify them into comfortable residences. Men such as Rhys ap Thomas who had supported Henry were lavishly rewarded and could spend huge sums on the refurbishment of their castles. Many others were merely abandoned, and by the time of the Acts of Union, which in 1536–43 brought about the political merger of a unified Wales with England, the effective military life of the castle in Wales ended.

There was an important swan-song for some strategically situated castles during the Civil War when they once more saw active service. In 1642, Parliament and King Charles took to arms and these castles were used as military bases and proved an effective method of defence and resistance. During the second war in

1648, Pembroke held out for so long that Cromwell himself had to come to the castle to direct the bombardment. The lesson was learnt, and after the war the 'slighting', or partial destruction, of all castles was ordered by Parliament to prevent them from ever being used militarily again.

105
Cilgerran Castle, Cardigan
Medieval masonry castle
12th–14th century AD
OS 145   SN 195431   R1   NT/Cadw

From Cardigan, take A478 Tenby road S for 2ml (3.2km). At crossroads, turn L (E) to Cilgerran (1ml, 1.6km). Walk down path to site, signposted. Standard hours; admission charge

Cadw Guidebook

Cilgerran Castle stands on a precipitous, craggy promontory overlooking the River Teifi where it merges with the Plysgog stream. The Teifi here is just at its tidal limit, so the castle was able to control both a natural crossing point and the passage of seagoing ships. We cannot be sure when this strong site was first fortified. It may be the same as a Norman castle called 'Cenarth Bychan' from which, we know, Nest, the spirited and beautiful wife of the Norman lord, Gerald of Windsor, ran off with Owain, son of the prince of Powys during a Welsh attack in 1109. Cilgerran is first mentioned by name in 1164, when the Lord Rhys captured the castle here. It was recaptured by William Marshal, earl of Pembroke, in 1204, only be be taken again by the Welsh during Llywelyn the Great's campaigns in 1215. However, eight years later, William's son, another William, regained control, and it was probably he who built the imposing masonry castle that we see today.

The form of the present castle may well reflect that of the earliest earthwork castle. The headland is cut off by a bank and ditch which encloses an outer ward, probably the original bailey. The ditch can still be seen, though much of it is cultivated as gardens.

The outer gatehouse survives as low footings only and is of uncertain date and there may have been another, perhaps later, gatehouse on the site of the modern entrance. Much of the existing outer ward wall is a thin modern rebuild; the collapse of the original wall was caused by slate quarrying on the cliff below.

Some 20m beyond the outer defences, another ditch encloses the inner ward, which William fortified in stone with two formidable towers and a strong gatehouse. An interesting feature in the ditch is the sally-port, which consists of a door through the wall next to the east tower, and another in the outer ward wall, which together gave access to the sloping ground east of the castle to enable defenders to slip around to take attackers in the rear. A drawbridge crossed the deep ditch in front of the three-storey gatehouse. The outer part of the gatehouse has fallen, but the portcullis grooves and the draw-bar holes for the gates can still be seen at either end of the gate passage. There was a vaulted room, perhaps a chapel, over the gate, and above this, a passage in the curtain wall, defended with arrowslits, connected the gatehouse with the two round towers to its east. Finally, at the top of the wall, a battlemented wall-walk gave the castle's defenders a second access route to the towers.

The strong, plain round towers protrude well beyond the curtain wall, and the outer defensive parts of their walls are much thicker than the inner sides. They are massive, unpretentious structures, designed with defence as the primary consideration; a series of arrowslits are the only openings on the outer side, to minimise the points of weakness against attack. Both towers have a ground floor and three upper storeys, the positions of which can be seen by the joist-

Aerial view of Cilgerran Castle, inner ward (right) and outer ward (left)

holes for the timber floors and by the fireplaces. The eastern tower was entered at first-floor level from the courtyard by a door which led to a newel or spiral stair; the ground-floor room had a separate entrance, and access to the upper floors was probably by a trapdoor. The west tower originally had a first-floor entrance reached by a stair from the inner ward; again, there must have been a trapdoor to give access to the ground floor which may have functioned as a strong-room or dungeon. Later, the ground-floor door was inserted and a newel or spiral stair was put in to give access above. The cross-wall was then built, so that the far side of the ground floor

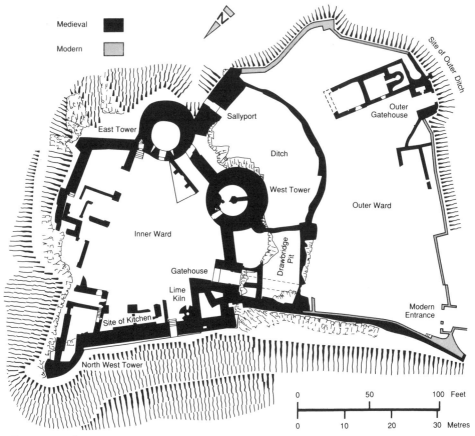

Cilgerran Castle

could continue in use as a strong-room.

The curtain wall and the remains of buildings along the north-east and north-west sides of the inner ward are a later build, probably dating to the second half of the 13th century, when the castle had passed through marriage from the Marshals first to the de Cantelupes, and then to the Hastings family. Some of the wall footings must belong to the hall and private apartments, and the kitchen lay against the western wall. A large square tower lay in the south-western corner. Near this is a round lime-kiln, and beyond, another well-defended sally-port to supplement the one in the outer ward.

In the 1370s an invasion from France was feared, and Edward III ordered that the now rather derelict Cilgerran be refortified. The north-west tower probably belongs to this period – it is clearly an addition, though so ruinous that it is difficult to date. After 1389, when the Hastings family died out, the castle passed to the crown, with which it was thenceforward closely associated. It may have been captured and held for a short time in 1405 during Glyndŵr's wars of independence; we known for certain that it was much damaged during the attack. But after that the castle's active military service came to an end. In the Tudor period, the Vaughan family were granted the castle by Henry VII, and they continued to occupy it until the early 17th century, when they built a new house nearby. The castle fell into ruin, but its picturesque setting made it an early favourite among tourists who, from the 18th century, could visit by boat from Cardigan.

106
Castell Nanhyfer, Nevern
Medieval motte and bailey
12th century AD
OS 145   SN 082401   U1/2

From Newport, travel E along A487 towards Cardigan for 1.5ml (2.4km). Take B4582 N (L) to Nevern. Turn L, signed Nevern Castle, and *follow road up hill. Site signposted on RHS 0.5ml (0.8km) out of village and reached by footpath (level but can be muddy)*

King and Perks 1951

The castle at Nevern is a fine example of a motte and bailey. It is made especially interesting by a short secondary development, after which it was abandoned, leaving the 12th-century plan unusually clear. It was the castle of the fitz Martins, the Norman lords of Cemais, but in 1191 the Welsh attacked and it was seized by Rhys ap Gruffudd, 'the Lord Rhys', who gave it to his son Maelgwyn. Three years later, Rhys himself was captured and briefly imprisoned at Nevern, or Nanhyfer as it was then known, by Maelgwyn and another son, Hywel Sais. The castle remained in the hands of Rhys's family after his death, though it lay far from the principal sphere of the family's possessions in the Tywi valley. In 1204 William fitz Martin re-established Norman influence in Cemais, but shifted his seat to the mouth of the River Nevern at Newport. Nanhyfer Castle seems then to have been entirely abandoned.

The castle stands on the western tip of a gorge in which the Gamman stream runs, near where it joins the Nevern river. The position is naturally defended by the gorge on the south-east, a small gully on the north, and the slopes overlooking the Nevern valley on the south. Only the western side is level. A high motte, or mound, was raised on the north-west, and two lines of banks run east–west and north–south to the lip of the gorge. On the north, the strength of the two banks was enhanced by the addition of a slight external counterscarp which may originally have continued on the west, where the modern road would have destroyed it.

On the eastern extremity of the site, a small, strong fortification has been formed by the excavation of a rock-cut ditch which cuts off a small level platform. This well-preserved ditch is still 6m deep, with smooth, vertical sides. The interior of the platform is ringed by the

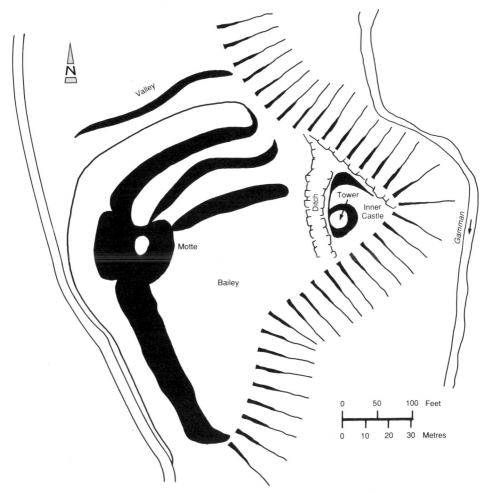

Castell Nanhyfer

remains of a stone wall. On the west is a large mound, which appears to have been formed by the collapse of a stone tower, originally perhaps around 10m square. The tower and bailey thus formed seem to have superseded the original western motte. It has been suggested that the building of this smaller stronghold on the east is the result of remodelling undertaken by Rhys to suit his very different requirements. Nevern thus changed from an important English castle, the '*caput*' or strong seat of the Norman lord, to a minor Welsh castle on the fringes of the family's sphere of influence.

107
Pointz Castle, St Davids
Medieval earthwork castle
12th century AD
OS 157   SM 831237   U1   NT

*From St Davids, take A487 SE towards
Haverfordwest for 5ml (8km). Drive up hill 2ml
(3.2km) beyond Solva, take 3rd track on RHS
through farmyard and park opposite site on
LHS*

Pointz Castle is a fine, though rather
overgrown, earthwork castle. The motte has a
classic flat-topped 'inverted pudding basin'
shape and on it originally would have stood a
timber defensive tower, or keep. The mound
is surrounded by a well-preserved ditch, and
there are traces of a slight counterscarp bank
beyond. If the castle originally had a bailey,
the earthworks have long since disappeared,
though the field to the west has traditionally
been called 'Parc y castell'.

In the mid-19th century, the south side of
the mound was dug into, and the resulting
scar is still visible. Apparently several bronze
coins were discovered. A pillar-slab with an
incised cross was also found on the motte,
and is now built into the modern farmhouse.

Though little is known for certain about the
history of the site, the castle may have been
the stronghold of Punchard, or Pons, a
Norman tenant of Peter de Leia, bishop of St
Davids from 1176 to 1190. The property was
retained by the bishopric and later became
one of its principal granges, though by then
the castle itself would have fallen into disuse.
A reference of 1326 mentions the place-name
'Castrum Poncii'.

108
New Moat Castle,
Maenclochog
Medieval earthwork castle
12th century AD
OS 145   SN 064254   U3

*From Maenclochog, 9ml (14.4km) N of
Narberth on B4313 Narberth–Fishguard road,
take minor road W toward Llys y Fran for 0.8ml
(1.3km), then turn L and proceed to New Moat
(1.2ml, 1.9km). Turn L in village and park by
stile in 1st field on LHS. Public footpath goes
over stile, across field past mound*

The tiny village of New Moat is dominated by
its two medieval monuments, the church
(now very rebuilt), and the earthwork castle.
The castle mound or 'motte' is a very fine
example, with a classic 'inverted pudding
basin' shape and flat top; it is now covered
with trees, but only sparsely, so that its shape
is clearly seen. It is about 5m high, with a
diameter of 17m at the top. The encircling
ditch now holds water, though it may have
been altered in fairly recent times. The motte
had a bailey which lies in the field to the west
of the motte. The low earthworks of the bailey
bank can be seen running parallel to the field
bank along the road-side, and are less well
preserved, but still just visible, on the two
short sides where the bank turns to join the
motte on the south and, in the garden, on the

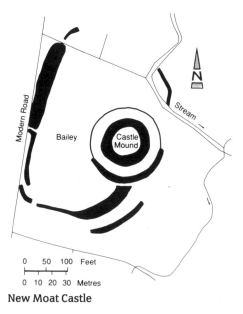

0   50   100   Feet

0   10   20   30   Metres

New Moat Castle

north. There is now no sign of any ditch. The bailey bank encloses an area of some 125m by 80m, and the entrance was probably on the south-west. The land to the east of the motte is marshy, and would have acted as an extra defence.

Henry's Moat, just to the north-west at SN 045275, also has a motte and church in close association, though the motte here is not so well presented.

109
Llawhaden Castle, Llawhaden

Medieval masonry castle

12th–16th century AD

OS 158   SN 073175   R1   Cadw

Llawhaden is 7ml (11.2km) E of Haverfordwest. On A40, turn N signed Llawhaden. At T-junction, stop at PO for key. Turn R, park along road, and walk L along signed path to castle

Cadw Guidebook

The bishops of St Davids owned extensive estates in south-west Wales and their lands in the Llawhaden area were particularly rich. Such important estates required protection, and Llawhaden Castle was built in the early 12th century for that purpose. The form of this earliest castle, a ringwork of earth and timber, may still be seen in the existing circular bank and ditch which would have protected the interior timber buildings of the bishop's residence. The bank has been reduced, and later stone buildings placed on top of it, but its plan is still clear. Originally, the castle would have been entered by a wooden gate and the bank was probably surmounted by a wooden palisade. Such was the castle that Giraldus Cambrensis saw when he visited his uncle, Bishop David fitz Gerald here in 1175. But the defensive capabilities of such castles were inevitably limited, and in 1192 the Lord Rhys, prince of Deheubarth, captured and destroyed the castle. The

earliest stone buildings probably date to the early 13th century when the bishops recovered Llawhaden; the foundations of the circular tower on the south-west, and the semicircular tower on the north-west still survive to demonstrate the strength of these new defences.

In the late 13th and early 14th century the castle was transformed into a great fortified mansion, more appropriate as the residence of men of the standing of the bishops of St Davids. It was now equipped both with quarters for a permanent garrison and with comfortable lodgings for important guests or the bishop's entourage. Earlier buildings and defences were dramatically altered or removed altogether – although the circular shape of the ringwork still remained, the bank became the base for large new residential buildings arranged around a central court. This work was probably carried out by Bishop Thomas Bek (1280–93) – who also founded the borough or market town of Llawhaden with a hospital for the poor and aged infirm – and his successor, Bishop David Martyn (1293–1328). After this, there were further building phases in the later 14th century when the imposing extension to the gatehouse and the chapel and chapel tower were built, and the early 16th century when the south range was remodelled and the chapel porch added. Tradition records that the castle was dismantled by Bishop Barlow in the mid-16th century, when the bishops moved their chief residence to Abergwili, near Carmarthen.

The outer part of the twin-towered gatehouse stands to parapet level, almost the full 14th-century height. The entrance is probably the most impressive part of the castle – the banded effect of the blue stone used in the masonry, the semicircular flanking towers with their heavy spurred bases and arrowslits, and the murder holes above the drawbridge combine to make the approach to the castle memorable. Behind the facade much of the gatehouse has fallen, but the passage still retains the slots for the portcullis, and the basements of guardrooms may be seen on either side. Originally, a large hall ran over the passage at first-floor level, and was probably used as the residence of the constable of the castle.

Across the courtyard, opposite the gatehouse, was the hall. The principal rooms were on the first floor, approached by an external stair from the courtyard; they lay above vaulted ground-floor store-rooms. Two wings were attached to the hall. That on the east housed the bishop's private apartments on the first-floor, while on the west was a kitchen; a bakehouse, which was built later,

lies adjacent.

On the east of the inner ward are the remains of the chapel, much of which has now fallen. The entrance was by a first-floor doorway fronted by a slender porch and stair which still stands; the outer doorway is decorated with a crowned male head and a female head with a wimple head-dress. The small, isolated rooms in the porch above the access to the chapel probably housed the exchequer, or finance officer, of the bishop. On either side of the main gatehouse are large rooms over vaulted basements. The eastern

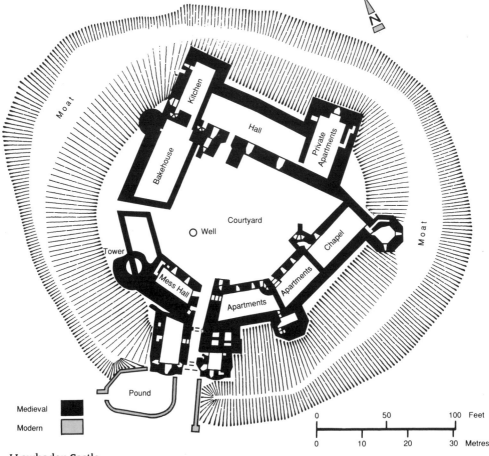

LLawhaden Castle

on the first and second floors of this tower the views of the castle courtyard are particularly fine.

110
Haverfordwest Castle
Medieval masonry castle
12th–18th century AD
OS 157   SM 953157   U1

The castle dominates Haverfordwest, and there are signs for foot access (to Castle Museum and Record Office) from town centre

The castle stands on a superb, naturally defensive position at the end of a strong, isolated ridge with a sheer cliff on the east. It was an English foundation, first established, reputedly, by Gilbert de Clare, earl of Pembroke, in the mid-12th century, and remained an English stronghold throughout its history. It is first mentioned by Giraldus Cambrensis as one of the places he visited in 1188 with Archbishop Baldwin. Of that castle, which must have been primarily of earth and timber, little now survives, except, perhaps, for the footings of a large, square keep in the north-east corner of the inner ward which may be late 12th-century. This is certainly the earliest surviving structure, and its position at the eastern extremity of the site, overlooking the river crossing, is significant. Some arrowslits in its vaulted ground-floor walls are still visible, half-buried in the ground.

The present form of the castle, divided into two wards, probably reflects that of the original 12th-century castle. The plan is a little difficult to make out, as the museum lies in the centre of the outer ward, while the former prison governor's house lies on the site of the inner ward gatehouse. The medieval castle was converted into a prison in the 18th century, but the buildings of the inner ward and the outer defences can still be appreciated. Haverfordwest was probably a strong stone castle by 1220, when it withstood an attack by Llywelyn the Great

Llawhaden Castle gatehouse

rooms are on two floors and probably served as the well-equipped apartments of important guests of the bishop; each set has a sizeable room with a fireplace, and a smaller bedroom with a lavatory housed in the south-west polygonal tower. The large room on the west may have been to accommodate the small garrison of armed retainers, kept at the castle by the bishops for their defence.

The later castle defences consist of the eastern and southern polygonal towers which gave a formidable appearance to the castle exterior, but in reality were built less for serious defence than to provide service areas and latrines for the apartment blocks within a military-style facade. Each tower has a vaulted ground floor and two further upper floors. In the east tower is a circular rock-cut dungeon with an entrance set into the ground floor, which presumably functioned as the castle's prison. From the octagonal apartment rooms

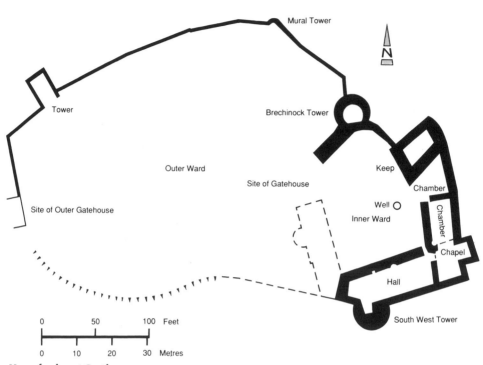

Dyfed

Mural Tower

Tower

Brechinock Tower

Outer Ward

Keep

Site of Gatehouse

Chamber

Site of Outer Gatehouse

Well ⟠

Inner Ward

Chamber

Chapel

Hall

South West Tower

0   50   100   Feet

0   10   20   30   Metres

Haverfordwest Castle

who had already burned the town. For some
reason, it was acquired in 1289 by Queen
Eleanor who immediately began building
there on a large scale, to judge from the
considerable sums of money recorded as
being spent on 'the queen's castle of
Haverford'. Much of the existing masonry is
late-13th-century in style and may well have
been undertaken during the one year before
her death in 1290.

The lofty inner ward has round towers on
the north-west and south-west corners, while
the south-east corner has a square tower with
an additional projecting turret. Presumably
the keep in the north-east still stood to defend
this corner, and the sharp angle in the curtain
wall marks the corner of the keep masonry.
The entrance lay on the west, protected by a
gatehouse of which no trace survives. The
remains of a spacious hall lie on the south,

with large windows built high enough in the
exterior wall to be safe from attack by
besiegers equipped with scaling ladders. The
east-range buildings were particularly
affected by the conversion of the castle into
the gaol. The large windows were blocked and
much of the masonry refaced. The private
apartments and the chapel probably lay on
this side. The south-west and south-east
towers have three storeys, the latter with a
basement equipped with a postern gate to
allow access to a small terrace which could be
used to counter-attack during a siege. The
internal arrangements of the north-west
tower have been made very confusing by the
insertion of a ventilation shaft for the gaol
partly over the spiral stair; at the same time,
much of the exterior masonry was refaced.
Even so, the wall-walk, carried on a row of
corbels on the east of the tower, is a well-

preserved feature on the inside, and from the outside of the castle the tower's remaining lights and arrowslits can be seen.

The outer ward has lost much of its medieval defences, but the curtain wall survives, albeit in a very rebuilt form, along most of the north side, with one small semicircular turret and a square tower further east. An outer gatehouse presumably lay near the present entrance on the west. This was the only side with no formidable natural defence, and would doubtless have been strengthened by an external ditch, though nothing survives here now.

In the 14th century, the castle was held by a series of owners including Edward, the Black Prince (from 1359 to 1367). In the hands of the crown from 1381 to 1385, the castle was repaired, and £129 was apparently spent on the castle, mill and weir. It was still strong enough to repulse an attack in 1405 during Glyndŵr's wars of independence. By the 16th century, however, it was derelict, but was hastily refortified during the Civil War. A story relates how, in 1644 the nervous Royalists abandoned the castle, mistaking a herd of cows on a nearby hill for a Parliamentary army, thus allowing it to fall to Parliament a few days later without any resistance! It was later recaptured and held for a year for the king, but finally surrendered after the battle of Colby Moor, just to the west (at SN 043174), when the Parliamentarians routed a Royalist army on the march.

Haverfordwest Castle

Medieval Haverfordwest was defended by town walls around the high ground near the castle, which were later extended as the town rapidly became an important market and trading place. Nothing remains of these town walls, although the three medieval churches of Haverfordwest do survive (see no. 140), and many of the shops in the town retain their medieval vaulted basements. One such basement, curiously divorced from its now-demolished upper storeys, stands opposite St Mary's church. It has fine decorated vaulting and must have belonged to a structure of some importance.

111
Wiston Castle, Haverfordwest
Medieval motte and bailey
12th–13th century AD
OS 158   SN 022181   U3

From Haverfordwest, take A40 towards Carmarthen. After 2.5ml (4km), take LH turn and follow signs to Wiston (1st L then R at T-junction). Park by church. Site on opposite side of road, over stile. Castle may soon come into state care, but until that time, request permission to visit from Manor Farm

Wiston must rank as one of the best-preserved motte-and-bailey castles in Wales. It is named after, and was probably built by, an early Flemish settler with the improbable name of Wizo (in Latin) or Gwys (Welsh). Wizo was dead by 1130, but the castle is first mentioned in documents in 1147 when it was taken by the Welsh. It was again taken by the Welsh in 1193, when it fell, apparently with the aid of treachery, to Hywel Sais, the son of the Lord Rhys, but was recaptured in 1195. In 1220, however, it was captured and destroyed by Llywelyn the Great, prince of Gwynedd, during one of his campaigns in south Wales. The local people were told to help William Marshal, earl of Pembroke, to rebuild it. Whether or not this rebuilding took

Wiston Castle

place is uncertain. The masonry shell-keep could be his work, but the style of the arch suggests an earlier date, and it is quite possible that the fallen masonry which still lies on the north was brought down during Llywelyn's attack.

Whatever happened after 1220, the castle was abandoned abruptly at an unusual and intermediate stage in castle development. The original wooden tower had been replaced by a stone shell-keep, but there were no further masonry additions, and thus the early stonework remains clear and unobscured.

The castle is situated on a high hill on the north side of the village of Wiston. The motte stands some 9m above the bottom of the deep encircling ditch, and is 18m in diameter at its summit. Upon the flat top of the mound is a shell-keep, or encircling stone wall, which would have formed the main defence, and within which would have stood other buildings, probably of timber. The shell-keep wall is circular internally, but externally the wall face is polygonal with 18 sides. Sections of the northern side of the wall have fallen toward the ditch. On the south side, facing the bailey, is the arched entrance on either side of which are deep draw-bar holes for securing the wooden gate. The wall varies from 1.5 to 2m in width and from 3 to 4m in height.

The large oval bailey is surrounded by an unusually well preserved bank which crosses

the motte ditch to abut the mound. The bailey ditch survives on the north and west, but has been filled in on the other two sides. The entrance through the bailey defences is on the north-east and is strengthened by an outer protective earthwork. This strongly defended bailey would have enclosed the main residence and ancillary buildings of the lord, which would almost certainly have been of timber.

There was an extraordinary military postscript to the castle's history during the Civil War. In 1643, the Royalists established a small outpost at Wiston, perhaps at the old motte. They withdrew, apparently without offering any resistance, when the Parliamentarians under Major-General Rowland Laugharne renewed operations in the area in 1644. A famous rout of the Royalists by a force of Laugharne's Parliamentarian troops took place at Colby Moor (SN 043174), just to the south-east of Wiston.

112
Pembroke Castle
Medieval masonry castle and town defences
11th–20th century AD
OS 158   SM 982016   R1   Private trust

Castle on W side of town. Park in town car parks, from which castle is easily accessible. Standard hours; admission charge. From castle, town walls and Barnard's Tower accessible on foot

King 1978; King and Cheshire 1982

The unsurpassed strength of this mighty Norman castle, sited on a high ridge between two tidal inlets, gave it the distinction of never having fallen to the Welsh. The strategic position, on a major routeway, was chosen early in the first Norman incursions into south-west Wales, when the castle was

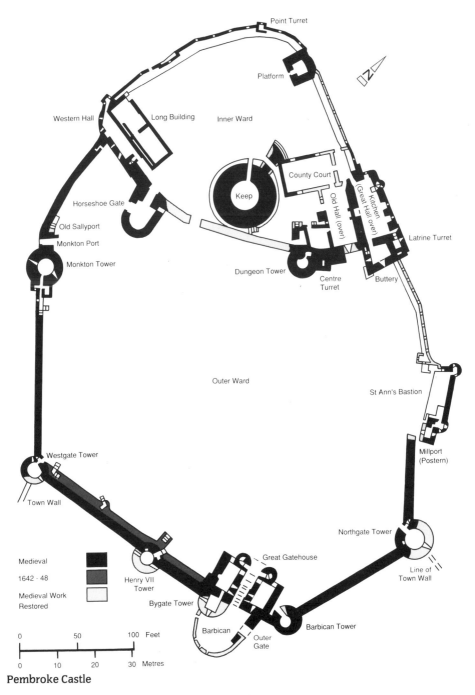

Point Turret

Platform

Western Hall
Long Building
Inner Ward

Horseshoe Gate

County Court

Keep

Kitchen (Great Hall over)

Old Hall (over)

Latrine Turret

Old Sallyport

Monkton Port

Monkton Tower

Dungeon Tower

Centre Turret

Buttery

Outer Ward

St Ann's Bastion

Westgate Tower

Millport (Postern)

Town Wall

Medieval

1642 - 48

Medieval Work Restored

Henry VII Tower

Great Gatehouse

Northgate Tower

Line of Town Wall

Bygate Tower

Barbican

Outer Gate

Barbican Tower

0   50   100   Feet
0   10   20   30   Metres

Pembroke Castle

141

founded by Roger of Montgomery in 1093, and it stood firm against Welsh counter-attacks in subsequent years.

Pembroke's strategic importance soon increased, as it was from here that the Normans embarked upon their Irish campaigns. In 1189, the castle came into the hands of William Marshal, who, over the next 30 years transformed the earth-and-timber castle into a mighty stone fortification. First to be built was the inner ward with its magnificent round keep, deservedly famous for its early date, height of over 22m and remarkable domed roof. The original entrance was on the first floor, approached by an external stair, the present ground-floor entrance being a later insertion. The keep had four floors, connected by a spiral stair which also led to the battlements. The large square holes at the top on the outside were to hold a timber hoard, or fighting platform. When the castle was attacked, the hoard could be erected as an extra defence, outside the battlements but way above the heads of attackers.

Enclosing the keep was the inner-ward curtain wall, to the south-west stood the large horseshoe-shaped gate, which only survives at footings level, and to the east was a strong round tower with a basement prison. Only a thin wall was required along the cliff edge; it had a small observation turret at the point, and the square stone platform on the north supported a huge medieval catapult for defence against attack from the sea. The domestic buildings on the west and east of the inner ward included William Marshal's hall and private apartments. These were improved and further buildings added in the later 13th century, when the new Great Hall was built with a towering mass of walling projecting over the south-east corner to enclose the mouth of a large cavern in the rock below which may have served as a boathouse (no. 2). At the same period, a large single-storey building was added near the keep to serve as the county court. By this time, the castle had passed to the de Valence family; the Hastings family then held it from

1324 to 1389, after which the castle passed into the hands of the crown.

Much of the building work in the outer ward may also belong to the early 13th-century work of William Marshal, and the main plan of the present defences remains as originally constructed. However, the apparently almost perfect preservation of this work is largely an illusion, as there was at the castle a systematic programme of restoration in the 19th and early 20th century. Much of the north-eastern defences, most of the curtain wall, the outer parts of the gatehouse and barbican, and most of the Westgate and Henry VII towers have been rebuilt from footings.

The fine series of four round towers, the north-east bastion and the remarkable gatehouse on the south made the defences of the outer ward wellnigh impregnable. There were postern gates on either side, defended by the St Ann's Bastion and Monkton Tower respectively, but the main gatehouse, with its two portcullises, stout doors, three machicolations, or murder holes, in the vaulting and its series of arrowslits, is one of the finest and earliest of its kind. The western Bygate Tower has a prison in its basement, then each gate tower has a ground and two upper floors reached by stairs spiralling in opposite directions. Doors lead from the upper rooms on to the wall-walk. The gatehouse is in essence a double-towered gate, with one of the towers moved along the curtain wall to clear the oblique entrance approach; its outer part is further defended by a fine semicircular barbican.

The castle was granted out by the crown with a series of short-lived tenancies, and fell into considerable disrepair. In 1405 Francis Court was hastily given munitions to hold the castle against Owain Glyndŵr's uprising. The castle later passed into the hands of Jasper Tewdwr, earl of Pembroke, and was apparently the birthplace of his nephew Henry, later King Henry VII. The room in the uncomfortable Henry VII Tower, in which tradition states that the future king was born, is a most unlikely birthplace, and it is to be

Pembroke Castle

hoped that his mother the widowed Lady Margaret Beaufort was given more consideration.

Pembroke declared its support for Parliament at the beginning of the Civil War, but in 1648, the town's mayor, John Poyer, disgruntled at his lack of reward, joined a disaffected group of Roundheads unwilling to be demobilised. Cromwell himself came to besiege the castle which only fell after seven weeks when the water supply was cut off and a train of siege cannon arrived to start a bombardment. After this defiance Cromwell blew up the barbican and the fronts of all the towers to prevent the castle ever again being used militarily.

The town of Pembroke still retains sections of its defences, which ran south from the Westgate Tower and east from the Northgate Tower. The northern line ran along what is now Millpond Walk. Little survives of the stretch nearer the castle, but further along are some well-preserved sections with crenellations still visible, but blocked by the raising of the walls, when stair ramps were built along them to give access to the town houses within. A small circular tower on the

north-east was originally attached by a now broken stretch of wall to 'Barnard's Tower', an impressive three-storeyed tower with a forebuilding over its entrance, defended by a bridge pit, portcullis and gate. The roof dome is intact, and the whole structure with its fireplace and lavatory is a strong, almost self-contained, defensive unit; this was probably necessary as it was isolated on the north-eastern end of the town, almost half a mile (0.8km) from the castle.

The wall (inaccessible) continues south from Barnard's Tower to Eastgate which formerly stood over Main Street. The only other surviving sections are a small fragment of a tower on Goose Lane and two small round towers on the south. They stand on a very rebuilt piece of town wall, and one has a later summer-house built on top. The southern town walls ran alongside a flat marsh, probably tidal in the 13th century. A fragment of Westgate survives opposite the castle entrance. The town defences, rather thin in comparison with others, are very early, and probably date to much the same time as William Marshal's late 12th- or early 13th-century work at the castle.

113
Carew Castle, Pembroke

Medieval masonry castle
12th–17th century AD
OS 158   SN 047038   R1
Pembrokeshire Coast National Park

*Carew is on A477, 3.5ml (5.6km) NE of
Pembroke. Turn N on to A4075. Castle
(signposted) 0.5ml (0.8km) further on LHS.
Open Easter–October; admission charge*

King and Perks 1962; Official Guidebook

Carew Castle is justly celebrated as one of the
most magnificent among the castles of Dyfed.
Its position is low-lying, but still prominent in
the flat land around the tidal reaches of the
Carew river. The castle stands at the end of a
ridge at a strategically excellent site

commanding a crossing point of the then-still-
navigable river.

The modern entrance to the castle is from
the east, following the medieval route
through the bailey, within which lie low
grassy footings of the later medieval service
buildings. These were protected by a
gatehouse, a wall and a massive rock-cut
ditch. Excavations have shown that this ditch
was in fact a recut of a much earlier one, dug
as part of a defensive system cutting off the
ridge in pre-Norman, perhaps Iron Age times.
The strength of these early defences suggests
that the site was important even in
prehistory, and settlement certainly went on
into the Roman period. But there is no
evidence to suggest any continuity between
this early settlement and the 12th century
when the castle was founded, early in the
Anglo-Norman conquest of south-west Wales.
Little now remains of the earth and timber

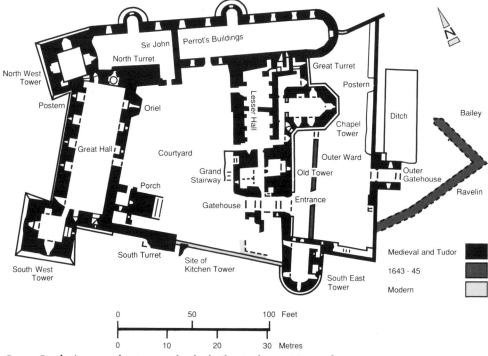

Carew Castle, inner and outer wards; the bailey to the east is not shown

Carew Castle

castle that was built here by the Norman Gerald of Windsor around 1100. It is first mentioned in 1212, when for some reason, King John seized it for a short time when passing through Pembroke on his Irish expedition. By this time it is probable that the first stone structure, the Old Tower, had been built to protect the original castle entrance through defences which may still have been earthen banks with timber palisades. The castle remained in the hands of the influential de Carew family who built, in various phases, the strong medieval castle that stands today. Its history, however, was without major incident until about 1480, when Sir Edmund Carew disposed of it to Rhys ap Thomas. Rhys, basking in the gratitude of King Henry VII for the support he had given him after his landing at Milford Haven, was able to spend significant sums on the castle, and set about converting it into a home worthy of an influential Tudor gentleman. It was he who built the gatehouse which leads from the bailey into the outer ward of the castle.

From this small, square gatehouse, there is a fine view of the outside of the inner ward. The early 13th-century 'Old Tower' is abutted on the north by the late 13th-century hall and polygonal, projecting chapel tower; the rounded end of Perrot's Elizabethan wing (see below) lies beyond, on the north corner. To the south lie the early 14th-century gatehouse and the late 13th-century south-east tower. Rhys ap Thomas later heightened some parts and much of the battlemented top is in fact his rather less-than-serious military work. The main gate into the inner ward is surprisingly unsophisticated. It has no strong projecting towers or outer portcullis, but only an outer door, five murder holes in the vault above, an inner door with no less than three bar-holes and a portcullis.

The castle was, in the late 13th and early 14th century, in the hands of Sir Nicholas de Carew who constructed many of the stone buildings which surround the small, compact inner ward. On the east (right) side is a now ruinous, three-storey tower in the corner which may have been balanced by a similar tower on the north-east, removed by the later Perrot wing (see below), but the early first-floor hall, built over a vaulted basement, and the fine, projecting chapel tower still stand intact. The courtyard elevation was, however, refaced entirely by Rhys ap Thomas to present a more uniform and decorative appearance. The fine windows on this courtyard side and the ornate fireplace inside the hall are also his work. The chapel was housed on the first floor of the semi-octagonal chapel tower and has an attractive cross-ribbed vaulted ceiling, and a *piscina* and an aumbry (cupboard) on either side of the east window. Above the chapel was a private room.

The curtain wall on the south was slighted after the Civil War and much of the present wall is modern. Of the Kitchen Tower, which originally stood on this side, virtually nothing remains. From outside the castle, however, the small rectangular South Turret can be seen, built by Rhys ap Thomas, who also rebuilt the upper sections of the adjacent curtain wall with thin battlements and no wall-walk, clearly added only for effect.

The early 14th-century western range consists of the Great Hall and two projecting towers, one at each corner. The Great Hall occupied the full length of the building at first-floor level over vaulted ground-floor storage rooms, which are now ruinous and open to the sky. The hall has a minstrels' gallery on the south, a fine series of windows and two fireplaces. Rhys ap Thomas confined his additions here to the oriel window on the north, and, on the south, the rich three-storied porch over the steps which led into the hall. On the porch are the arms of Henry VII, of Arthur, prince of Wales, to the left, and of Arthur's wife, Catherine of Aragon, to the right, probably put there as a courtesy to the royal family who attended a great tournament held by Rhys at the castle in 1507. This splendid and costly event was undoubtedly one of the most lavish entertainments in the history of Wales.

The magnificent north wing was the last major addition to the castle. It was built by Sir John Perrot, to whom the castle was granted by the crown in 1558 after the downfall of Rhys ap Thomas's descendants. The building necessitated the destruction of the north-east tower and northern curtain wall. The range consisted of five great rooms, the second floor being occupied by one enormous long gallery over 40m in length. The facade of the building is typically Elizabethan with two rows of great rectangular mullioned and transomed windows and two big oriel windows supported on massive tower-like semicircular bases. Magnificent though it was, the building was not occupied for long. Sir John was convicted for treason in 1592 and died (of natural causes) in the Tower. Thereafter the castle was let out to tenants, who probably found the great mansion too expensive to maintain, and the castle was abandoned in about 1686.

During the Civil War the castle was refortified and the angular 'redan', or 'ravelin', for the guns still survives as a low, grassed bank immediately outside the middle gatehouse. It is worth walking around outside the castle to see the two early 14th-century drum-towers on the north- and south-west corners with their massive spurred bases. From the north, across the bridge, look back at the castle's ornate Elizabethan range with its extraordinary expanse of windows. Carew Bridge is also very fine, and the early tidal mill and millpond and the magnificent early medieval cross (no. 94) contribute to the memorable setting.

114
Manorbier Castle
Medieval masonry castle
12th–20th century AD
OS 158   SS 065978   R1   Private trust

From Pembroke, take A4139 E towards Tenby for 5ml (8km). Take B4585 R (S) to Manorbier. Park in beach car park, walk up hill to castle entrance. Open Easter week, then mid May – end of Sept 10.30–5.30; admission charge

King and Perks 1970; Castle Guidebook

Manorbier is famous as the birthplace of Giraldus Cambrensis, the Welsh ecclesiastic

who in 1188 accompanied Archbishop
Baldwin on his tour of Wales to recruit for the
Third Crusade. Giraldus' subsequent books
describe Manorbier as 'the pleasantest spot in
Wales', a description with which it is easy to
agree. The castle overlooks the valley and the
beach and nearby are the remains of a mill
with its millpond and a dovecote (no. 131),
while, from the high ground to the south, the
church overlooks the castle to complete this
pleasing complex.

The secluded charm of the village now and
in the medieval period owes much to the
relative lack of political importance of the
family to whom the castle belonged. The de
Barrys, taking their name, Giraldus tells us,
from the Barry in South Glamorgan, were its
owners by 1146 when the castle is first
mentioned, and the earliest masonry at the
castle, that of the hall block and the tower
next to the gatehouse, could date from then.
Whether or not any earth-and-timber castle
preceded this stone one is therefore
uncertain. Giraldus tells us that the castle was
'excellently well defended by turrets and
bulwarks' and describes most lyrically the
fishpond, orchard, vineyard and hazel wood
which lay around the walls. The more
important estates of the de Barry family lay in
Ireland, taken during their participation in the
conquest of that country in the 12th century,
and Manorbier passed from generation to
generation quite peaceably. It did see some
action in about 1327, but only in an
unimportant family dispute between Richard
de Barry and his nephew David.

In the later 14th century, the castle passed
to Sir John Cornwall, who in 1403 was ordered
by the English king to fortify it in case of
attack by Glyndŵr; however, no such attack
occurred. After 1475, Manorbier became
crown property, and had a number of
occupiers, among the most illustrious of
whom was Margaret Beaufort, granted the
castle for life by her son Henry VII. But by
1630, the castle was disposed of, eventually
to the Phillips of Picton Castle, who still own it
today. In 1645, early on in their ownership,
the castle was taken by Major-General

Aerial view of Manorbier Castle

Rowland Laugharne for Parliament during the
Civil War, and, although it is doubtful if he met
with much resistance, earthworks associated
with a Civil War refortification still survive.

Manorbier owes much of its rather
domestic charm to its unusual later history.
Farm buildings, constructed in both inner and
outer wards, suggest a more workaday
agricultural use by the 17th and 18th
centuries, but in 1880, J R Cobb, a castle
enthusiast, leased Manorbier, and built the
present house in the inner ward. He added
floors in the North and Round Towers and in
the gatehouse which was also roofed.

The castle that Giraldus knew may have
included the present hall and Old Tower. The
rectangular hall block is on the west, and in its
north end the private apartments lie on the

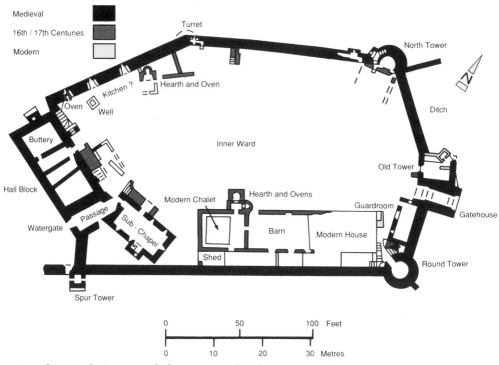

Dyfed

Medieval ▨

16th / 17th Centuries ▨

Modern ▢

Turret

North Tower

Hearth and Oven

Kitchen ?

Oven

Well

Buttery

Inner Ward

Ditch

Old Tower

Hall Block

Modern Chalet

Hearth and Ovens

Guardroom

Gatehouse

Watergate

Passage

Sub - Chapel

Barn

Modern House

Shed

Round Tower

Spur Tower

```
0            50           100  Feet
├────────────┼────────────┤
0      10     20      30  Metres
```

Manorbier Castle, inner ward; the outer ward to the east is not shown

top floor of what is here a three-storey building. The dividing wall between hall and apartments has now fallen. The hall itself lay over vaulted ground-floor basements, curious in that they were unlit save for the lampstands in the northern ones. The southern two were bricked up in the 13th century and even now the southernmost is inaccessible, though the other has been breached. The hall was entered from an external stair from the courtyard. The scant foundations of a building on the north-west may be the remains of the kitchen, though this cannot be certain, for the hearths within it are secondary insertions. The large square well is here also. The Old Tower, the other 12th-century structure, has partly fallen and seems to have been only crudely built. It is on the east, adjacent to the gatehouse and

indeed probably defended an earlier gate on the site of the present one. It is best seen from the outer ward, but its interior is inaccessible.

These two 12th-century structures were probably connected by an earth bank and palisade, replaced by the present stone curtain wall in about 1230. The early 13th-century defences then consisted of a low wall, a plain gate with a portcullis and two towers. Of these two towers, the four-storey Round Tower in the south-west corner, with its well-preserved domed roof, seems to be slightly earlier than the semicircular three-storey North Tower. The more sophisticated gatehouse was probably added soon after this. It had a drawbridge over the ditch and was further protected by two portcullises. Of the two rooms over the gate passage, the well-appointed second-floor room may have housed the castle's constable. To the south of the gatehouse is a rectangular vaulted guardroom, now altered and used as a shop.

The original low curtain wall and towers were later raised and strengthened. The earlier, lower battlements can be seen in several places, such as between the gatehouse and the North Tower. These were accessible from the old wall-walk, retained to allow for a two-tiered defence. A turret at wall-walk level at an angle on the north wall was used in defence and for observation and also served as a double latrine.

Around 1260, a large, ornate chapel was built near the hall. It was at first-floor level over a vaulted basement and was reached by an external stair. The chapel is itself covered with a fine high-pointed vault. Its windows have been altered and one has been blocked by a later fireplace, but enough remains of their tracery, along with the *sedile* and traces of wall paintings, to suggest that this must have been an impressive building. Later in the 13th century a building over a watergate passage was squeezed into the space between the hall and chapel. It served to connect the two earlier buildings, and the rooms on its first floor probably replaced those in the hall block as the family's private apartments. The building of an extension to the south to provide latrines cut off two curious dark courts on the south and west. At some unknown but probably quite late date the western curtain wall was demolished, leaving the west side of the hall block as the only defence on this side.

The outer ward, now only fragmentary, was clearly built after the inner ward: the postern gate near the ditch on the north, the rectangular and the semicircular towers on the north, and the fragment of tower on the south near the ditch may be 13th-century in date. The Civil War earthwork or 'redan' consists of a stone-revetted terrace which runs across the ridge in front of the medieval ditch. The modern entrance to the castle passes through the right-hand face of the central salient. A late barn is built against the other side.

115
Tenby Castle and Town

Medieval masonry castle and town walls

12th–15th century AD

OS 158   SN 137005   U1

Tenby is on A478, 27ml (43km) SW of St Clears. Park in town car parks (crowded in summer). Castle above harbour

Laws 1896; Turner 1970; Thomas 1962

Tenby Castle stands on a high rocky headland, in a position of great natural strength, connected to the mainland by a narrow isthmus. Only isolated stretches of the castle walls remain, perched above sea cliffs, and perhaps a complete circuit of walling was considered unnecessary. Little now remains of the defence of greatest importance, the wall across the neck of the headland, but on the north, a short stretch of well-preserved wall has arrowslits, embrasures and wall-walk surviving, and on the south a similar length lies adjacent to the gate and barbican. A more fragmentary, much-repaired piece lies next to the museum, itself built on to a medieval domestic building, probably the hall.

The entrance to the castle is only a simple square gate through the curtain wall, but it is further protected by an impressive D-shaped barbican which sits astride the sloping approach road. Inside the castle, at the highest point of the headland, is a watch-tower, formed by two small towers joined together. Low footings of what may well be other medieval domestic buildings lie on the landward side of the watch-tower.

Most of the castle masonry is 13th-century or later, but we know that there was an earlier earthwork castle here, as there is a record of its capture by the Welsh in 1153. Later attacks on the town of Tenby do not seem to have affected the castle which had probably fallen into disrepair by the 14th century. It did see action in the Civil War when, together with the

Tenby Castle and walled town

town, it remained in Parliamentary hands for most of the war, despite two attempts by Sir Charles Gerard to recapture it. In 1648, a unit of Royalist rebels held the castle for 10 weeks but was finally starved into submission by Colonel Horton's besieging forces.

While the castle at Tenby is impressive because of its striking position, the medieval town defences are magnificent in their strength and the extent of their preservation. The landward defences along what is now South Parade and St Florence Parade and the shorter northern stretch along White Lion Street are almost complete, save for the North Gate which was demolished. A hotel now stands on the site, at the northern corner of the medieval town. From here, a probably

rather flimsier line of wall ran east along the sea cliff to a gate outside the approach to the castle. Another sea wall ran along the east side of the town, but, save for one round tower on the middle of the east line, both sea walls and the gate have now disappeared, or have suffered drastic rebuilding. Of the three gates and twelve towers that originally defended the town, one gate and seven towers survive.

Tenby was attacked in 1187, and again in 1260, when Llywelyn the Last sacked the town during his campaigns in the south-west. It was probably after this, in the late 13th century, that the walls were built. The landward walls have been altered by successive rebuildings, and strengthened by a series of towers and by a barbican built around the South Gate. Originally, the walls were lower and had a low series of arrowslits which could be defended from the banked-up ground inside the town. There was then only one tower, that on the north-west corner, and the South Gate was a simple opening. At a later stage, perhaps associated with a royal grant of tolls for murage in 1328, the famous D-shaped barbican was added to defend the gate. Four of its 'Five Arches' are post-medieval rough breaks, and the one original door can be distinguished as the only one with dressed stonework and a portcullis groove. The D-shaped towers north and south of the gate were also added at this time. In the mid-15th century, the barbican was heightened so that, now, two tiers of arrowslits run around the front of the barbican. These are higher than those on the town wall and were reached by open stairs. They allowed defenders to fire both outwards from the wall, and into the interior of the barbican – an important asset if invaders had already broken through the barbican gate but not through the town gate itself. At this stage, the round 'Imperial Hotel' tower was the southern termination to the defences.

In 1457, a rather unusual arrangement was agreed upon between Jasper Tewdwr and the townspeople, whereby each agreed to pay half of the sum required for refortifying the defences. The moat, which ran outside the walls where St Florence Parade is now, was widened to 30ft, the walls were heightened and a second, higher series of arrowslits was built, reached by a new parapet walk. This wall-walk was supported on arches, so that the original lower arrowslits could still be used from below. The lower embrasures were blocked by the heightening and the scar left by their blocking can be seen in the masonry, while the two levels of arrowslits remain open. Some sections of the arched wall-walk survive, too, but are hidden in the gardens within the town. It was at this later stage that the square tower was added to the clifftop on the south of the town, and the large rectangular bastion two towers further north

was built with its key-hole gun-ports, fireplace and latrine. A later feature of interest is a date stone near the 'Five Arches' which refers to a rebuilding during the Spanish Armada scare.

116
Banc y Beili, St Clears
Medieval earthwork castle
Late 11th–13th century AD
OS 158   SN 281154   U1

St Clears is on A477 Carmarthen–Haverfordwest road, 8ml (12.8km) W of Carmarthen. From main road, turn off into town centre, following signs to Laugharne on A4066. Motte on LHS (E) of road 0.5ml (0.8km) further on, through gate with small parking area in front

King 1983

Banc y Beili, the motte-and-bailey castle at St Clears, is situated on the junction between the Taf and Cynin rivers, probably at the limit of navigable water for the shallow-draught boats that the Norman settlers would have used. The substantial motte, 8m high and an oval 20m by 10m across its top, lies on the north of the site and is well preserved. However, both the ditch which originally would have surrounded the motte and the defensive banks and ditches around the bailey have been rendered inconspicuous by the dumping of soil on to the adjacent areas in modern times. The large, rectangular bailey extended 50m south of the motte (as far as the house on the far side of the site). There are reports of stonework being visible on the summit of the motte, suggesting that it carried a masonry structure in its later history.

The castle was probably founded in the late 11th century, judging from the fact that a Cluniac priory was established at St Clears around 1100 and this would almost certainly have been after the foundation of the castle. The present church, situated to the north of the castle, was the priory church, though of the remainder of the monastery nothing now survives.

The early history of the castle is obscure. It may be the castle called Ystrad Cyngen which we know was captured in 1153 by Rhys ap Gruffudd, later famous as 'the Lord Rhys' of the south-Wales royal house of Deheubarth. Giraldus Cambrensis mentions St Clears Castle by name as the home of 12 archers who had murdered a young Welshman who was 'devoutly hastening to meet' the archbishop, presumably to offer himself as a crusader. This was a terrible sin and the 12 Englishmen themselves later took the cross as penance. The tables were turned when the Lord Rhys took the castle from the English a year later in 1189 and gave it to his son Hywel Sais, but it was recovered by William de Braose II in 1195. In 1215 it was one of the castles taken by Llywelyn the Great during his sweeping campaigns into south Wales, but was in English hands again by 1230 when William Marshal the younger, earl of Pembroke, took charge. Thereafter it appears to have remained in English hands until the 14th century when decay set in. St Clears does figure briefly in the Glyndŵr uprising in 1405 when it was besieged and presumably captured along with the castle at Carmarthen.

117
Laugharne Castle, St Clears
Medieval masonry castle
12th–17th century AD
OS 159   SN 302107   R1   Cadw

Laugharne is 4ml S of St Clears on A4066. Car park at bottom of hill S of castle. Castle closed for repairs; projected opening date 1993 (admission charge and standard opening hours)

Avent 1988

'The castle, brown as owls' – Dylan Thomas's description of Laugharne Castle in his 'Poem

in October' – is apt, as much of the structure is of an old red sandstone which gives it a distinct and attractive mellowness. It stands on a low cliff by the side of the Coran stream, overlooking the estuary of the River Taf. The castle may be the Abercorram mentioned in about 1116 as the castle of Robert Courtemain, but the first definite reference to the Norman castle is in 1189 when, after the death of King Henry II, it was seized by the Lord Rhys, prince of Deheubarth. It attracted further hostility from the Welsh in 1215 when it was destroyed by Llywelyn the Great and later, in 1257, when it was again taken and burnt.

The early 12th-century castle was probably a ringwork, and traces of an important building with a large hearth have been found during excavations at the site. The castle was remodelled in the second half of the 12th century: the interior of the ringwork was partially filled in, new defences were constructed and a large rectangular hall was built on the north. By the time of the Welsh attack in 1257, the castle was in the ownership of the de Brian family and it was Guy de Brian IV who, evidently determined to create a much more defensible structure, started to build the strong masonry castle which we see today.

The de Brians remained as the lords of Laugharne until the end of the 14th century and, during their long occupancy, carried out considerable additions and repairs. In 1349 the lordship was inherited by the distinguished Guy de Brian VII, who greatly improved the overall standard of accommodation within the castle. Guy de Brian's death in 1390 was followed by a long period of decline and in the late 15th and early 16th century only parts of the castle were occupied, and much was in ruins. However, a real change came about in the castle's fortunes when, in 1575, Elizabeth I granted it to Sir John Perrot, an important dignitary who converted the old medieval castle into a comfortable Tudor mansion, rather as he did at his main residence at Carew (no. 113). Unfortunately for the castle,

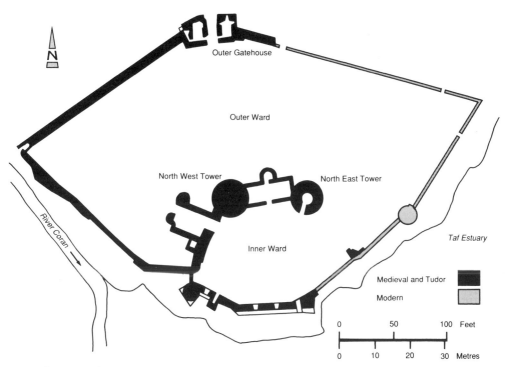

Laugharne Castle

Perrot became too powerful for royal comfort, and in 1592 he was sentenced to death for high treason; he died, though from natural causes, in the same year. An inventory made in 1592 suggests that Perrot's building was of rather poor quality and that the castle 'is like within few yeares to run to utter ruin again'.

The castle ruins are, therefore, the end result of a long development from earthwork castle to Tudor mansion. This complex history makes the castle, at first sight, difficult to understand. Little visible now remains of the ringwork bank, nor of the first stone hall; the bank was reduced in height when the hall was built, and the hall itself was demolished, probably in the late 12th century. The next phase in the castle's history, the rebuilding by the de Brians in the late 13th century, is far more evident within the standing remains. The two strong round towers on the north were built at this time along with the curtain wall, some of which still survives. The impressive north-western tower still retains its fine medieval domed roof, though the topmost sections of the wall with the battlements were reconstructed earlier this century. The tower acted as a keep and also as a guardian for the simple entrance through the curtain to its south. The other tower, a solid three-storey structure, has partly fallen, and the section through the tower exposed by the collapse gives a good view of the two extra storeys and the circular stair added in the Tudor period. A new hall was built in stone against the south curtain wall during this late 13th-century rebuilding, and the outer ward, if not already in existence, may also have been added then, but probably only with timber defences at this stage.

At the end of the 13th century, the defences were further strengthened. A forward-projecting gatehouse was built against the earlier, simple entrance into the inner ward. As this was constructed over the earlier ditch, the opportunity was taken to incorporate a basement beneath the main entrance passage. This arrangement is made all the more unusual by the postern placed at the front of the basement to give access to the edge of the inner ward ditch. In addition, a new round tower with deep spurs was built at the south-west corner of the inner ward and the defences of the outer ward, including the outer gatehouse, were rebuilt in stone.

The castle had so far been constructed entirely in red sandstone, but in the mid-14th century Guy de Brian VII used for his building a distinctive green stone, which is quite easy to detect. The whole south-western corner of the inner ward, including the round tower and the inner gatehouse, was considerably heightened. This building phase is particularly clear on the outside of the castle, where the green-stone heightening of the south-west tower and adjacent curtain wall with a well-preserved trefoil window can be easily distinguished from the older masonry. The south-east corner was remodelled at this period, and a postern door, giving access out to the estuary, was inserted. Finally, the outer gatehouse was also rebuilt, again using the green stone.

Sir John Perrot drastically altered this medieval castle by converting it into a substantial Tudor mansion. The old hall against the south curtain wall was completely remodelled and the curtain wall heightened with mock battlements. The scar of the roof-line of the mansion can be seen high on the wall, but the building has completely gone and its magnificence must be left to the

Laugharne Castle

imagination. Ranges of Tudor buildings extended around the south and east of the inner ward and, on the north, the curtain wall between the two round towers was demolished and replaced by the large rectangular accommodation block. Its upper floors were reached by a splendid projecting semicircular stair tower. The Tudor ranges looked over a central cobbled courtyard, on which, we are told by contemporary accounts, a fountain played. The inner gatehouse, too, was made more impressive by being considerably raised to its present height and gardens were laid out in the outer ward.

Following its slighting in the Civil War, the castle was left as a romantic ruin during the 18th century and at the turn of the 19th century, the outer ward was laid with formal gardens. The gazebo overlooking the estuary was used in the 1930s and 40s by the author Richard Hughes, who leased Castle House during this period. No one can visit Laugharne without becoming aware that it was also the home of the poet Dylan Thomas, whose house, the Boathouse, is open to visitors. Little now remains of the medieval town of Laugharne save its church (no. 97) and castle, though we know roughly the line of its defences and the position of the town gates.

118
Llansteffan Castle
Iron Age fort and medieval masonry castle
6th century BC and 12th–15th century AD
OS 159   SN 351101   U2   Cadw

Llansteffan is 8ml (12.8km) SW of Carmarthen. On A40, just W of Carmarthen, take B4312 S to Llansteffan from where car park signed to L. Walk up (steep) path to castle

Official Guidebook; Guilbert 1974

Llansteffan is one of the great scenic castles of Wales, situated on a high ridge overlooking

the Twyi estuary, and commands wonderful views over the surrounding countryside. As is often suspected on other sites, but here has been proved by excavation, the strong position was also used in prehistory: the promontory was first defended in the 6th century BC when a double bank and ditch were thrown across the neck to form a promontory fort with an 8ha interior. The far field hedge to the west of the castle is probably an outer earthwork representing a later extension to the Iron Age fort.

When the promontory was reoccupied in the early 12th century, the earlier defences, now presumably grass-grown earthworks, were refurbished and a castle of earth and timber was constructed within. At the highest point, a circular bank was raised to form the inner, upper ward, separated from the remainder of the defended promontory which formed the bailey or outer ward. This ringwork-and-bailey castle was apparently built by the Norman Marmion family, and then passed to that of the de Camvilles. Its early history was stormy indeed. It is first mentioned in 1146 when it was captured by the princes Cadell, Maredudd and Rhys of the royal house of Deheubarth, and the chronicles relate how the young Maredudd held the castle against the English, throwing their scaling-ladders down into the ditch. Nonetheless it returned to English hands, only to fall again to Rhys in 1189, and again in 1215, when Llywelyn the Great invaded south-west Wales. The building of the first masonry structures dates to the late 12th and early 13th centuries and is probably associated with these attacks. The inner stone curtain wall with its wall-walk was built then, with the well-preserved square gatehouse on the north defended by portcullis and doors. The room over the gate passage could only be reached from the wall-walk, but a stair led from there to the second-floor room. A little later the curtain wall was heightened, and, in places, was provided with a wider wall-walk supported on vaults. The lower courses of a small round tower and further buildings also date to this 13th-century work.

Dyfed

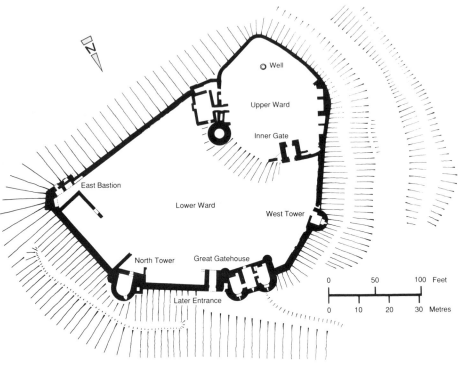

Llansteffan Castle

In 1257, the English were heavily defeated at the battle of Coed Llathen by the forces of Llywelyn the Great, and the Welsh quickly pushed home their advantage by capturing a number of castles in the area, including Llansteffan. When the de Camvilles regained control the castle was strengthened to the extent of a major remodelling. The defences of the bailey now assumed a far greater importance. Two strong D-shaped towers were built on the north and west along with a complex bastion on the east, accessible one to another by the wall-walk which surmounted the new stone curtain wall. The tower on the north was relatively spacious with fireplaces and with separate stair and latrine turrets, and it probably provided the private accommodation for the lord. A hall

may have stood on the north-east, of which nothing now remains. A little later, the separation of the castle into two wards broke down with the partial demolition of the inner ward wall. An impressive double-towered gatehouse was then built to dominate the all-but impregnable northern side, thus completing the strong defences of the castle as we see it today.

The Great Gatehouse, modelled on the East Gate at Caerphilly Castle, with which it has several features in common, has now been blocked, and a smaller gate inserted alongside, but the original plan is still clear. In the gate passage can be seen marks of the seatings for the gates, grooves for a portcullis at front and rear and two sets of five murder holes in the vault above. The conspicuous outer machicolations above the gate (because of the later blocking of the passage, they can only be seen from outside) are especially reminiscent of Caerphilly. A guardroom lies on either side of the passage. Each of the upper floors of the gatehouse forms a single great room, both spacious and well appointed despite the lower one having to accommodate the portcullis in its raised position. The upper of the two rooms probably served as the new private apartment of the lord, the fine, large fireplace on the south wall having decorated 'sconces', one of which retains its carved female head.

After the death of the last male de Camville in 1338, the castle evidently declined in importance. In 1377, it passed into the hands of the crown. The threat posed by the Glyndŵr uprising in 1405–6 caused the crown to order the tenant, Sir John Penres, to strengthen the castle which may have been captured and held by Glyndŵr for a short period. Later, Henry VII conferred it on his uncle Jasper Tewdwr who held it until his

death in 1495. The alteration to the entrance may well date to this time; the blocking of the gate to convert this awesome military structure into a comfortable residence, and the building of the small, weak gate to the side shows clearly that by this date a Tudor gentleman had no need of such a formidable entrance, but merely a strong front door to dissuade a mob from forced entry. After this, the castle sank into further obscurity, and the gables along the north-east side are of an agricultural building in use as recently as 1860.

119
Kidwelly Castle
Medieval masonry castle
12th–15th century AD
OS 159   SN 409071   R1   Cadw

Kidwelly is on A484 Carmarthen–Llanelli road 10ml (16km) S of Carmarthen. Castle

Llansteffan Castle

(signposted) on N of town. Car park, standard hours, admission charge

Cadw Guidebook

Kidwelly is a mighty and imposing monument to Norman power. It is also a beautiful example of castle development, as the castle was dramatically altered on a number of occasions to conform to the latest thinking in military science. Roger, bishop of Salisbury, the justiciar of England, established Norman power in the area and the ringwork castle that he built here was one of a series of strongholds designed by the Normans to secure the new conquests in south Wales by commanding the river passes here and at Laugharne (no. 117), Llansteffan (no. 118) and Loughor. The ringwork at Kidwelly was constructed on a steep ridge overlooking the River Gwendraeth at its upper tidal limit. No further strengthening was needed on the riverside, and the present semicircular bank and ditch formed the 12th-century defences which would have been supplemented by a timber palisade on the bank, probably further strengthened by towers and certainly by a gate. In the interior would have been the timber domestic buildings of the lord. This castle fell to the Welsh on a number of occasions in the late 12th and early 13th centuries, including once in 1159 when Lord Rhys took it and burnt it. He is later credited with rebuilding the castle in 1190. By 1201, however, it was back in Norman hands and remained English from then on, despite periodic attacks.

In the mid-13th century the de Chaworth family gained possession, and began the long work of building the mighty stone castle that we see today. The earliest parts are best viewed from the centre of the castle, as they consist of the square inner ward with the four large round corner towers and simple portcullis gates to north and south. By building this inner ward, set as it is within the outer ward, Pain de Chaworth converted

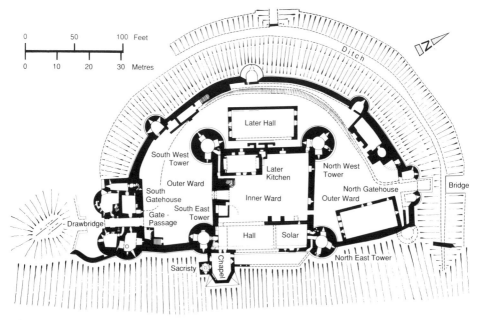

Kidwelly Castle

Kidwelly Castle

Kidwelly into a strong 'concentric' castle, with an inner and outer ring of defences.

Kidwelly passed by marriage in 1298 to Henry, earl of Lancaster, who quickly set about upgrading the accommodation to suit his status. A large first-floor hall reached by a semicircular external stair was built on the east; this has largely fallen, though the wall footings and a fireplace can still be seen. The chapel, housed in a projecting tower overlooking the river, was also built at this time, and the massive spur buttresses of the tower are a distinctive feature of the castle and are best seen from the outside. The chapel has white Sutton-stone mouldings around doors and windows, *piscina* and *sedile*, making it one of the finest parts of the castle. A small building on the south of the chapel housed the sacristy above the priest's bedchamber. Its fine cruciform roof can be seen from the wall-walk leading from the Great Gatehouse.

In the early 14th century, the present mighty outer defences were constructed. The stone curtain wall with its wall-walk and series of mural towers was built, or, more probably,

an existing wall was considerably heightened. On the north was a small gate with a drawbridge over the ditch, while on the south the Great Gatehouse was constructed, achieving a hitherto unattainable strength. The four inner towers had to be heightened also to maintain an effective field of fire. The marks of the early crenellations may still be seen, now blocked by the later, heightened stonework.

The Great Gatehouse took at least a century to complete. It was evidently unfinished at the time of the Welsh siege in 1403 during the Glyndŵr uprising. Despite the fall of the town to the Welsh, the castle resisted the siege for three weeks until an English army arrived to give assistance. By this time, the castle was in the hands of the crown, and the 15th-century refurbishment after the damage caused by the siege cost over £500. It was not until 1422 that the building finally received its lead roof. The gate passage has a tower on either side with basements which could have functioned as store rooms or as prison cells as their doors are secured by draw-bars on the outside only. The ground floors may have housed porters or guards in the front rooms, while one of the back rooms has a large, bare, dark beehive-shaped prison. On the first floor, over the gate passage and tower rooms, was a massive hall, well-appointed despite its having to accommodate the inner portcullis and murder hole, the slots for which may still be seen in the floor. The private apartments of the owner, or perhaps the constable of the castle, were on the second floor above the hall.

The gatehouse was extremely well defended, and indeed was designed so that it could be held independently if the remainder of the castle had fallen to besiegers. A small room in front of the hall housed the outer portcullis and murder hole, and the rooms above must have held the mechanism for lifting the drawbridge. The gate displays a fine array of defensive features. On the towers are a series of arrowloops to defend the entrance; above the arched doorway is the rectangular recess into which the drawbridge would have been drawn, raised by chains running through the small holes in the corners; above the entrance are three arches, or 'machicolations' through which missiles could be dropped on to the hapless invader; on the top of the gatehouse would have been battlements, now mostly gone though their supporting corbels still survive providing for a wider wall-walk for the defenders behind. Within the gate passage were an outer portcullis and gates, three murder holes in the vault above, and an inner portcullis and gate.

The last significant addition to the castle was at the end of the 15th century when a large hall was built on the west of the outer ward with a connecting kitchen within the inner ward. Another building and a bakehouse were added, probably the work of Rhys ap Thomas who was granted the castle by Henry VII. In the early 17th century the judicial court was held in the castle, perhaps in the new hall, but by that time the castle's life as a fortification was wellnigh over and it played only a minor part in the Civil War, lying as it did far away from the central area of the struggle.

A walk around the exterior of the castle is recommended, as its dominating position within the town is best appreciated from outside. Kidwelly retains the street pattern of the medieval walled town, and though the walls themselves have disappeared, the early 14th-century South Gate of the town still stands on the main street opposite the castle. The line of the town defences survive as hedge lines and property boundaries, and the northern outworks are particularly well preserved. The foundation of the town was an early one, only shortly after that of the castle, and a small priory was established for the Benedictines at the same time, in 1114.

120
Carmarthen Castle
Medieval masonry castle
12th–14th century AD
OS 159   SN 413200   U1

Castle in centre of Carmarthen. Park in town car parks and walk to Dyfed County Council offices. Castle W of Council car park, in Nott Square

James 1980, 1989

The castle at Carmarthen, on its rocky eminence overlooking the River Twyi, must have dominated the medieval town just as, a little way to the east, the Roman fort must have dominated the Roman town a thousand years before. Giraldus Cambrensis tells us that even in the late 12th century, parts of the strong walls of the 'ancient city' of the Romans were still standing. The castle was converted into a prison in the 18th and 19th centuries, and the building of the Council offices has also not helped its appreciation as a military entity. However, enough remains to make a visit worthwhile.

The castle is first mentioned in 1094, when the name Rhyd y Gors is used. This earliest castle, built by the Norman William fitz Baldwin, may have been sited elsewhere perhaps further down river. After 1105, the annals refer to Carmarthen by name, so by then certainly, this Norman castle was on its present site. The castle evidently became important early on, and passed into the hands of the crown. Carmarthen quickly became the administrative centre of south-west Wales as it had been under the Romans, and inevitably underwent a series of attacks and rebuilding episodes during the turbulent struggles between Welsh and English in the 12th and 13th centuries. Among these episodes was the capture and destruction of the castle by Llywelyn the Great in 1215 after

which extensive rebuilding work was undertaken by William Marshal the younger, earl of Pembroke, who had recaptured the castle in 1223. It may have been at this period that the massive stone defences were built on the site of the original motte. This renewed strength enabled the castle to survive another formidable Welsh siege in 1234, which lasted three months.

A survey of the castle of 1275 refers to a dungeon, a great tower, a gatehouse, hall, kitchen and chapel, all of which apparently needed repair, and from 1288–9 much rebuilding took place; this probably included

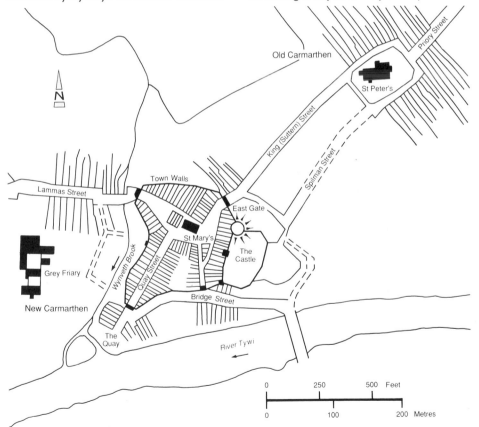

Conjectural plan of Carmarthen Castle and medieval town, showing the possible property boundaries within the two urban areas; St John's Priory to the north-east of Old Carmarthen is not shown

the construction of the stone curtain wall. By 1308, a number of new residential and administrative buildings filled the bailey. Further buildings were added in the 14th century including the present gatehouse and the south-west tower. It seems from documents that the castle had an inner ward by then, and a map of 1610 suggests that part of the old bailey had been separated from the rest by a stone wall. The castle remained important in the 15th century and required considerable repair after being sacked by Glyndŵr in 1405. By 1456, Edmund Tewdwr (father of Henry, later Henry VII) had gained possession of Carmarthen Castle as the king's representative, and he died here in that year.

The castle became the county prison in 1789 and this conversion, along with the rebuilding of the gaol in 1869, effectively destroyed the open space of the outer ward. However, it would not be very misleading to imagine the present Council car park and office building as presenting the outer and inner wards of the castle, defended at first by an earthwork bank with a timber palisade, a wooden keep on the high motte on the north and a timber gate. Later these wooden structures were replaced by a stone curtain wall with mural towers, stone defences on the old motte and the gatehouse on the west.

It is probably best to look first at the earliest surviving structure, the motte. The exterior of the motte may be seen by leaving the car park by the vehicular entrance, and walking along the small path by the side of the old gaol wall to the left. The stone-revetted motte is immediately in front of the path, and two of the semicircular corner towers are visible. The lower parts of the stone wall and towers presumably retain the old earthern and rock motte, which explains the lack of lights, slits and other features. Further along the path are two late buttresses, which are known to be on the site of another of the towers, this one probably rectangular. The curtain wall, evidently much rebuilt, connects the motte with the gatehouse.

Now go back through the car park and out through the small, modern door to the

Carmarthen Castle gatehouse

gatehouse. The 14th-century gatehouse has been partially blocked internally, though the old arch above the gate passage is quite evident in the masonry. The outer portcullis groove and the arches over the murder holes can be seen from the outside. On either side of the passage are two gate towers with battlements supported by a corbel table. The upper floor of the gate housed the constable of the castle, and the trefoil-headed windows in the towers must be associated with his lodgings.

Return through the gate into the castle and turn right. At the corner, only partially visible, stands the south-west tower with its fine buttressed base, built in the 14th century to defend this corner of the castle. Beyond this, a small, square tower with a vaulted basement stands with a stump of the old curtain wall attached. Both towers are unfortunately largely inaccessible, being concealed by walls to the front and houses behind.

Surprisingly few traces survive of the medieval town of 'New' Carmarthen, which grew up around the castle. The town walls and four gates, the Augustinian priory and the Franciscan house of the grey friars have all disappeared, though material from excavations on the latter two sites may be seen in the museum at Abergwili. The parish church of St Peter's was certainly in existence around 1100, when it was granted, along with the priory, to Battle Abbey. It is one of the largest parish churches in the diocese of St Davids and houses the splendid tomb of Sir Rhys ap Thomas and his wife, moved here from the friary church at the time of the Dissolution.

We know that the population of Carmarthen rose dramatically in the mid-13th century as the town grew in administrative importance. It was used by Edward I as the centre from which men and supplies for his Welsh campaigns were organised. On the site of the Roman town, a settlement known as 'Old' Carmarthen grew up around the Augustinian priory of St John, and administratively it formed a separate lordship under the prior. Both Old and New Carmarthen continued as urban centres with their own charters, and the relationship between the two towns was frequently rather strained, due to competing economic pressures.

A small section of the Civil War defences, thrown up by the Royalists, survives on the south-west of the town (near Tesco's supermarket). They are known as 'The Bulwarks' and consist of an earthwork bank and a well-preserved four-sided bastion.

121
Newcastle Emlyn Castle
Medieval masonry castle
13th–15th century AD
OS 145   SN 311407   U1

Newcastle Emlyn on A484 11ml (17.6km) SE of Cardigan. Castle and car park on NE side of town, signposted from town hall

Parry 1987

The new castle of Emlyn, from which the town takes its name, lies on a low promontory skirted on two sides by a looping meander of the River Teifi some 16m below. The inner ward is on the point of the promontory while the larger outer ward lies on the open west side. A bank and ditch, now rather eroded, defended the exposed western approach to the outer ward, while the steep slopes on the north and south required no man-made defence. Nothing now remains of any medieval structures within the outer ward, but on the far side, just outside the gatehouse, is the curving earthwork of a Civil War 'redan'. This was a defended gun emplacement constructed during the 1640s. There is documentary evidence to suggest that the inner ward was originally defended by an external ditch, but this has been filled in, possibly before the construction of the redan.

The twin-towered gatehouse, which stands on the west side of the triangular inner ward, is the dominant feature of the castle. According to a record of 1336, its construction was begun in the reign of Edward II (1307–27) but it was not completed until 1349. Much later, about 1500, it was altered by Sir Rhys ap Thomas who inserted the large windows, as by then defence was of less importance than comfort. The gatehouse towers are semi-octagonal outside and rectangular internally and have latrine shafts on the north and south, which may be later insertions. In the floor of the north gatehouse room is a manhole cover which blocks the slanting entrance passage of an extraordinarily well-preserved vaulted cellar. Access to the upper floor of the gatehouse was via an external stair adjacent to the east wall of the north tower, which may also have served as an access stair to the wall-walk on the curtain wall.

South of the gatehouse are two blocks of masonry which belonged to a square tower, probably 14th-century in date like the gatehouse. A length of ruinous curtain wall runs from the tower along the south side of the inner ward for some 23m. The inner-ward

Newcastle Emlyn Castle

curtain wall followed the slope of the promontory and further fragmentary sections have been excavated at the east end, but have now been covered over.

From a survey of 1532 we know that the hall lay near the gatehouse, probably on the south side. The survey further tells of a chapel which adjoined the hall and lay at first-floor level over a kitchen and larder. Another large building was apparently situated on the eastern side of the castle. No traces of these buildings now remain above ground level, nor of the bakehouse and stables that we know stood in the outer ward.

The castle was probably founded by Maredudd ap Rhys around 1240, and if this is so, it is one of the few castles in Dyfed built by the Welsh in stone. His son, Rhys ap Maredudd, held the castle in 1287, and the castle changed hands three times during his successful revolt against the English crown

from 1287 to 1289. After Rhys had finally been defeated and killed, the castle became crown property and remained so until 1349. During this period, three refurbishments are recorded, during which time the gatehouse was constructed and a new town was founded outside the castle walls. In 1403, the castle was taken by Owain Glyndŵr, but was described as being 'in ruins' by 1428. Sir Rhys ap Thomas acquired and repaired it in about 1500. It changed hands a number of times before the Civil War during which it was held for Parliament until its capture by Sir Charles Gerard in 1644. Major-General Rowland Laugharne besieged it for Parliament in 1645 but was routed by Gerard in a fierce engagement below the castle walls. After the general surrender of the Royalists, the castle was blown up to make it indefensible and, according to a source of 1700, the castle was 'plundered and ever since neglected'.

122
Dryslwyn Castle, Llandeilo

Medieval masonry castle

12th–15th century AD

OS 159   SN 554204   U2   Cadw

Dryslwyn is 2.5ml (4km) W of Llandeilo, reached either by A40 or B4300 Llandeilo–Carmarthen roads. From either road, take B4297 (signposted Dryslywn Castle). Car park opposite castle by riverside, short walk up steep hill to castle

Caple 1990

Within the wide, flat valley in which the River Twyi gently meanders are a number of abrupt, rocky hillocks. Dryslywn Castle sits on one such isolated hill, from which are commanded extensive views of the valley. This was a good strategic asset in the early 13th century when a castle was founded here by the Welsh rulers of Deheubarth (south-west Wales). There are no references to the castle in the historical record before 1245, and it seems to have played no very large part at least in military history before 1287, when it passed into English hands. We know, however, that it was an important seat of the princes of Deheubarth, and that in 1271 the lord of Dryslwyn, Maredudd ap Rhys, died here and was succeeded by his son Rhys. In 1281, Rhys was granted a charter to hold a four-day fair at Dryslwyn around St Bartholomew's Day, so we may assume that by this time the township of Dryslwyn, situated at the foot of the castle, had been in existence for some time.

In 1287, Rhys ap Maredudd rose in revolt against King Edward I. In consequence, the castle was besieged by a large army led by the earl of Cornwall, and so well-documented and dramatic was this siege that it has captured the imagination of history. An 11,000-strong force was mustered for the attack which was aided by a siege engine, and quarrymen and carters were used to equip it with stone shot. In the 10 days following 20 August, 26

sappers were employed to undermine the defences, so that the walls would collapse; the sappers evidently miscalculated, as the walls collapsed sooner than was expected and killed some of the besiegers. The castle was taken soon afterwards, and Alan de Plucknet was made custodian; he raised money to pay for the small garrison and the necessary repairs to the castle by selling produce from the estate which included livestock (cattle, lambs and pigs), cereals, hay, apples, nuts and ox-hides.

Dryslwyn Castle remained in the hands of the English crown for much of the 14th century, and building records suggest that its series of constables kept the structure in reasonable repair and there are other references to the township. In 1402 Rhys ap Gruffudd was appointed constable, but in the following year he joined Owain Glyndŵr in his rebellion against English control. Perhaps the castle was destroyed during this rebellion, or perhaps dismantled soon afterwards, but in any case it plays no further part in history.

The approach to the castle is from the west, and the first, rather breathless view is of the flat area of the township on the left, the outer ward of the castle to the fore, and the inner ward on the higher ground to the right. The town lay on the lower part of the hilltop enclosed by a large, deep defensive ditch and a wall which now survives as a low bank; against the latter are still visible the earthworks of some of the small rectangular houses and gardens. The occupation of the town seems to fit into the 13th–15th century time-span of the castle: documents of 1356–9 show that at this time the town itself contained 34 plots of land or 'burgages' with a further 14 outside the walls. In 1391, the burgesses were given equal status with those of 'English' boroughs like Carmarthen, but the town seems not to have been inhabited much beyond the mid-15th century.

The hub of the castle was the inner ward. The small, high point of the hill was crammed with buildings defended by an angular enclosure wall. The earliest visible remains are those of the circular keep on the north-

Dyfed

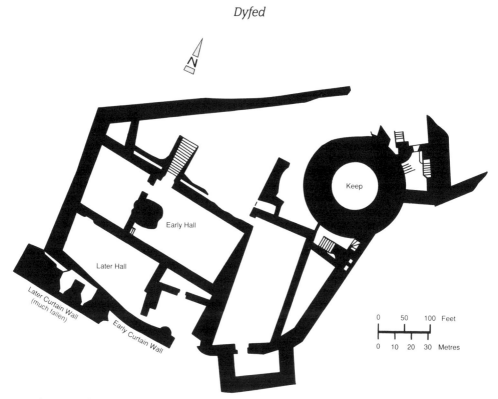

Dryslwyn Castle, inner ward; the outer wards and town to the north are not shown

east, and the curtain wall which enclosed the ward; only the lower courses remain of these early 13th-century structures. Archaeological excavations have revealed a series of clay floors of probably wooden buildings which were contemporary with this early phase of activity. The large hall block was built slightly later, along with another building with a hearth, perhaps a kitchen, to the south. Against the east side of the hall, another large, rectangular building was constructed later in the 13th century.

Sometime in the late 13th century, probably after the capture of the castle by the English, the original polygonal curtain wall was demolished on the south and east and the present mighty wall constructed; a new grander accommodation building with large windows was built against it, and the old hall was converted into a two-storey structure;

the large stone pier in the centre probably supported a hearth on the first floor. A chapel was built in a projecting rectangular tower on the south-east. The old, lower curtain wall can be seen to underlie the new massive wall in places, where the rough foundations of the new wall sit uneasily on the facework of the older curtain. This also gives some indication of the amount of levelling up of the ground within the inner ward that accompanied the rebuilding.

After this major reconstruction, later building episodes seem to be confined to minor repairs, followed by the abandonment of the castle, its destruction by fire, and its deliberate slighting in the early to mid-15th century.

Between the inner ward and the town lay the middle ward which in its later stage at least appears to have been filled with

166

buildings constructed against the surrounding wall. Further north-east again lay the outer ward where a few pieces of upstanding masonry tempt speculation about the nature of so-far unexcavated buildings and towers – some are probably associated with the original medieval entrance which seems to have woven a twisting path through the town defences and the outer ward.

123
Dinefwr Castle, Llandeilo
Medieval masonry castle
12th–18th century AD
OS 159   SN 612218   R2   Cadw/
Dyfed Wildlife Trust

Park in Llandeilo. Just N of river bridge on S of town take path by lodge. Go through gate and follow Dyfed Wildlife Trust path across fields, following badger footprint signs, through churchyard, across a field stile, and up wooded path to castle, a steady 20mins climb. Castle under repair but due for partial opening soon (Tel. Cadw for information)

Dinefwr is of paramount importance in Welsh history as the seat of the Welsh rulers of Deheubarth, the medieval principality of south-west Wales. The rocky crag with its commanding view over the wide Twyi valley may have seen occupation in prehistoric periods, and Roman artefacts have been uncovered from various parts of Dinefwr park. The place-name appears in the Welsh law codes which suggest that, early in Welsh history, the site was the principal possession of the south Wales royal house. The early importance of Llandeilo (no. 99) as the probable site of St Teilo's monastery gives further weight to Dinefwr's claim to be an early medieval centre of political power.

In 1163 the castle was in the possession of the Lord Rhys, who ruled over Deheubarth at a time of stability and harmony, a time, moreover, of a renaissance of Welsh culture, music, poetry and law. After the death of this great ruler, conflict over the succession arose between his sons, and thereafter the important castle figures repeatedly in the turbulent years of dynastic struggles between the Welsh princes, and the wars between the Welsh and English in the late 12th and early 13th centuries. We are told, for instance, that Rhys Grug, the son of the Lord Rhys, was forced to dismantle Dinefwr Castle by Llywelyn the Great, prince of Gwynedd who became pre-eminent in the area in the early 13th century. The first building in stone may have followed this supposed dismantling as the circular keep is of a type traditionally dated to this time.

Later in the 13th century the English crown had to respond to the threat of the increasing power of Llywelyn the Last of Gwynedd, and the resulting battle with the Welsh at Coed Llathen near Llandeilo was a devastating English defeat. Dinefwr at that time belonged to Rhys Fychan and, after his death, to his son Rhys Wedrod. It may well have consisted of the great round keep, the polygonal curtain wall and the round north-west tower of the inner ward, while the outer ward probably contained timber service buildings.

After the death of Henry III in 1272, Edward I came to the throne and within five years had destroyed the power of the Welsh princes. In 1276 an English army under Pain de Chaworth was assembled at Carmarthen, and Welsh resistance crumbled. Rhys Wedrod placed Dinefwr in the king's hands, and from this time the castle remained largely in the possession of the English crown. The castle was put into the custody of a constable, and building accounts inform us that repair work was undertaken in 1282–3 when the ditches were cleaned out, the tower, bridge, hall and 'little tower' were repaired, a new gate was built and five buildings were erected within the outer ward. Further repairs were carried out in 1326, and it may be that it was around this time that the rectangular hall, projecting beyond the north curtain wall, was constructed. Comparatively little was spent on the castle during the remainder of the 14th century, and the great tower is described as being on the point of collapse in a document of 1343. However, it was still able to resist a siege by Glyndŵr in 1403. In the Tudor period, Sir Rhys ap Thomas gained possession of the castle and carried out some alterations, especially to the hall on the north, before abandoning the castle for a new house built to the north, on the site of the present Newton House. The castle was deliberately converted into a 'romantic ruin' during the 'picturesque period' and a summer-house added to the top of the keep to provide views to delight 18th-century visitors to the estate.

The approach to the castle is from the east, through the defences of the outer ward at the probable site of the outer gatehouse. The defensive bank and deep rock-cut ditch enclose the lower part of the hilltop, where stood the castle's domestic and service buildings such as, perhaps, the stables, smithy and bakehouse. The path continues through the fragmentary remains of a middle gate and a long, narrow entrance passage protected by a high wall to the inner gate. Despite considerable alteration during several building phases, the joints of the original, large entrance arch can still be seen in the masonry. Inside the inner ward, little remains of the gatehouse save for the lower courses of the masonry to either side of the gate passage and consequently the style of this probably later 13th-century structure is unknown.

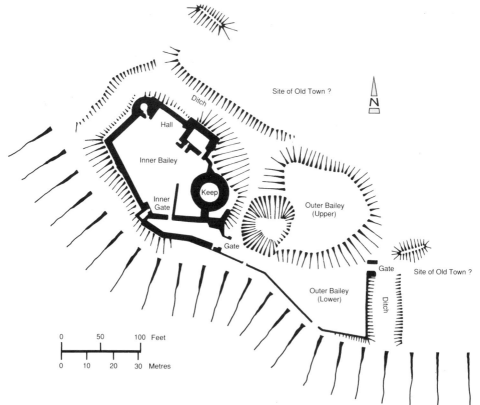

Dinefwr Castle

Aerial view of Dinefwr Castle

Arrowslits which would have defended the passage from rooms on either side, and the ornate stops for the gates may be seen low down in the stonework. Above this, the masonry has been rebuilt, and, on the east, the ground level has been raised in post-medieval times to form steps to the wall-walk.

The inner ward is enclosed by a high, angular curtain wall, much repaired and equipped with iron railings in recent times to create a safe, pleasant walk. Dominating the interior of the castle is the great round keep on the east, with its battered base and heavy roll-moulded string course. The present ground-floor entrance is a later insertion, and the original door was on the first floor. This is now blocked by the later arched bridge leading from the steps, but the outline may be still seen from the inside, high in the wall on the south; the door was presumably entered from an external stair on the courtyard. A trapdoor in the floor probably provided the sole access to the large, dark basement, floored with slabs laid over the bedrock, and lit only by a series of three small slits with stepped bases (two of these were enlarged in later, more secure times). A larger, first-floor window which overlooked the courtyard on the north, was also blocked during 18th-century work on the tower, though, like the door, its outline is still visible in the masonry. It is now difficult to know how much taller the keep would have been before it was so drastically modified by the addition of the summer-house on the top, but it may well

have had at least one further storey. The summer-house, with its conical roof, became a famous landmark, and it still retains its door and large windows designed to give splendid views over the park.

The curtain wall probably continued around the keep on the east but has now fallen, and the walling on the north-east corner is modern. The circular three-storey tower on the north-west may have been built by the Welsh princes but the rectangular tower on the north was probably constructed after 1277. It has a latrine on its west side, and a deep basement. The tower and the adjacent rectangular hall, the inner wall of which has now fallen, were substantially modified in the early Tudor period, when the castle was owned by the wealthy and influential Sir Rhys ap Thomas. By this stage, the military significance of the castle was minimal, and comfort and appearance was of greater importance. Of unknown date are the (probably) timber buildings which evidently lay against the curtain wall on the west. Built into the wall on the south is a latrine chamber with a corbelled roof, and adjacent to the gatehouse is a small turret which was transformed into another summer-house in the 18th century.

The Welsh town of Dinefwr lay in the immediate vicinity of the castle; its precise position is uncertain, though the flat ground just to the north of the castle is a distinct possibility. In 1298 King Edward founded a new English settlement at Dinefwr, and the two communities seem to have coexisted, along with the nearby town of Llandeilo, until at least the early 15th century. The new Tudor mansion may have been built over the site of the English town, and now the positions of both settlements remain obscure.

The new Dynevor Castle, or Newton House, is a drastic refacing (in 1857 by Penson) of a mid-17th-century house built by Sir Edward Rice on the site of the earlier 16th-century mansion. The grounds in which it stands form a superb park landscape associated with Capability Brown, which has been admired by visitors since the 18th century.

124
Carreg Cennen Castle, Llandeilo

Medieval masonry castle

12th–14th century AD

OS 159   SN 668191   R2   Cadw

From Llandeilo, take A476 Llanelli road S to Ffairfach (0.5ml, 0.8km). Turn L (E) and then immediately R and follow signs to Trapp and Castle (3ml, 4.8km). Walk up steep hill to castle. Admission charge; standard hours

Cadw Guidebook

The spectacular limestone crag of Carreg Cennen towers 90m above the valley of the River Cennen which separates it from the high range of the Black Mountains to the east. Finds of 1st- and 2nd-century coins on the hill suggest that the Romans may also have taken advantage of this wonderfully defensive position, but we know nothing about the form of this occupation. Nor do we know much about the earliest medieval castle on the crag, save that it was a Welsh stronghold belonging to the rulers of the kingdom of Deheubarth and closely associated with their other possessions at nearby Dinefwr and Dryslwyn. The history of the 12th- and early 13th-century castle is bound up with the dynastic rivalries of these princes and their changing alliances and fortunes. But the later stone castle has obliterated the remains and even the form of this early stronghold.

In 1277 the castle fell to Edward I during his Welsh campaigns and remained in English hands apart from brief periods of recapture in 1282, during the last episodes of the struggle of Prince Llywelyn ap Gruffudd against the English crown, and in 1287, when Rhys ap Maredudd rebelled against English rule. The castle had by then been granted to the king's supporter, John Giffard, the owner of Llandovery Castle (no. 125). He and his son remained in possession from 1283 and 1321, save for the two years immediately after the 1287 rebellion, when Edward I gave it to the earl of Hereford to defend. Most of the buildings belong to these 38 years, and the castle remains a good example of an almost single period of construction.

The nucleus of the castle is the inner ward with its gatehouse in the centre of the north side, flanked by the circular north-west and square north-east corner towers. Both towers were accessible from the gatehouse by a wall-walk on the curtain wall. The south side of the castle lies directly on the precipitous limestone cliff and required less defence; a curving projection and a corner turret sufficed to protect the south-west and south-east corners. The main living quarters were on the east of the inner ward, at first-floor level over a series of ground-floor basements which were probably used for storage. The hall was in the centre, entered by an external stone stair, and the kitchen with its large fireplaces was conveniently adjacent on the north; the chapel was also accessible from the hall, and was housed in a small, square tower which projected beyond the inner-ward wall. Two doors on the south of the hall led to the owner's private apartments, which have at some later date been substantially altered. Accounts of repair work carried out in 1369, when John of Gaunt had the tenure of the castle, mention the repair of the entrance and the reroofing of the hall, and one of these private rooms is said to have been 'walled up'. Two cisterns at the back of the gatehouse probably held the castle's water supply.

A most interesting feature of the castle is in the south-eastern corner of the inner ward, where steps lead down to a postern from which a narrow, vaulted passage runs along the cliff edge to a natural cave. This cave was, we know, used in early prehistory, as four human skeletons and a pendant made from a horse's tooth were found within, under a layer of stalagmite. The mouth of the cave is partly walled up, and the masonry pierced by holes used as nesting boxes for pigeons, kept during the medieval period for fresh meat in winter months. At the end of the cave is a small, natural reservoir, but neither this limited water source, nor the dovecote, were

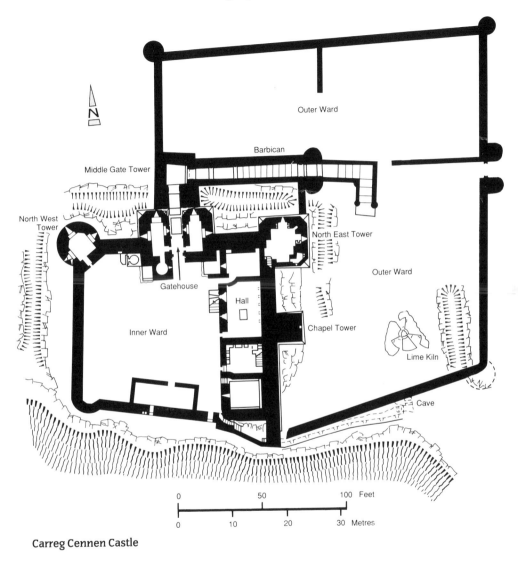

Carreg Cennen Castle

the reason for this elaborate passageway. The open cave could have been a source of weakness, allowing an enemy a base from which to infiltrate the castle or undermine its walls. The passage was therefore a device to include the cave within the castle defences.

After the downfall of the Giffards in 1321

due to their participation in a rebellion against Edward II, the castle passed through various hands and eventually became crown property in the later 14th century. It was taken by Owain Glyndŵr after a lengthy siege, after which, back in English hands, it required further substantial repair in 1416. The castle

Carreg Cennen Castle

was garrisoned by the Lancastrians during the Wars of the Roses, when an account of 1455 mentions sums of money spent on refortification. A military feature which may well date to this phase in the castle's history is found in the north-west tower, where one of the ground-floor arrowslits has been blocked and a gunport inserted. After the Yorkist supporters, Sir Richard Herbert of Raglan and Sir Roger Vaughan of Tretower, had eventually persuaded the Lancastrians to surrender, the castle was demolished by 500 men 'with bars, picks and crowbars of iron' in order to prevent 'inconvenience of this kind' happening there in future.

So dramatic a landscape feature as Carreg Cennen could not, of course, be forgotten, and, later, tourists came in increasing numbers to view the ruins. In response, in the 19th century, the owners, the earls of Cawdor, carried out extensive repairs which in places, such as the north-east tower, have rather confused the original plan. However, their work can normally be distinguished from the medieval because the blue-grey stone used looks unweathered – this can be clearly seen, for example, in the upper courses of the curtain wall.

The outer ward and entrance barbican were built as a secondary phase of the main building work of 1283–1321. The outer ward encloses ground on the east and north to provide an extra defence on this, the only level approach. The curtain wall with small, solid drum towers at the angles and gate, would originally have protected service buildings such as stables and the smithy but now there only remain some internal dividing walls and a lime kiln with a quarry ditch used to provide lime for mortar during building work. From here exterior features of the castle, such as the fine projecting chapel tower and latrine shaft on the east, are best appreciated.

The elaborate barbican defended the entrance to the inner ward by way of a narrow, stepped angular ramp guarded by two gates each with a moveable bridge over deep pits. On the corner, in front of the gatehouse, are the remains of a tower with a basement, referred to as a prison in a building account of 1369. Between this and the main gatehouse was a drawbridge to cross the ditch which defended the inner ward on the north, west and north-east sides. The gatehouse, the hub of the castle's defences, was a battlemented, three-storey structure which could be defended from the arrowslits in the projecting gate towers and by a portcullis and doors at either end of the gate passage. Above the entrance can be seen the remains of machicolations, or slits through which missiles could be dropped on to invaders.

125
Llandovery Castle, Llandovery
Medieval masonry castle
12th–13th century AD
OS 146   SN 767342   U3

Llandovery is on junction between A40 Llandeilo–Brecon and A4069/A483 Swansea–
Llanwrtyd Wells roads, and 12ml (19.2km) NE of Llandeilo. Castle on S of town by market car park

Though the masonry of Llandovery Castle is late 13th-century in date, the site clearly retains the form of the motte and bailey of the original castle built here in the 12th century. A high rocky hillock overlooking the Afon Bran has been scarped to form a motte on its western end and a lower sub-rectangular bailey on the east. The motte thus stands some 15m above the surrounding area, though most of this height is natural outcrop.

The surviving masonry consists of a strong D-shaped tower on the west, with part of a twin-towered gatehouse with a well-turret to the north, and sections of the curtain wall around the motte. The bailey has a low bank surrounding it. Two outlying banks, forming an outwork some way to the west, were destroyed years ago during the construction of the car park.

The castle was an English foundation, perhaps of Richard fitz Pons who was confirmed in this small and rather vulnerable

Llandovery Castle

lordship of Cantref Bychan by Henry I in 1116. This was difficult country for the Normans and the early history of the castle was stormy. The castle is first mentioned in the same year, 1116, when it was attacked by Gruffudd ap Rhys. In 1158 it fell briefly to the Lord Rhys, but from 1159 to 1161 the English king Henry II, recognising the dangerous weakness of the strategically important castle, spent a considerable sum of money on its repair. This did not prevent it from capture by Rhys again in 1162, and thereafter it remained in Welsh hands for over 100 years. From 1195 to 1213 the castle figured in a series of repeated skirmishes during the dynastic quarrels of the southern Welsh princes, but in 1277 it fell to the English king Edward I, and remained English apart from its temporary capture by Llywelyn the Last in 1282.

The masonry almost certainly dates from after 1282 when Edward I granted Cantref Bychan to John Giffard who had assisted the English king in his wars against Llywelyn. Giffard was ordered to strengthen the castle 'on account of the present disturbances amongst the Welsh'. In 1403, there was evidently enough remaining of the castle for it to be besieged by Owain Glyndŵr.

The picnic tables on the bailey and the adjacent children's playground and car park, while not enhancing the medieval atmosphere of the castle, make it a suitable venue for a family outing.

126
Aberystwyth Castle
Medieval masonry castle
13th–17th century AD
OS 135   SN 579815   U1

Castle sited prominently on sea-front on W of town. Park on promenade and walk up to castle

The powerful castle at Aberystwyth was built by the English king Edward I during his campaign against the Welsh in 1277. It is,

therefore, quite a late construction in the history of castle building in Wales. The present masonry castle was the first fortification to be built on this site and was not preceded by any earthwork castle. However in the histories of the 12th-century struggles between the Welsh and English there are many references to a castle in the vicinity. The earliest, built by Gilbert de Clare in 1110, is almost certainly the ringwork at Rhyd y Felin, some way to the south of Aberystwyth (see Appendix). But there were different considerations for the siting of the Edwardian castle; proximity to the sea was all-important for the supply of the isolated English garrison.

Edward's decision in 1276 to act against the threatening power of Llywelyn resulted in an extensive programme of castle building in Wales. During the next 20 years no fewer than 10 new castles were built, some also with substantial new town fortifications. As well as this, several existing castles were refurbished. The new castles at Builth and Aberystwyth were the first to be started. The building accounts for these royal castles have survived, and we know far more about the construction of Aberystwyth than of any other castle in Dyfed.

The plan of Aberystwyth castle, as finally constructed at least, is that of two concentric diamond shapes standing diagonally across the neck of a slight promontory, the point of which formed an outer enclosure. It seems, however, that this concentric design was not the original plan as excavations have revealed the footings of an early wall which, had it been completed, would have extended the west side of the inner ward toward the sea. Initially, the building of the castle was in the hands of Edmund, the king's brother. Masons, labourers and smiths were brought from the west of England by ship from Bristol via Carmarthen to carry out the work. The headland was owned by Strata Florida Abbey (no. 150) and the land had to be acquired and the existing tenants removed, though they were compensated with grants of land elsewhere. Work on the castle began on

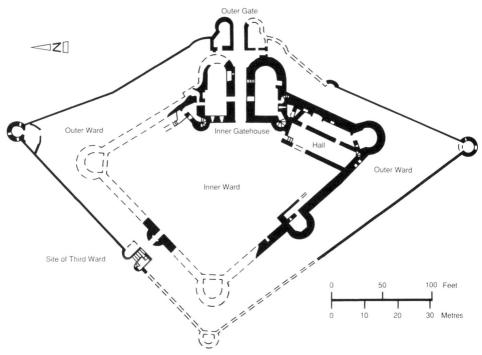

Aberystwyth Castle

1 August 1277; before the end of that year a new town of Aberystwyth was made a free borough, and was later defended by a wall and ditch – but, sadly nothing of these town defences now remains.

Construction work was not without its problems, and numerous letters were sent from officials at the castle complaining about shortages of money or labour. In 1280, the influential justiciar of west Wales, Bogo de Knovill, was made keeper of the castle; he visited Aberystwyth and wrote that there was a severe shortage of skilled masons, provisions and arms. The gates of the town had no locks, and shipments of Tenby limestone for mortar were urgently required 'for no other stone in the country would serve to make lime except this'. Also the work was behind schedule, as parts of the castle were proving very difficult to construct. 'The gate

tower' had, apparently, been placed too near the castle ditch and was 'shaken day in and day out by the great crash of the waves'. The castle was still incomplete in 1282 when it was temporarily taken and burned by the Welsh, but building work resumed and was finished in 1289. When, in 1294–5, the Welsh besieged the castle, it stood firm, relying on continuing supply by sea. The building had taken 12 years and had cost at least £4,300.

Most of the defences of the medieval castle survive at least at low level to reveal the concentric diamond-shaped plan. On the central angle is the twin-towered great gatehouse with a small gate to the rear and a stone barbican. Originally there were round towers on every corner on both internal and external wall circuits, and most still survive, though that on the north remains unexcavated. The highest tower, still standing almost to its original height, is an inner-ward wall tower which provides access through a postern gate to the outer ward. Paths now run along the castle ditches.

Building surveys of the 14th century suggest that the castle was by then suffering from lack of maintenance. It was taken in 1404 by Glyndŵr during his Welsh rebellion, and was only recaptured by the English in 1408 when Prince Henry, later King Henry V, brought artillery to pound the castle. During the Civil War, the castle was garrisoned for the king, and, along with the town, was attacked several times. Excavations have revealed a gun emplacement dating from these encounters. It finally surrendered to Colonel Rice Powell's Parliamentary army on 14 April 1646 and afterwards, like many other castles, was blown up to end its life as a military fortification. We know that a number of buildings were constructed within the ruins in the 17th century, among them a Royal Mint which was removed to Furnace, a little way to the north, during the Civil War. The castle was restored by the Victorians, whose masonry can be detected in several places (in the gate passage, for instance, built as plain facework above portcullis grooves or arrowslits), and who built numerous small pillars to provide support for weak stonework. Later still, an Eisteddfod bardic circle was erected within the inner ward.

127
Castell Gwallter, Aberystwyth
Medieval earthwork castle
12th century AD
OS 135   SN 622868   U2

Aberystwyth Castle

From Aberystwyth, take A487 N toward Machynlleth for 4ml (6.4km). Turn L on to B4353 into Llandre, then 2nd L over level crossing, and follow road round to L, to ask permission for visit from owner in Ael y Bryn (house set back on RHS of road opposite Garth y Clyn), who kindly allows access on request. Return to road fork (by Sanctuary). Follow road to L for 0.4ml (0.7km) up steep LH bend, to road fork. Park by stile (tight), follow public footpath over stile through field. Site in next field on LHS

O'Neil 1946-7

This is a very fine, unusual castle mound with a double bailey, a strong sub-rectangular bailey lying on the north and a larger, but less well preserved, one on the south. Castell Gwallter is situated on a hilltop with steep slopes to the north and east. The motte is 5m high with a wide encircling ditch and high external counterscarp bank.

The west bank of the smaller, northern bailey is well preserved, the east less so, and the severe natural slopes necessitated no further defence on the north. The larger, southern bailey is less clear as its banks have been incorporated into field boundaries, and this may always have been the weaker of the two. The natural approach to the castle is on the level south-west, and the gap in the counterscarp bank on this side is probably the site of the original entrance. To the east of the castle the gently sloping ground outside the man-made earthworks is bounded by steep natural slopes, and might itself have functioned as part of the castle.

Castell Gwallter was built by Walter de Bec during the period of Norman ascendancy in Ceredigion between 1110 and 1135, but was destroyed in 1136 by the north Welsh royal princes Owain and Cadwaladr. It must have then been rebuilt, as in 1151 it held out for the north Welsh royal house against an attack by the southern princes Cadell, Maredudd and Rhys. However, two years later, it was finally captured by Maredudd and Rhys. They may have destroyed the castle, as no subsequent mention of it appears in any documentation.

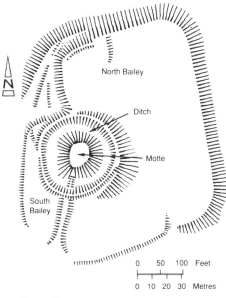

Castell Gwallter

128
Domen Las, Machynlleth
Medieval earthwork castle
12th century AD
OS 135   SN 687969   R2   RSPB

Eglwys Fach is on A487 12ml (19.2km) N of Aberystwyth, 6ml (9.6km) S of Machynlleth. In Eglwys Fach take track signed RSPB, and drive to RSPB centre (1ml, 1.6km). Entry charge payable at reception where there is map of reserve. Walk along marked track towards Estuary Hide, then Marian Mawr or Domen Las Hides. Latter hide adjacent to site. NB: site not accessible to visitors during heron nesting season, February–July

Domen Las motte stands on the point of a rocky ridge which overlooks the extensive marshes on the bank of the Dyfi estuary. The mound is 7m high and the diameter across the flat top is 10m. It is surrounded on three sides by a wide, deep rock-cut ditch and on the fourth by the marsh. On the north-east is a roughly rectangular area bounded by a steep scarp and separated from the motte by a deep ditch. This irregular area may possibly be the remains of a bailey.

The motte is probably the castle recorded as being built at Aberdyfi by the Lord Rhys in 1156 as a precaution against an attack by Owain Gwynedd of north Wales, who at the time was threatening Ceredigion with a large army. This threat came to nothing, but two years later the castle was taken and rebuilt by the Norman Roger de Clare, earl of Hertford. It was recaptured by Rhys probably in the same year, and thereafter is not heard of again.

Carswell medieval house

129
Carswell and West Tarr Houses, St Florence
Medieval houses
Late 14th–15th century AD
OS 158   SM 098011   U2   Cadw

From Tenby, take B4318 W towards Pembroke, for 3ml (4.8km) then turn L towards St Florence. At St Florence take Penally road. After 1ml (1.6km), turn down Carswell Farm drive (at sharp RH bend in road), park near farmhouse and walk through farmyard. Site in small paddock on LHS

Smith 1988; Cadw Guidebook

These two houses stand in this guide as the sole representatives of the later medieval farmhouse in Dyfed. Though there still survive a fair number of the small, stone-vaulted structures so typical of the medieval buildings of the south-west, most are inaccessible.

Both farmhouses lie on a slight eminence overlooking the Ritec valley, originally a tidal creek – which may have given Carswell one element of its name, as 'gors' means 'marsh'. The two farms were closely associated with one another and the first known references to

them, in the 14th century, show that they belonged at that time to the estates of the earl of Pembroke. The tenants would have been yeoman farmers of moderate means. The buildings are difficult to date because of their simplicity and lack of ornament, but are generally thought to have been constructed in the 15th century.

Carswell House has a vaulted ground-floor room with an entrance at one side, and two small slit windows; one of these has been blocked and the other enlarged to form a second entrance. The great hearth which extends the full length of one end of the house has also been altered by the addition of a short piece of walling designed to reduce its vast size. The circular oven is a later addition, as is the stone 'table' built against one side. The room has a workaday feel, a combined kitchen and living room, like many a farmhouse kitchen today. Excavations showed that unfortunately no evidence remained of the earliest floors, so whether they were flagged or were perhaps just of beaten earth is unknown. The first floor housed the more important 'hall' or living room, and has a smaller, decorative fireplace and small windows, one of which has been enlarged at a later date. This room evidently had a timber pitch roof, and the two gable ends are almost complete, showing its original height and shape. There was no internal access to the hall from the room below, but via a stair, of timber or of stone, which led to the rectangular-headed door in the corner.

From the outside, the enormous size of the chimney can be appreciated. These large stone chimneys are a feature of the local building style, and a number, either rectangular as here or, more commonly, circular, may be seen in the area. On the end of the house opposite the chimney are the marks of timbers from a roof which once was incorporated into the farmhouse. It is uncertain whether or not these small houses were ever complete buildings, and it may be that the vaulted structure was only part of a larger house even as originally built. Excavations on the site provided no clue, as there had been late clearance of the area down to the bedrock. However, another vaulted building of roughly similar size stands on the other side of the farmyard, and this may have been an outhouse or perhaps another farmhouse.

West Tarr House (SN 089008) is in the farm of that name, two farms back down the road towards St Florence. Access is down a footpath (park on road) between the entrance to East and West Tarr Farms. The building is soon to pass into state care, though at present it is private and permission to visit should be requested from the owner of West Tarr Farm.

A little way along this lane on the left are two tiny buildings. The first is not vaulted, but its small windows and similar build suggest that it may have been a farm building associated with the farmhouse which stands nearby. The main building is similar in size to Carswell, but, instead of the timber pitch roof, has a first-floor stone vault with a slate roof. Thus we have here two vaults, one above the

other, each of a different form: the lower one is rounded, the upper one more pointed. The house also complements Carswell in the position of its chimney. West Tarr has a lateral chimney on the uphill side of the house, and the small hearth and flue on the end is a later addition. The original chimney has been much damaged and a new door cut through the side, but the original layout remains quite clear.

The entrance to the house was at first-floor level, the door, which can be seen at one end, now being blocked. However, at West Tarr communication between the two floors was provided by a stair in the opposite corner. At this point there are clear signs that there was here a low roof, as at Carswell, and the end wall of the lower room has gone. The footings of adjacent stone walls suggest that at one stage at least the standing building was only part of a larger structure. The future consolidation, survey and perhaps excavation of the site will doubtless help us understand the complex history of these buildings.

130
Rosemarket Dovecote, Haverfordwest
Medieval dovecote
?13th–14th century AD
OS 158   SM 954082   R2

From Haverfordwest, take A4076 Milford Haven road for 0.5ml (0.8km). At Merlin's Bridge, take LH turn and follow signs to Rosemarket (4ml, 6.4km). Site near church, in private garden. Owners kindly allow access on request; information panel outside bungalow

The small, circular dovecote at Rosemarket now stands curiously isolated in a field known as Pigeon Hay. Great House to which it belonged has not survived, though its ruins were still standing in the 19th century. The dovecote is built of local sandstone; its walls are some 1m in thickness, and a single row of projecting flat stones serves as the top course, below the circular, domed roof. The exterior of the building and the roof stands intact, but the rows of over 200 nesting boxes built into the interior are beginning to deteriorate, as is the single, small doorway. Originally an internal ladder would have provided access to the boxes to allow the keeper to take eggs and young birds as a supplement to the diet.

The church and village of Rosemarket were granted to the Knights Hospitallers of Slebech (no. 142) in the 12th century, and it seems probable therefore that the dovecote would have been built by them. Dovecotes are difficult to date as their form remained unchanged for centuries, but there is little doubt that the building at Rosemarket is medieval. After the Reformation, it probably passed into the hands of the owners of Great House.

Manorbier Dovecote

131
Manorbier Dovecote, Manobier
Medieval dovecote
?13th century AD
OS 158   SS 062978   U2

Follow directions to Manorbier Castle (no. 114). From car park, cross road and walk along track opposite to N, alongside stream, past ruinous mill and through gate. Site on LHS of path over stile

An essential building on any medieval estate was the dovecote, as young birds and eggs were regarded as a useful source of food. The small, circular dovecote at Manorbier was undoubtedly originally part of the castle estate of the de Barry family. It is particularly well preserved and retains its corbelled roof, formed by thin slabs of overlapping stone, with the central opening in the top to allow access for the doves. The large number of nesting boxes in the walls are also intact, and it is possible to see (with a torch) or feel how

the holes for the boxes are built to curve around into the masonry. There is one small door on the east. Originally a ladder would have allowed the keeper to get to the boxes to extract the eggs or young birds.

The low marshy ground between the dovecote and the castle originally held fishponds and, although the area is now silted up and overgrown, it is not that difficult to imagine the ponds in use, providing the castle inhabitants with another source of foodstuff.

132
Pont Spwdwr, Kidwelly
Stone bridge
?15th century AD
OS 159   SN 434059   U1

From Kidwelly, take B4308 Trimsaran road for 1.9ml (3km). Just after bridge over railway, site on RHS of road, to one side of modern road bridge. Now used as footbridge

Pont Spwdwr

Pont Spwdwr, or Spudder's Bridge, carried the main road over the Gwendraeth Fawr until comparatively recently. It must be one of the most ancient bridges in south Wales after the great medieval Monnow bridge in Monmouth. In 1571, Daniel Vaughan of Trimsaran left 40s. in his will towards the repair of the bridge, which presumably was of some age then. A further 20s. for the same purpose was given by Daniel's nephew, Griffith ap William Vaughan, 16 years later.

The bridge has six pointed arches, three large and three small, though the river now only passes beneath two of them. There are four cutwaters with recesses on each side. Protruding stones under the arches in the side of the masonry may have held the timber forms around which the stone arches were originally built.

The bridge over the Gwendraeth Fach in Kidwelly is also of interest. Although much rebuilt and altered, it still contains within its structure part of the ancient bridge which may have been built at the end of the 15th century. It is only by close examination from the path by the riverside that the older pointed arch may be seen, mostly encased in more recent masonry.

8

The Medieval Church

The Normans' strong instinct for organisation was not confined to the secular aspects of life. Despite their celebrated warlike nature, they also possessed a conventional piety and must have regarded the existing Welsh church as sadly anachronistic and isolated. Accordingly, they swiftly set about remodelling it so that it conformed with the mainstream Latin church on the Continent, with which they were familiar. First of all the religious settlements established by some of the more influential 6th-century saints were reorganised into the territorial dioceses of Bangor, Llandaff, St Davids and, a little later, St Asaph, and for the first time each had its own clearly demarcated boundary. The outlying churches were then incorporated into a parish system which defined the area of responsibility for each church. Impressive new cathedrals were built at each of the sees, and gradually, and not without protest, the four Welsh dioceses were made subject to the authority of Canterbury. The first Norman church at St Davids was built by Bishop Bernard in the early 12th century, though it was destroyed by fire in 1182, and the earliest work in the present-day cathedral is the fine late 12th-century nave of Bishop Peter de Leia. New and larger churches were built to serve the parishes, and, as stone was now more commonly used for their construction, many of these early buildings survive, albeit usually in a heavily modified form.

The new system that the Normans imposed not only brought the Welsh church into mainstream Christendom, but also allowed them to control the activity of the church by the election of suitable English bishops; with few exceptions, the medieval bishops of St Davids were Englishmen. The bishops built up enormous power and wealth, and acted as Marcher lords in their own right, with responsibilities for administration and for the exercising of justice in their lordships. Their estates were extensive and productive, and like any other lords, the bishops built palaces and castles for their own private use and for the defence of their properties. The bishop's palace at St Davids is a magnificent structure as it stands, in its 14th-century form, built as a reflection of the temporal power of these great men. Similarly the palace at Lamphey (no. 146), tucked away in a favoured and productive valley, wanted for nothing, and the castle at Llawhaden (no. 109) combined an imposing appearance with a serious military intent.

The Norman Conquest influenced monastic life too. The Celtic *clas* was not so much a monastic community as a grouped enclosed hermitage, belonging to no

Reconstruction drawing of Cathedral Close, St Davids, in the early 16th century

particular order and isolated from the reforming movements which were sweeping through monasteries on the Continent. The Normans were not prepared to allow these idiosyncratic Welsh communities to continue in their old way of life. Here too they sought control, and attached the ancient religious sites to Continental reformed foundations with their regulated discipline. The Celtic monastery of St Dogmaels (no. 133), for instance, was granted to the Tironensian order, a reform of the Benedictines. Other monasteries, like that at Pembroke, were founded on new sites near the *caput* or capital, of the Norman lord.

This new monasticism was slow to be adopted in 'pura Wallia' and it was only with the coming of the Cistercians that the Welsh princes began to give their patronage. The Cistercians, with their emphasis on the importance of labour and a disciplined life of rural simplicity, provoked a sympathic response among the Welsh. The founding of Whitland Abbey near Carmarthen in about 1140 was a landmark, for 8 of the 15 Welsh Cistercian monasteries were offshoots from this great house. Notable among these was Strata Florida (no. 150), which became renowned as a centre of Welsh culture and learning, providing the principal copyists and custodians of Welsh history and poetry. Another offshoot from Whitland was the Cistercian house at Llanllyr, founded by Rhys ap Gruffudd as a daughter house of Strata Florida, and the only nunnery to be established in Dyfed.

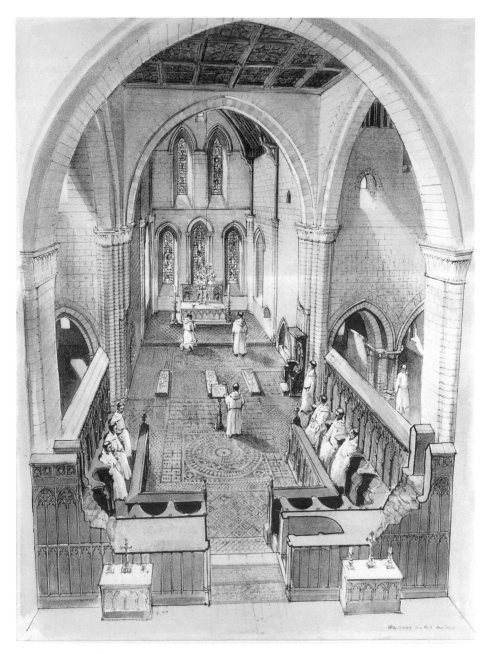

Reconstruction drawing of a scene in a Cistercian monastery church

The foundation of new monastic houses was at its height in the late 12th and early 13th centuries, and it is to this period that the principal monasteries in Dyfed belong. The Cistercians at Strata Florida, the Premonstratensians at Talley (no. 149) and the Augustinians at Haverfordwest (no. 140) and Carmarthen built their new monasteries at the invitation of both English and Welsh lordly families who would continue to provide support for their foundations, thereby shrewdly combining piety with a measure of control. The new monasteries needed not only the initial grant of land for the monastic buildings, but required further gifts of land to provide income from rents and agricultural produce. These estates were often far away from the monastery to which they belonged. Nearer to the house would be the mills, gardens, orchards and fishponds the monastery would require for its own daily needs. Some orders, such as the Augustinians, concentrated less on rural frugality and more on the fulfilling of parochial duties, hence the tendency of their houses to be situated near towns. The spiritual incomes, tithes and other money derived from the appropriation of parish churches were another important source of income.

The monastic day, ordered along Continental lines, was a strictly laid down timetable of church services, periods of work and of leisure, mealtimes and sleep. There were several variations in tradition, observance and way of life between the Celtic church and the new monasteries, which had to be ironed out, sometimes by means of synods or conferences. Discipline was enforced by the leading clergy of the appropriate order who would visit monastic houses for this purpose, and the lists of problems or laxities encountered make entertaining reading. It is clear that some of the smaller and more remote houses, such as Talley, exacted particular censure for failure to adhere strictly to the orthodox discipline of the order, especially in later medieval periods.

Fundamental to monastic life were, of course, the monastic buildings, which were laid out to an established pattern. The 'cruciform' or cross-shaped church normally lay on the north of the monastery, aligned east–west, with the high altar at the east end of the presbytery, a choir in the centre where the monastic services would be sung, transepts in the short arms of the cross, and a long nave on the west. The cloister was the nucleus of the monastery and combined the functions of study and thoroughfare, being composed of a central open garden, surrounded by a walkway which was normally covered by a pent-roof but was open on the garden side. The range of buildings on the eastern side of the cloister would be largely taken up with the chapter house, where the business of the monastery would be conducted, and the monks' dormitory lay on the first floor above. On the south side of the cloister lay the refectory, with the kitchens beyond, usually in a separate building to lessen the risk of fire. The abbot or prior had his apartments on the west side, along with a dining room and further apartments for the entertainment of eminent guests, one of the responsibilities of the head of the house. In Cistercian houses, however, the west range was used for the refectory and dormitory of the 'lay brothers', men used by the monks to carry out building work, grow the food and tend the flocks and herds. Other orders used paid servants to act, as time went on, in an increasing variety of ways, from porters to butlers and cooks, from washerwomen and sewing-women to servants for the infirmary to help with the sick or aged monks.

The 13th century was generally a prosperous period for monasticism, but the wealth of the monks was beginning to attract criticism. The arrival in Britain of the Dominican and Franciscan friars with their fundamental mission to serve the laity was timely, and attracted great interest. There were, however, only two friaries founded in Dyfed, at Haverfordwest and at Carmarthen, and, sadly, there are no surviving remains at either site. There were also established in Dyfed a number of other religious houses which did not belong to the more commonly found groups of monasteries. The Knights Hospitallers were an international order set up to care for the sick and, later, to provide escorts of mounted knights to protect pilgrims to the Holy Land. Their house at Slebech (see no. 142) was an important possession and become famous for its hospitality. A hospital was founded in 1287 at Llawhaden (see Appendix) by Thomas Bek, bishop of St Davids, and continued in its service of the sick under the authority of a prior until the 16th century. Finally, the pre-Norman *clas* at Llanddewi Brefi was refounded as a secular college of clerks bound to service in the church.

Monasticism suffered its first painful setback when the bubonic plague, the 'Black Death', struck in the mid-14th century. Economic and religious unrest followed and the consequent social upheaval, together with a lengthy period of war, contributed towards a general decline in intellectual and religious life in England and Wales. The Church, still enormously wealthy and influential, was failing to attract men and women into the monastic life and the numbers of brethren in monastic houses had fallen drastically. When, in 1536–40, Henry VIII undertook his famous Dissolution of the Monasteries, the buildings of most religious houses were stripped of their valuables, including the lead from their roofs, and were either allowed to fall into ruin, or were demolished and the land built on anew. Sometimes the monastic churches were reused as parish churches, and in some places such as St Clears, this is all that remains above ground. At other sites, such as Haverfordwest, extensive ruins of the monastic enclosures remained untouched through the centuries, save for the depredations of stone robbers. Now, the trowels of the archaeologist and the stonemason together are at work to breathe a new life into such ruins for the benefit of the student, the nearby resident and the tourist, reflecting the very different interests and requirements of our own age.

133
St Dogmaels Abbey, Cardigan
Medieval monastery
12th–16th century AD
OS 145   SN 164458   U1   Cadw

*St Dogmaels is 1ml (1.6km) SW of Cardigan on
B4546 road to Poppit Sands. Abbey
signposted on LHS of B road. Park in front of
abbey gates*

Cadw Guidebook

The Tironensian movement, with its simplified
liturgy and austere life-style based on the rule
of St Benedict, was very successful in
Scotland. In England and Wales, however, less
than 10 houses were founded altogether;
most were dependent priories and only a few
were granted the status of abbey. Among
these was St Dogmaels, the 'mother house' of
two nearby priories, Caldey (no. 147) and Pill
(no. 143). This remote cluster of three houses,
like all Tironensian monasteries at first at
least, remained closely bound to the abbey of
Tiron.

A priory was founded at St Dogmaels
around 1115 by Robert fitz Martin, the
Norman lord of Cemais. Thirteen monks were
brought from France to bring Continental-
style monasticism to this site, where,
formerly, the ancient Celtic *clas* (or
monastery) of Llandudoch had stood. No
trace remains of the *clas*, though the early
Christian stones (now in the parish church)
presumably belonged to it. Five years after its
foundation, St Dogmaels was made an abbey,
and was given three dependent priories: at
Pill, on Caldey Island (given to the abbey by
Robert's mother, Geva) and at Glascarreg in
southern Ireland. It also held property in the
locality and in Devon, from which the abbey
derived income. We know little of the history
of the abbey itself, though during its life it
underwent many modifications, probably
reflecting the changing political fortunes of
the Norman lordship.

The cruciform church lies on the north and
was originally planned to have an aisled nave,
transepts with apsidal chapels and a short
presbytery with an eastern apse. This plan
seems never to have been completed,
perhaps because of the political troubles of
the time. In any case, the church was
considerably remodelled in the early 13th
century to its present form with a simple nave
and square-ended presbytery over a crypt.
This was achieved by blocking the arcade of
the southern aisle to become the new south
nave wall. The cloister was then extended
further north to disguise the assymetry. The
monks' choir lay in the crossing, separated
from the nave by a stone screen or *pulpitum*.

The church saw three further stages of
modification. In the 14th century, there was a
major rebuilding programme (necessary,
perhaps to repair damage inflicted during the
troubles associated with the Edwardian
conquest of Wales), during which the cloister
and refectory were also substantially altered.
The nave was remodelled, as the large west
window and the fine decorated door on the
north show. Also the vaulting in the crypt was
rebuilt over capitals with reeded and stiff-leaf
foliage decoration. The crypt vaulting clearly
rose above the floor of the adjacent
presbytery, so presumably the high altar was
set on a raised floor above the crypt.

The second episode of rebuilding took place
in the 14th or 15th century, when the plain
tiled pavement and the rood screen were
added, and the *pulpitum* was strengthened,
the latter perhaps for the insertion of an
organ in the gallery above.

The church saw a final, and major, series of
alterations in the 16th century, when the
north transept was extensively modified and
given an elaborately vaulted roof, with
decorated corbels to support the timbers: an
angel for St Matthew, a lion for St Mark, and
the Archangel St Michael. A similar corbel of
an eagle for St John, found during
excavations, can be seen in the stone display.
Despite the modifications, designed, perhaps,
to provide a special chapel for the founder's
family, elements of the earlier transept may

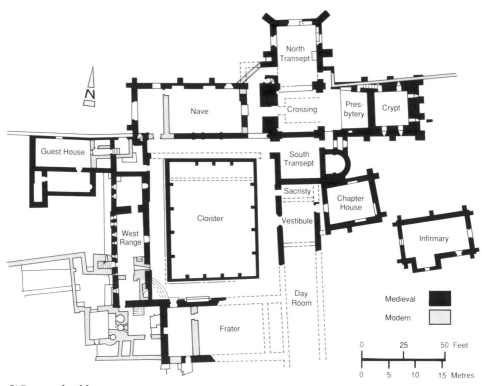

St Dogmaels Abbey

still be seen, including the *piscina* on the east. The base of a small stone altar lies against the east wall, and there are two tomb recesses in the north-east corner. The stone 'cadaver', or skeleton, now in the stone display, may have come from one of these recesses. After the Dissolution, the church was altered to become the parish church. The rood screen was given a central door, and new walls blocked off the west end of the nave to form a porch.

South of the nave lies the cloister. The present walls are 13th-century, and held arcades to support a timber pent roof over the pavement. East of the cloister the now fragmentary sacristy lies between the church and the vestibule of the chapter house, rebuilt in the 14th century at rather an odd angle to

fit in with the infirmary to the south. Parts of the remarkably well-preserved infirmary stand to roof level, and within it have been set for protection decorated stonework from the abbey, which shows the original richness of the abbey buildings. There are plans to move these stones to a permanent exhibition elsewhere on the site. The dormitory for the monks presumably lay at first-floor level over the east-range buildings.

Little remains of the refectory which once formed the south range, and the confusing masonry in the south-west corner is that of the late 16th-century rector's house remodelled from the monks' kitchen and the abbot's house after the Dissolution. The west range would have been used for storage on the ground floor and probably for the abbot's apartments on the first floor. In the 14th century, a guest house was built projecting west from the northern end.

134
Llanllawer Well, Fishguard
Medieval holy well
?13th/14th century AD
OS 157   SM 987360   U2

From Fishguard, take B4313 SE towards Gwaun Valley for 2ml (3.2km). At Llanychaer, take L turn towards Llanllawer for 0.3ml (0.5km), then park at pull-in, just beyond church on LHS. Site over stile in field adjacent to church

The holy well at Llanllawer, constructed to cover a small stretch of open spring water, is a simple, unadorned stone structure standing in the corner of a field near to the medieval church of St David's. The rectangular well-chamber is corbelled to form a pointed vault 2m high. The interior is original, but the exterior masonry has been unfortunately restored. It is comparable in appearance with Higgon's Well (no. 141), though there is no evidence that there was ever an adjacent well chapel – perhaps the proximity of the church

Llanllawer Well

made this unnecessary. The well is of so simple a construction that it is almost impossible to date it with any precision, but vaulted wells like this are usually thought to have been built in the medieval period.

The site had a reputation for miraculous healing as late as the 18th century, when there are references to people visiting the well and throwing in straight pins if they wished good, crooked pins if they wanted evil. The water was supposed to be particularly beneficial for sore eyes. A stream still flows here, emerging from the well to run down towards the hedge.

The adjacent church of St David's has two cross-inscribed stones (no. 89).

135
Bishop's Palace, St Davids
Medieval bishop's palace
Late 12th–15th century AD
OS 157   SM 750255   R1   Cadw

Site on W side of St Davids, signposted. Admission charge; standard opening hours

Cadw Guidebook

According to tradition, St David founded his *clas* or ecclesiastical community in the 6th century near Whitesands Bay – 1.5ml (2.4km) to the north-west. But for some reason, the monastery was soon transferred to its present position on the bank of the River Alun, near the south-western point of this remote and rocky peninsula. Nothing remains now of the modest buildings that would have housed the Celtic religious community, and indeed the Viking incursions on these coasts in the 10th and 11th centuries may have brought about the destruction of the settlement. But such was the fame of its founder that it quickly became a leading Welsh monastery and the seat of a bishopric. After the Norman Conquest, it was adopted by the English church and reorganised along English lines.

Dyfed

In the 12th and early 13th centuries, the building of the cathedral was the main concern of the bishops, and their accommodation buildings were probably of no great size or richness. Indeed, in 1172, when King Henry II visited St Davids, the resources of Bishop David fitz Gerald were strained to the limit by the necessary lavish entertainment. Although the buildings of the western range are the earliest on the site, their plainness makes it difficult to date them accurately, or even to understand their function. They may have replaced earlier timber structures, or may be the only survivors of a complex of contemporary buildings. It was not until the late 13th century, probably during the bishopric of Thomas Bek (1280–93), that a degree of grandeur was introduced into the residence with the building of the gatehouse, a chapel on the south-west, and a long, vaulted range of buildings on the east of the courtyard which probably housed the hall and private apartments of the bishop.

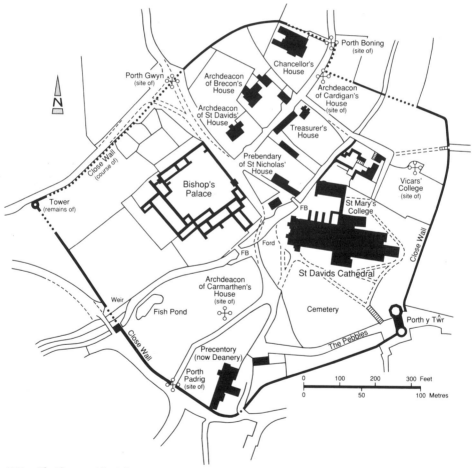

St Davids Close, with Bishop's Palace

The palace of Bishop Bek and his immediate successors, then, was approached from the north and defended by a vaulted projecting gate with a room above to give access to the wall-walk on the enclosure wall. The west-range buildings on the right were used, perhaps, for guest accommodation on the first floor and storage below. On the left was the vaulted range with the hall and private quarters on the first floor. The hall was served by a kitchen, now gone, which we know lay to the south-east side of the hall. The chapel lay opposite the gate and was again entered at first-floor level by an external stair. The traceried windows in the north and the square bellcote with its attractive octagonal spire are original features, while the decorated eastern window and the ornate *piscina* date to alterations made in the time of Bishop de Gower.

At this period, the palace was probably skirted by the River Alun which flowed in a much wider course close to the eastern walls of the hall and immediately adjacent to the eastern wing which housed the latrines for the bishop's private apartments. The entire cathedral close was also surrounded by a boundary wall which Bishop Bek ordered to be built for the protection of the houses of the clerics. We know that some sort of enclosure with gates existed at the time of Henry II's visit in 1172, as he was met by the cathedral canons 'at the white gate'. But it seems probable that the walls that survive today, albeit in a very repaired and altered form, date back to those built by Bishop Bek. Of the four original gates, Porth Boning, Porth Gwyn, Porth Padrig and Porth y Twr, only the last still stands, used as the bell-tower for the cathedral.

In 1328, Henry de Gower was elected bishop. He was an eminent man, a scholar, an able administrator, and above all a great builder. By this time the bishops of St Davids were among the wealthiest and most important landowners in Wales, with vast estates and considerable power both in religious and temporal affairs. Gower evidently considered the existing palace buildings an inadequate expression of this prestige, and built on the south side of the courtyard a large imposing rectangular hall over a series of vaults. The hall, with its rich porch decorated with statues of seated figures and its fine traceried windows, is still a magnificent sight. The east gable was flanked by rectangular turrets, one of which carried the stair to the wall-walk, and between them was built a fine wheel-window. Strangely enough, there is no fireplace in the hall, and there must have been a central hearth with a louvre in the roof for the smoke.

A new first-floor kitchen with large hearths was built on the south-east to serve the new hall, to which it was connected by a covered corridor. North of the kitchen, the east range was substantially modified to become the bishop's private quarters, approached by a stair with an ornate porch. Further north again, a new chapel was built in a slightly cramped position in the corner of the courtyard near the gate. A decorative arcaded parapet was built along the wall tops of the entire south and east ranges supported by corbels, carved with a wonderful profusion of subjects – male and female heads, winged grotesques, a mermaid, and a sow suckling her piglets, to mention just a few. This richness was further enhanced by a chequer-board pattern of a white stone and the purple Caerbwdi stone which is used generally on fine stonework on the palace. Similar decorated corbels may be seen in the rooms of the east range.

It was perhaps at this time that the River Alun was canalised, and a new boundary wall built on the east. This has now disappeared, but the later garden wall, with peculiar pillars intended to support trellises, stands on roughly the same line. New service buildings may have been built on this reclaimed land.

Gower's great building scheme may well have been finished after his death, but by 1350 the palace had been completed, to remain until 1536, when Bishop Barlow, who wanted the seat of the bishopric removed to Carmarthen, stripped the lead from the roof of the great hall. Thereafter the palace lost all significance and by the end of the 17th century was derelict.

From the east gate, the 'Porth Y Tŵr', the fine battlemented close wall, is accessible to the north-east corner where it turns to bridge the River Alun. At the other side of the close, the sluice-gate tower straddles the Alun, controlling its flow perhaps to regulate water through the adjacent fishponds. The close wall was too long for realistic defence; it would have deterred a casual raid, but was more concerned with presenting a prestigious appearance. We know from a survey of 1326, the 'Black Book of St Davids', that within the close were the residences of important ecclesiastical dignitaries such as the archdeacons of Brecon, Cardigan and St Davids. We also know that even in the medieval period the close was semi-rural, with fishponds, orchards and grazing land. The removal of the bishop's residence to Carmarthen, and the reduced demand for development here, have resulted in the unique survival of the rural tranquillity of this most atmospheric place.

136
St Non's Chapel, St Davids
Medieval chapel and well
?8th–16th century AD
OS 157   SM 752243   U3   Cadw

Chapel lies 0.5ml (0.8km) down track going S from St Non's Hotel, St Davids, and is signposted. Car park at end, chapel through stile and across field

Cadw Guidebook

This must be one of the most idyllically situated monuments in Dyfed, overlooking, as it does, the rocky coastline above St Non's Bay. A visit to the chapel ruins can be extended to a longer walk on to and along the coastal footpath west as far as the Merryvale road, which leads back to St Davids.

The ruins lack any distinguishing features to help date the building, and the earliest reference to a chapel here is in a document of 1335. However, an early excavation reports the uncovering of 'stone coffins' which might in fact have been slab-lined graves of the early Christian period. Also the presence here of the pillar-stone (see no. 91) with its incised Latin cross, roughly datable to the 7th to 9th century, is suggestive of a early medieval foundation for the chapel, although unfortunately, there is no firm evidence that the stone originally came from the site.

The chapel is a simple rectangular building, with an entrance on the west. The north–south orientation of the building is unusual, and is probably best explained by the foundations having been laid out to suit the severe slope. The massive masonry on the southern, downhill end was presumably put

St Non's Chapel

down as part of a foundation platform, to help level the site. The position of the altar is marked by a step at the north end. The chapel is traditionally held to mark the place where St Non or Nonna gave birth to St David.

The chapel was one of the more important sea-shore chapels in the area; two pilgrimages to St Davids were held in the medieval period to equal one to Rome, and pilgrims to the chapel gave money 'by the dishful', which was taken to the cathedral. After the Reformation, pilgrims ceased to come to St Davids, and St Non's passed out of religious use. It was converted into a dwelling house, and later into a vegetable garden.

The holy well, just to the east of the chapel, continued to be a famous place for healing after the Reformation, and there are antiquarian references to the pious offering pins and pebbles at the well on 2 March, St Non's Day. In the 18th century, the present stone vault was built over it, though this may have replaced an earlier well building.

137
City Cross, St Davids
Medieval preaching cross
14th century AD
OS 157   SM 754253   U1

Cross stands very conspicuously on one side of a small park which forms a roundabout in the centre of St Davids. In winter, park on road adjacent; in summer, use Quickwell Hill car park

This cross stands on a large, square, stepped base formed of flights of six steps made of the local purple sandstone from Caerbwdi Bay. The fine socket stone has worn decoration of 14th-century style on the corners. The cross itself has a wheel-head and a tapering octagonal shaft. It was heavily restored in the 19th century and there is an inscription on the steps commemorating this repair work. The cross is probably in its original position, and perhaps functioned as a preaching cross

in the heart of the medieval cathedral city. It is still an impressive and picturesque monument to St Davids' medieval past.

138
St Justinian's Chapel, St Davids
Medieval chapel
14th–16th century AD
OS 157   SM 723252   R1

Site is 2ml (3.2km) W of St Davids down minor road signed St Justinians. Park at car park near end of road. Chapel in field by RHS of road near harbour; private ownership, view from road only

The ruins of St Justinian's chapel lie on the coast, overlooking the harbour. The walls of this simple rectangular structure stand almost to full height, and show many details of interest. The chapel has three doors, one on the west and two on the north; there are also three windows, small apertures on each side of the nave and one at the east end. Around the wall top on the outside is a corbel table, which is cut into by the east window. An antiquarian refence to the chapel describes a bell tower at one end, but nothing now survives of this. A step runs across the chapel

St Justinian's Chapel

dividing it into two equal sections. On either side of this step is a hole in the wall, which probably held the beams for a rood screen.

The building of the present chapel is attributed to Bishop Vaughan, bishop of St Davids from 1509 to 1522. There are, however, references to a chapel here in 1492, which mention the income it generated for the cathedral. The foundation of the first chapel on the site must date back many centuries before that. Excavations on the site in 1926 revealed the foundations of an earlier, probably 12th-century building, and several burials, some of which may belong to the early medieval period. The dedication to St Stinian, an obscure Celtic saint, also suggests a pre-Norman foundation.

The harbour at Porth Stinian was used as a landing place for travellers to and from Ireland, and the chapel may have served as a place of worship for those embarking on or returning from the sea voyage.

139

St Teilo's Chapel and Well, Maenclochog

Medieval chapel
?13th–14th century AD
OS 158   SN 099269   U2

From Maenclochog (N of Narberth), take Crymmych road E for 0.2ml (0.3km); take RH Llangolman road for 1ml (3.2km), then 1st R on to Llanycefn road. Park by 1st farm on LHS (Llandilo Isaf). Right of way passes through farmyard to right, and site is through gate to RHS of path

Very little remains of the old church of St Teilo, and it is chiefly remembered as the findspot of three important related early Christian stones (no. 88), two of which are now in Maenclochog church, nearby. However, the dedication to this early saint, the presence of the inscribed stones, and the circular shape of the graveyard all point to

this church being a very early foundation. In its overgrown state it certainly has a romantic charm, surrounded by the headstones of burials made when the church was used for parish worship. It was abandoned early in the 19th century and all that now survives are the wall footings of a simple rectangular building comprising a nave, chancel and south door. A round-headed chancel arch, which was still standing in the early years of this century, has now collapsed. A low stone bench apparently ran around the nave wall, but this too has become ruinous and overgrown. The graveyard is surrounded by a low, circular stone wall which has been substantially repaired and realigned on the north. About 100m to the north-east is a rough stone well. The water had, until quite recently, a widespread reputation for healing, especially of pulmonary complaints, and pilgrims were supposed to drink the water from the human skull provided, stoutly reported, despite the inherent improbability of this, to be the skull of St Teilo.

140

Haverfordwest Priory, Haverfordwest

Medieval monastery
13th–16th century AD
OS 157   SM 958153   U2   Cadw

From A40 roundabout on E side of Haverfordwest, follow signs to town centre and cross river bridge. Take 1st left (Quay Street) and after 0.2ml (0.3km) park on RHS of road opposite gate and stile. Site over stile

The ruins of Haverfordwest Priory lie on the banks of the River Cleddau on the outskirts of the town. Robert fitz Richard, lord of Haverford, founded the priory for Augustinian canons in about 1200. The Augustinians, with their commitment to work in the parishes among lay people, were a suitable choice for this town which was quickly becoming an important mercantile centre.

Though Haverfordwest soon outgrew its original boundaries and further stretches of town walls were built, the priory remained outside the defences, in a suburb known as Parva Haverford (or 'Small Haverford').

Augustinian houses tended to build up possessions in their own borough and Haverfordwest Priory derived much of its income from rents from its considerable local properties. As an important landowner, the priory had considerable influence in

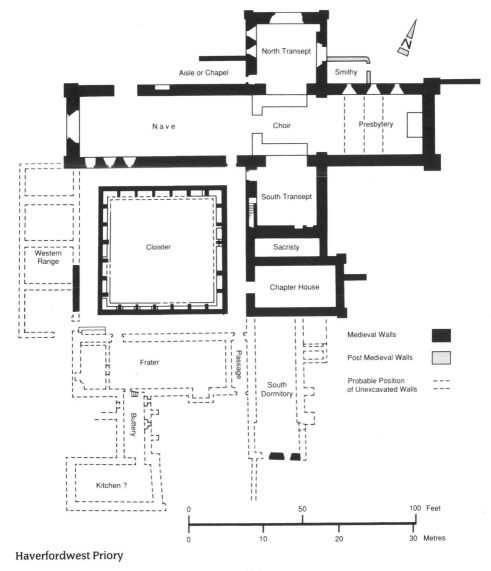

Haverfordwest Priory

Haverfordwest. Here the inevitable tensions between the two communities of main town and suburb seemed to be restrained, in contrast to Carmarthen where the settlement around the Augustinian priory of St John became almost a rival town at some periods. Haverfordwest Priory appropriated the three medieval churches within the town and a number of smaller churches in neighbouring villages, and these possessions would have brought the priory further income from tithes.

Little is known of the history of the priory itself. It seems to have escaped damage from war or accident, and the buildings so far excavated have shown no evidence of destruction or fire. The ruins themselves have been substantially robbed of their decorative stonework, but the quality of the fragments of tracery and carving found during the excavations suggests that the priory was reasonably well off. Its annual income at the time of the Dissolution was assessed at £133, indicating a moderate wealth by the standards of Welsh monastic houses.

Until 1981, the priory ruins were obscured by ivy and scrub growth, since when repair work has revealed the standing masonry and excavations have shown that footings of most of the monastic buildings survive below ground. As the area has never been developed, eventually it should be possible to excavate and display the complete priory, including its service buildings, hospital, gardens and roadways.

The modern entrance to the priory is from the north, and the high walls of the north transept are the first to be seen. The church is of one simple cruciform build. The presbytery walls were robbed to below floor level, but have now been built up slightly (over a line of red tiles inserted between medieval walling and the modern stonework above). The earliest floor in the presbytery may have been on one level, but at some later stage the series of three steps was built, raising the floor from the crossing towards the high altar which was set against the east wall.

The north and south transepts both had chapels built into them, but while that in the south transept is sufficiently well preserved to have retained its altar, chapel wall and stepped floor, the north transept was considerably damaged. The south transept was lit by windows on the east, south and west, and on the south are the remains of the *sedile* and *piscina*. Within the west wall is the door leading to the night stair from the dormitory, which the canons would have used for the night services. The north transept has a niche in the corner which evidently held a slab, possibly for an altar before the chapel was inserted. Both transepts were divided from the crossing by the stalls of the canons' choir, where the monastic services would have been sung. We know from early drawings of the priory that a square tower stood at the crossing but this tower had fallen by the early 18th century. A screen wall or *pulpitum* with a splayed doorway divided the choir from the nave which was lit by a series of windows on the south and a great window on the west. The north wall has now fallen. The church has massive buttresses on all corners and in the north-west corner buttress is a small spiral stair for access to the roof.

Outside the south transept, the long narrow room with a little cupboard in its south wall was probably used as a sacristy. Its door into the church has been blocked by a pillar, built perhaps around 1900 to support some weak masonry. The room was covered by a plain barrel vault, and below the floor was a drain taking rainwater away from the cloister. Next to the sacristy lay the chapter house; the bench around the walls survives intact, as does the buff and green tiled floor, though this has been covered for protection. The fine doorway to the cloister had a window on either side, only the sills of which now survive. Decorated stonework found during the excavations suggests that the chapter house was modified in the late 14th century when an ornate ribbed vaulting was inserted, supported on richly decorated corbels. A plinth in the floor marks the grave of an important benefactor of the priory, and around it were found the broken pieces of a

13th-century effigy of a knight in armour.
Beyond the chapter house was a vaulted
ground-floor room probably given over to
storage, and the dormitory lay at first-floor
level over the entire east range. The refectory
was on the south of the cloister but has not
yet been excavated, though part of the large
stone *lavatorium*, the basin in which the
canons would have washed their hands
before meals, was found near the main
doorway in the south-west corner of the
cloister. The grassy footings of outer
buildings, kitchens, the infirmary and the
prior's house lie further to the south. The
west range, probably used for guest
accommodation, also awaits excavation, but
the cloister has been uncovered to reveal the
tiled pavement of the cloister walk, which
would have been covered by a pent roof;
rainwater would have been collected in the
surrounding drain, to be carried away down
to the river. A garden would have lain in the
centre. The cloister, used by the canons
primarily for study, was evidently substantially
remodelled in the 14th century, and parts of
the earlier decorative masonry was broken up
and used as building stone in the later walls.

The main cobbled road from the town
into the monastery lay just outside the
west end of the church, but there was another
flagged path along the riverside, with a gate
through the boundary wall. The path led
around the west and south of the church,
by the side of the canons' cemetery. Of
the three medieval churches in Haverfordwest,
St Mary's, in the main street, is especially fine,
with decorated stonework similar to that
found at the priory.

Higgon's Well

*From A40 roundabout on E side of
Haverfordwest take minor Uzmaston road to S
and branch off immediately on to unmarked
road on RHS to car park. Follow footpath
through gate signed Higgon's Well to 1st house
on LHS. Well in private garden; for closer look,
seek permission at Higgon's Well House.*

Higgon's Well, a remarkably intact medieval
holy well, has had a chequered recent history.
For many years it was completely engulfed in
the bushes and scrub from the adjacent slope,
and it was assumed to have been destroyed
at some point after the 18th century when it
had been drawn by the painter Charles Norris.
Happily, it was rediscovered quite recently,
and has now been repaired.

The vaulted well is a small, rectangular
structure, built, like Haverfordwest's priory
and castle (nos 140 and 110) of the local
millstone grit. The exterior has lost much of its
facework, but the arched opening over the
downstream side remains. It is intact
internally, and has stone benching around the
sides. It still contains water and the stream
which supplies the well apparently never
dries up. On the far side, built up against the
slope, a well chapel was added at some later
stage, but of this only the now much altered
shell survives. The well had a great popular
reputation for healing in the medieval period.

141
Higgon's Well,
Haverfordwest
Medieval holy well
?13th–14th century AD
OS 157   SM 962151   U1

142
Slebech Church, Haverfordwest

Medieval church of Knights Hospitallers

12th–16th century AD

OS 158   SN 032139   U2

From Haverfordwest, travel E along A40 for 7ml (11.2km). Turn R on to A4075; after 0.2ml (0.3km) turn R; after 0.6ml (1km), park near Blackpool Mill entrance (or in its car park to visit mill or café). On RHS of mill, cross bridge

and follow track (L at T-junction). After 1.5ml (2.4km) turn L at crossing, through gate and follow track by water's edge to site

The order of the Knights Hospitallers, or the Knights of St John, was probably founded in the early 12th century. The brethren were originally infirmarians whose main duties were caring for the sick and poor, but later they provided escorts for pilgrims to the Holy Land. It was an international order with a Grand Master to whom the brothers were subject. The order was first introduced into England around 1144, and soon attracted grants of churches and land. In order to

Slebech Church

administer this property, small monastic houses called preceptories were set up, each under the charge of a resident knight or preceptor.

The Knights apparently received gifts of land and property in south-west Wales early on in the Norman conquests of the region. The Norman lord, Wizo, whose seat was at Wiston Castle (no. 111) had, by 1115, granted all the churches in his barony to the Benedictine abbey of Gloucester, and among these, it seems, was a church at Slebech. Walter, either the son or grandson of Wizo, later granted the church to the Knights, to whom it passed, not without some legal wrangling, probably in the 1160s. Slebech quickly became established as the headquarters of the order in west Wales. We know that in 1338 it had 1 preceptor, who by this time was known as the 'commander', 2 serving brothers, 1 chaplain, 10 officials and servants and 2 lads, as well as other servants elsewhere. It was famed far and wide for its hospitality, and annually distributed 40 quarters of barley and 15 of beans and peas to the poor, as well as giving food and shelter to all travellers. This service became increasingly burdensome as time went on, apparently being abused by strangers 'who come and go in great numbers from day to day'. The commandery drew most of its supplies from the considerable amount of rich arable land which it owned to the south, on the other side of the Eastern Cleddau, and contemporary documents complain about the difficulties of access across this treacherous piece of water.

Only the church of the commandery now remains. It is a cruciform structure, much altered after the Reformation when it became the parish church. The south transept in particular was considerably modified when the Barlow family converted it to provide a family pew. The round windows of yellow stone inserted at that time scarcely blend with the medieval work elsewhere, but are themselves not without interest. The north transept arch and the decorated niche below are fine medieval work, and in the walls of the

chancel may be seen the blocked remains of tomb recesses. The main entrance is on the north, through the vaulted ground floor of the square tower.

The church was deliberately ruined by the first Baron de Rutzen, who built the modern parish church at a more convenient position 1ml (1.6km) further north on the A40. Two 15th-century effigies which were originally in the medieval church were brought to the new church when it was built in the early 19th century. Opposite the commandery church, standing in the water of the estuary, are two tree-covered mounds which have been variously described as Bronze Age burial mounds or Civil War defences. They could conceivably be associated with a causeway which was at least planned by the knights to give easier access across the water to their farmland on the south.

143
Pill Priory, Milford Haven
Medieval monastery
13th century AD
OS 158   SM 903073   U1

From Milford Haven, travel N on A4076 Haverfordwest road. At Steynton turn L on to Thornton road. After 1ml (1.6km) take 2nd R signed Lower Priory. Site 1ml (1.6km) further on LHS. Ruins in private garden, but visible from road and pub. For closer view, seek permission at house adjacent to ruins

The priory at Pill was founded probably around 1200 by the Norman Adam de Roche as a dependent priory of St Dogmael's Abbey, near Cardigan (no. 133). It belonged to the Tironensian order, closely allied in way of life to the Benedictines, and was dedicated to St Mary and St Budoc. It was a small and relatively unimportant house, but seems to have been adequately endowed by the founder, having acquired, by the end of the 13th century, an estate of well over 1,300 acres in the rich arable land of the cantref of

Dyfed

Pill Priory, chancel arch

Rhos. In 1504, the priory is recorded as having a prior and five monks.

Very little remains of the 13th-century priory buildings, but the site has great charm in the way it nestles inconspicuously in the valley, and the passer-by almost stumbles across it. The church's lofty chancel arch is an imposing sight from the road, and on the masonry can be seen the 'springers', or the first side stones of the arches which divided the two transepts from the crossing. In the east face of the wall adjacent to the chancel arch is a spiral stair leading to a mural passage, which would have given access to the roof.

The east end of the church, the nave and the north transept have fallen completely, but the south wall of the south transept still stands nearly to full height. A slender arched doorway led from the church into the building to the south of the transept; nothing now remains of this structure, but it was presumably one of the normal east-range rooms such as the sacristy. The house, which is adjacent to the transept wall, itself incorporates a fine barrel vault running east–west which may well have been the chapter house. The monks' dormitory probably lay over this at first-floor level, as this position for the dormitory is more or less standard in medieval monastic houses.

Almost all of the east, south and west ranges, which would have housed dormitory, refectory, guest and the prior's accommodation, have disappeared, though wall footings may well survive below ground. It is interesting that the road curves around what must have been the end of the nave of the church and the west range buildings, and much of the modern garden lies where the cloister probably once stood.

144
Jeffreston Cross, Pembroke
Medieval preaching cross
14th century AD
OS 158   SN 089065   U1

Jeffreston is 8ml (12.8km) E of Pembroke, along A477 Pembroke–St Clears road. From A477, take B4586 N towards Haverfordwest, then turn R into Jeffreston, to church

Jeffreston Cross

200

This 14th-century preaching cross stands near Jeffreston church in the churchyard. It has a square, two-stepped base of rough masonry and a large, undecorated socket stone. The tapering shaft is octagonal in section with a decorated base. The head is an equal-armed cross, the arms of which widen slightly at the ends. It has been repaired in the past with two large rivets.

In the church porch stands a tall, narrow slab on which is an incised ring-cross with slightly splayed intersecting arms. There is an irregular continuation of the shaft of the cross below. The cross probably dates to the 7th–9th century. It was discovered early this century built into the porch threshold.

St Govan's Chapel

145
St Govan's Chapel and Well, and Bosherston Cross, Pembroke

Medieval chapel, holy well and preaching cross
?13th–14th century AD
OS 158   SR 967929   U2

From Pembroke, take B4319 Castlemartin road for 3.7ml (6km), then turn L on to Bosherston road. Go through Bosherston, and drive to car park at end of road. Site signposted on coast path. NB: road from Bosherston closed during army firing periods (see local press or 'phone National Park for details)

The chapel and well at St Govan's Head are deservedly celebrated for their dramatic position in a narrow fissure in precipitous cliffs just above high water. They are reached from the cliff top above by a flight of approximately 70 rough steps (by tradition, they are impossible to count). The dedication to St Govan, a Celtic missionary, suggests an early date for the founding of the chapel, but the vaulted building that stands on the site now is rather later, perhaps 13th or 14th century.

The chapel is built against the rock face and has doorways on the north and west, three small, single-light windows, and one larger, square window in the south wall. On the east is a stone altar with its original altar slab, and beside it is a door leading up some steps to a small chamber, or anchorite's cell, contained in the living rock. A stone bench runs along the north and south sides and along the east wall south of the altar. On the left of the entrance is a holy water stoup, and there is an 'aumbry', or cupboard, in the south wall. The chapel has a slate roof, with a bellcote on the west end.

The tiny well, inconspicuous among the fallen rocks, is further down the cliff, and only accessible through the chapel. It is covered by a small stone vault which has been reconstructed in modern times. The well was renowned for its powers of healing as late as the 19th century. Writings by 18th- and 19th-century antiquarian travellers refer to cripples coming from all over Wales to bathe their limbs; some apparently left their crutches as a votive offering on the altar of the chapel. The water source has now disappeared and today the well is dry.

Bosherston Cross stands in the churchyard in the village of Bosherston, 1ml (1.6km) north of St Govans. It has a large square base of three rough masonry steps and a plain, tapering octagonal shaft. At the intersection of the arms is a much- weathered human face in high relief, presumably representing Christ. The cross is probably of 14th- century date. The head of the cross and the shaft are of different stone and evidently originally belonged to two different structures. The shaft probably belonged to a larger cross, which explains the rather stumpy appearance of the present composite structure.

146
Lamphey Bishop's Palace, Pembroke
Medieval bishop's residence
12th–16th century AD
OS 158   SN 018009   R1   Cadw

Lamphey is 1.5ml (2.4km) E of Pembroke, on A4139 Tenby–Pembroke road. Lane to site signposted from A4139. Car park, standard opening hours, admission charge

Cadw Guidebook

Though the buildings are now ruinous, the secluded charm of the palace at Lamphey remains and it is easy to understand why this was the favoured rural manor of the bishops of St Davids. At Lamphey the bishop could become a country gentleman, surrounded by his gardens and orchards, fishponds and deer park, far from the centre of his diocese at St Davids and his castle at Llawhaden (nos 135 and 109). But Lamphey was very important financially as well. A survey of 1326 known as the 'Black Book of St Davids' describes the productive lands of the manor and mentions two watermills, a windmill and a dovecote on this fertile site, by the side of a small stream.

The origins of the palace probably go back to Celtic times: the church's dedication to St Tyfai, a nephew of St Teilo whose homeland was at nearby Penally, links Lamphey with the important early *clas* or monastery there (no. 95). But nothing now remains to help us visualise the appearance of any Celtic

buildings, or, indeed of the earliest Norman buildings, though we know that there was a residence here in 1096 belonging to Wilfred, bishop of St Davids. The earliest masonry at Lamphey is that of the old hall, built in the early 13th century, slightly earlier than the spacious building which was added to its west. The two buildings looked north into a courtyard, which presumably was protected by a boundary wall and gatehouse.

The old hall is a simple two-storeyed building, now largely ruinous. The main room was, as usual, on the first floor and was entered by a door on the north with an external stair. When the chapel was built 300 years later, this door was blocked; the hall by then had doorways leading to it from de Gower's hall, from the chapel, and from the adjacent building on the west. This larger building was probably built for Bishop Richard Carew (1256–80) to replace the old hall, which may then have become private apartments. It survives well, and, like the earlier hall, lay at first-floor level, entered through a richly-carved door on the north. The original 13th-century ornate lancet windows may still be seen from inside the hall, though they were altered in the early 16th century when square-headed windows were inserted. Other noteworthy features are the decorated fireplace, and the painted plaster on a window in the south-east corner. On the south is a small projection which houses the latrine.

In 1328, Henry de Gower became bishop of St Davids, and during the next 19 years, Lamphey reached the height of its glory under the care of this powerful and able man. It was he who built the new, larger hall to the south-east which was surmounted with a less ornate form of the arcaded parapet that he had built at St Davids. There were by this stage at least two courtyards within the palace; the inner courtyard lay just in front of the bishop's hall, entered through the inner gatehouse and surrounded by a wall which has now mostly fallen. The outer court must have run, to judge from early drawings of the site, far beyond this, to cover the whole of the

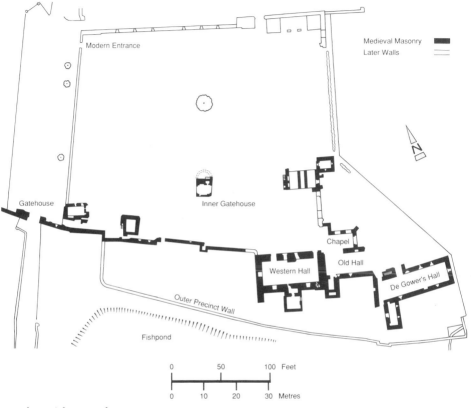

Lamphey Bishop's Palace

present walled garden and beyond. It was entered through the outer gatehouse on the west and was surrounded by a battlemented wall. Wall footings against this wall on the south and other structures to the north may have belonged to buildings such as barns to store the agricultural produce of the manor, stables and storehouses, bakehouses and brewhouses essential for the servicing of the palace of so eminent a person as the bishop of St Davids.

Bishop de Gower's hall lay on the first floor of a large two-storeyed block, built at a slight angle to the rest of the buildings. Like the earlier halls, it too has a vaulted ground-floor room which would have been used for

storage or servants' quarters. An external flight of stone steps on the north led into a long hall which had six windows of two-trefoiled lights; the arcaded parapet and the arrangements of the roof are clearly visible from within. On the south of the hall is a projecting wing with latrines.

The only major additions to the palace after the death of de Gower belong to the early 16th century, perhaps to the time of Bishop Edward Vaughan (1509–22). It was at that time that the chapel was remodelled. There must, of course, have been a chapel at the palace from the beginning, and the present building, with its fine east window, must have replaced an earlier one. At the same time, the western hall was adapted to incorporate an additional third storey, perhaps for guest accommodation, and new windows were inserted.

These careful but relatively plain alterations suggest that by this time the opulence of the medieval palace was proving unnecessary, even unmanageable, and economy was an important factor. Certainly after the Reformation, the manor was surrendered to the crown and, for a short time in the late 16th century, was the home of the Devereux family. Hence Robert Devereux, the earl of Essex, famous as the favourite of Queen Elizabeth, stayed here as a young man. During this period, additions were small and modest, aimed at adapting the structure to a comfortable Elizabethan home – for instance, additional hearths and latrines were inserted. But despite these efforts, the old palace was soon abandoned as a dwelling, and became used for farm buildings. In the 19th century, the courtyard was adapted to serve as the kitchen garden for the impressive new house of Lamphey Court to the north, and the battlemented wall was constructed to serve as its western boundary, enhanced by the planting of the palm trees which give Lamphey a strangely exotic appearance.

147
Caldey Priory, Caldey Island
Medieval monastery
12th–16th century AD
OS 158   SS 141963   U2

Boats to Caldey Island go from Tenby harbour, from Easter to September. Follow path from island jetty, passing modern abbey on LHS. Site on RHS of path, signposted

The presence of the modern abbey in the centre of the island gives the ruins of the old priory at Caldey a very special sense of enduring Christian tradition. The old priory church remains in use as a place of worship. The east- and west-range buildings also still

stand, and are under repair and often inaccessible. The modern abbey was built by Benedictine monks, but in 1929 it was taken over by a community of Cistercians, who now own the medieval priory.

There was probably a Celtic *clas* as early as the 5th century at Caldey, then known as Ynys Pyr ('Island of Pyro') after its first abbot. Nothing now remains of the buildings of this first community, dedicated to St Illtud, and indeed even the identification of Caldey as Ynys Pyr is not completely certain. However, inside the church is an inscribed stone, recorded as having been found in the priory ruins. It has an Ogam inscription: '*(The stone) of Maglia-Dubracunas, son of. . .*' which may be 5th- or 6th-century in date, and this supports Caldey's claim to be Ynys Pyr. On the face of the stone is the Latin inscription: ET SINGNO CR/UCIS IN ILLAM / FINGSI ROGO/ OMNIBUS AM/MULANTIBUS / IBI EXORENT/ PRO ANIMAE / CATUOCONI, /or: *And by the sign of the cross (which) I have fashioned on that (stone) I ask all who walk there that they pray for the soul of Catuoconus.* This inscription, and the two Latin crosses on the face and side, were added later probably in the early 9th century.

Pyro was succeeded as abbot by St Samson, to whom the modern Cistercian abbey is dedicated. We know little else about the early community, and it is only after the Norman Conquest that we regain sight of the island. It was granted in 1113 by Henry I to Robert fitz Martin, the Norman lord of Cemais, who then granted it to his mother, Geva. She founded a priory on Caldey under the abbey of St Dogmaels (no. 133), recently established by Robert for the Tironensians. But it is doubtful whether it was a permanent convent. Geraldus Cambrensis states that only one monk was living at Caldey in the late 12th century, and its income, according to a record of 1291 was only £1.10s. 0d. At the Dissolution, too, there was apparently only a single monk present here.

The simple and compact 13th-century priory church lies on the south of the cloister. The western entrance is through the tower

N

Site of
Modern House

Prior's Tower

Refectory

Guest
Accommodation

Dormitory

Cloister

Gatehouse

Church

| 0 | | 25 | | 50 Feet |

Caldey Priory

| 0 | 5 | 10 | 15 Metres |

which has been the victim of subsidence, giving the spire on the top rather an eccentric lean. The presbytery has a plain barrel vault and the church has an attractive cobbled floor. To the west is the gatehouse, and adjacent is a building used for storage on the ground floor and for guest accommodation above. The eastern range housed the monks' dormitory on the first floor reached by a stair in the west wall. The prior's accommodation lay on the north-east corner, over the ground-floor kitchen; his chambers were provided with a latrine in a small tower on the north-

east. The buildings of the east and west ranges may only be viewed from the outside. The refectory lay on the north of the cloister, but nothing of this now stands. After the Dissolution, parts of the monastic buildings were incorporated into a house which has now been demolished. But the sense of enclosure imparted by the buildings still standing to full height on three sides of the cloister is unique among the medieval monastic remains of Dyfed. The medieval fishponds outside still survive, now used as watercress beds.

148
Old Church of St Michael, Llansteffan

Norman Church and grave slabs
12th–15th century AD
OS 159   SN 302133   U4

From St Clears, drive along A40 E towards Carmarthen for 1ml (1.6km). After Forge Restaurant, turn R on to minor road labelled Llansteffan. After 1.5ml (2.4km), at sharp LH bend in road, take unlabelled road straight on past Foxhole, and leave car near gate to Trefenter. Walk through farmyard to L, to far gate directly opposite farmhouse, follow track obliquely across field to gate, walk down slope of near field, keeping field hedge on R, to gate to site

The charming ruins of St Michael's church stand isolated in fields near the point at which the Afon Cywyn flows into the Taf estuary. It was the parish church until 1848 when a new one was built in a more convenient location. The church was probably founded by the lords of the 12th-century motte-and-bailey castle, the remains of which stand near Trefenty Farm (which would explain this now lonely position).

The church consists of a nave, a narrow square-ended chancel and a western tower. The nave is probably early 13th-century, while the chancel was substantially remodelled in the 15th century when the tower was built or perhaps rebuilt. The stairs in the small projection in the north wall of the nave were for access to the rood screen, which separated the nave from the chancel. The fine Norman font is now in the modern church on the main road.

Six graves lie in the graveyard near the church, their positions marked by decorated grave slabs and headstones. These are difficult to date but are usually thought to be late 12th- or early 13th-century. Two of the slabs are the so-called 'hog-backed' form, and are decorated with a cross, the long arm

A 'pilgrim's grave' at the old church of St Michael, Llansteffan

of which runs along the ridge of the stone. The other four are flat slabs. Two of these show female figures, one of which is full-length, the other of which occupies only half of the stone, the remainder being decorated with a lattice pattern (see illustration). This latter figure holds a rod in one hand, and there is an animal on either side of the head. The figure on the third slab is too broken to allow identification, but his knee-length tunic and the horseman with a lance in one hand, depicted on both head and foot stones, suggest that the occupant was a male, perhaps a knight. The fourth figure is small, dressed in a long skirt, and appears to be standing at a barrier. Its small size suggests that it may mark the grave of a child. All the slabs, save for the last, have short, round-headed stones at head and foot with crosses and cable decoration on them.

Perhaps these graves shelter members of the Norman family who lived in the castle nearby. Tradition, however, holds that the graves are those of pilgrims, and the church is often known as the Pilgrims' Church.

149
Talley Abbey, Talley
Medieval monastery
12th–13th century AD
OS 146   SN 633328   R2   Cadw

From NE side of Llandeilo, take B4302 N for 5ml (8km). Turn L into Talley. Site on RHS, signposted. Admission charge, standard hours

Cadw Guidebook

The abbey at Talley is unique in Wales in being founded for the monastic order of the Premonstratensians, or White Canons. The canons had a constitution and way of life based on Cistercian lines, even adopting the same white habit, but followed the Augustinian canons in their undertaking of duties within the parish. The order was well

supported in England at the end of the 12th century, and Henry II's chief justiciar, Ranulf de Glanville, was prominent among its patrons. It may well have been this man who influenced Rhys ap Gruffudd, the Lord Rhys, in his choice of the White Canons for the new house which he founded at Talley in the late 1180s, a time of peace and concord between the Welsh prince and the English crown. The downfall of Ranulf soon afterwards may in turn have had some bearing on the fact that no other Premonstratensian houses were ever founded in Wales, and that Talley was only poorly endowed.

The princely descendants of the Lord Rhys continued to support the abbey, and his great grandson, Rhys Fychan, was buried there in 1271. The endowments made through the years to the abbey included grants of land both near to Talley and further afield in Ceredigion, Gwent and the Gower, and the rents from the estates brought in much-needed income. Of great financial importance to Talley were the canons' 'spiritualities', income generated from tithes and other receipts of those parish churches, including the church of Llandeilo, which it had appropriated. Nevertheless, the monastery was never wealthy. Indeed, soon after its foundation, the canons were involved in an expensive lawsuit against the abbot of the Cistercian house at Whitland, who evidently regarded Talley as a dangerous rival. This may have been the reason for the abandonment of the original ambitious building plan of the church.

Talley was taken into royal control on a number of occasions during its history because of its impoverishment, due either to the ravages of war, or to the neglect of successive abbots. The canons seem to have attracted particular criticism from outside authorities who were suspicious of a house which was isolated not only through geography but also because of its predominantly Welsh community. In 1284, the community was under investigation for loose living, and Edward I stated in a letter that the immorality of the canons would

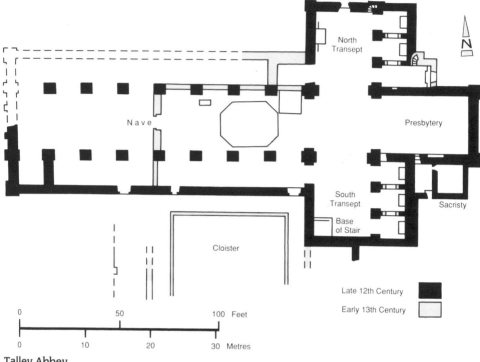

Late 12th Century	■
Early 13th Century	□

North Transept

Nave

Presbytery

South Transept

Sacristy

Base of Stair

Cloister

0   50   100 Feet

0   10   20   30 Metres

Talley Abbey

result in their expulsion and replacement with those 'of the English tongue who are able and willing to observe the religious life'. The abbey was made a daughter house of Halesowen, but it is uncertain still how strictly control was exercised. In the late 15th century, canons from Premonstratensian houses in England were transferred to Talley in an attempt perhaps, even at this late date, to bring it more closely into the English Premonstratensian fold. However, the abbey continued in existence until the Dissolution, after which the chancel of the church was used for parish worship. In 1772, a new parish church was built and the abbey buildings were left to decay.

The remoteness, which contributed so much to the relative poverty of the community, now adds to the peace which surrounds the abbey at its site at the head of the two lakes from which the village takes its name (Talyllychau means 'head of the lakes'). Much of the monastic building has fallen and now only the abbey church, dedicated to the Blessed Virgin Mary and St John the Baptist, and part of the cloister remain. The modern entrance leads into the church from the west, but immediately below the entrance gate, the stone footings of walls on the right, and of three pairs of columns ahead belong to the church that was begun but never completed. In the event, only the eastern four bays of the nave and south aisle were actually built higher than foundation level, and of the planned north aisle, only the easternmost bay was built as a small room accessible from the north transept.

The early 13th-century church, then,

consisted of a short nave of four bays, a south aisle, north and south transepts each with a series of three eastern chapels, and the presbytery. There was a tower over the crossing, and it is the east and north sides of this tower with their supporting arches that still stand so dramatically almost to roof height. High within these walls are passages which allowed access to the roof space above the chancel and transepts, and to a room high in the tower. The joist-holes for the floor of this room can be seen in the tower wall from the west.

In the north transept, a spiral stair in the north wall led to a passage within the walls of the tower, transepts and nave. The southernmost chapel is longer than the others and has another stair built into its north wall; a *piscina*, for washing sacred vessels, can be seen on the south. All six chapels in the transepts were probably divided from one another by openwork screens placed within the dividing walls. In the south-west corner of the south transept lies a square stone base. This supported a stair to the canons' dormitory, which would have run south from the south transept at first-floor level. The dormitory building would have formed the east range, the refectory the south range, and buildings on the west would probably have been used for guest accommodation. All these would have stood around the central cloister. Now there remain only the footings of the northern half of the cloister, accessible from the church via two doors leading from the south aisle.

Little detail survives in the presbytery, but a recess in the south wall probably housed the *sedile*, and the adjacent door led to a small room and thence to the sacristy. Excavations in the church uncovered several burials, some in lead coffins, and all these remains have been reburied in the nave; a stone plinth stands to mark the place. Through the churchyard of the modern church is a path to the shore of the lake, from where one may contemplate the surrounding quiet countryside.

150
Strata Florida, Pontrhydfendigaid
Medieval monastery
12th–16th century AD
OS 135   SN 746658   R1   Cadw

From Pontrhydfendigaid, on junction of B4340 Tregaron–Aberystwyth and B4343 Tregaron–Devil's Bridge roads, take road E, signed to abbey. Site on LHS. Car park, standard hours, admission charge

Cadw Guidebook

The first abbey of Strata Florida, founded by the Norman Robert fitz Stephen in 1164 for the Cistercians, lay 2ml (3.2km) away from the present site, by the banks of the Afon Fflur from which Strata Florida (Vale of Fflur, or 'flowers') derives its name. It was a daughter house of the great Cistercian abbey at Whitland, and the first colony of monks would have come from there. We do not know why or when the abbey was moved to its present position on the banks of the River Teifi, but politics may have played a major part, as in 1166 the Welsh prince of south Wales, Rhys ap Gruffudd, conquered Norman holdings in Ceredigion and took control of the area. The Cistercian order, committed to a life of rural simplicity, was very successful in Wales, and Rhys was happy to take over the new foundation. Indeed he later even became known as the founder of Strata Florida, for which he indeed had a special affection.

The building of the new church began apparently in 1184. The abbey received continued support from the princely Welsh descendants of Rhys, who granted the abbey extensive estates in the surrounding rich pasture lands, and further afield in Carmarthen and Powys. These lands, used for the large flocks of sheep for which the Cistercians became famed, produced much of the income for the running of the abbey. Perhaps due to this patronage, the abbey, with its series of Welsh abbots, soon became renowned as a centre for Welsh scholarship. The Welsh annals later known as the *Brut y Tywysogion* (Chronicle of the Princes) may have been compiled here. They record the close association between the abbey and the royal house of Deheubarth, and the fact that, during the late 13th century, many of its princes were brought to the abbey for burial. The abbey had a great cultural influence in medieval Wales and even now its name is associated with Welsh scholarship.

Strata Florida was not immune, however, from the ravages of war and accident. In 1212, King John threatened the abbey with destruction, as he considered it to be a partisan Welsh establishment 'which sustains our enemies', though troubles elsewhere diverted him from this task. In 1285 the church was damaged by lightning, and the buildings suffered further in struggles between the Welsh and English 10 years later. The abbey was taken over by the military

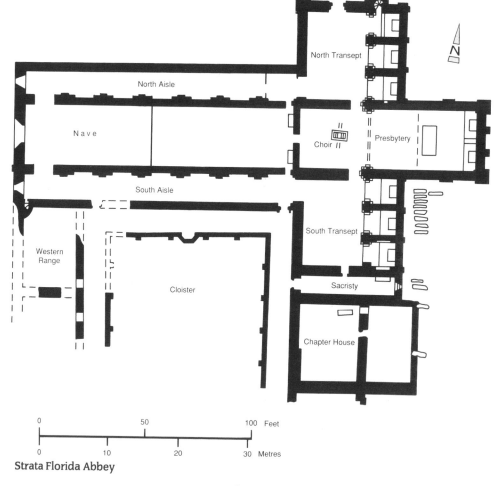

Strata Florida Abbey

during Glyndŵr's war of independence. After the Dissolution, the monastic buildings were abandoned. They were excavated in the 19th century by Stephen Williams, a remarkable man who fell in love with the site when working as an engineer on the construction of the railway which used to run along the valley nearby.

The artistic achievement of Strata Florida is still reflected in some noteworthy survivals amidst the ruins. One is the richly decorated, round-headed west door of the church. This justly celebrated doorway was originally flanked by a pair of lancet windows, but only one now survives. The cruciform church was built mainly in the late 12th and early 13th centuries. It has a long nave of seven bays with two aisles divided from it by walls linking the pillars but with doorways at both east and west ends. The monks' choir, where the monastic services would have been sung, was built in the late 14th century, and the irregular stepped sunken basin in the centre of the crossing may be a late medieval, or even post-medieval, insertion.

The presbytery floor rises towards the east with three steps, on the middle of which is the high altar. Two small chapels lie against the eastern wall of the presbytery, which was extended in the mid-13th century. This internal arrangement is quite late; the original 13th-century floor was probably level and the high altar was positioned against the east wall. The transepts each had a series of three chapels, and their stepped floors, laid with richly decorated tiles, are a glorious reminder of how different the church must originally have looked. The tiles have incised decoration glazed or slip-inlaid, with a variety of devices, including 'the man with a mirror' which probably represents vanity, a griffin, patterns of stylised flowers, leaves and crosses, and heraldic shields. The pavements probably date to the 14th century, and those on the south have been covered with a modern roof to protect them. The floor of the entire church east of and including the choir would originally have been tiled, and other smaller sections of a plain tiled floor are preserved in various parts of the church. The less important nave and aisles apparently had floors of local slate.

In the south wall of the south transept, a door led into a narrow sacristy. The chapter house, to the south, was, in its original mid-13th-century form, quite a large structure, but it was halved in size in the 14th century, when it was rebuilt at a higher level, perhaps after the destruction caused during the 1294 Welsh uprising. A single decorated grave slab survives in the floor.

The graves of the Welsh princes lie outside the church, east of the south transept. Their decorated headstones and grave slabs must mark the graves of two of the Lord Rhys's sons. Tradition has it that Dafydd ap Gwilym, the greatest poet of medieval Wales, was also buried within the precincts of the abbey, and a memorial slab commemorating him stands in the north transept.

Nothing now remains of the dormitory, refectory and service buildings that must have been arranged around the cloister, though footings of the northern half of the cloister wall still stand. The cloister was rebuilt in the 15th century, and set within its north wall is a polygonal alcove, used for a lectern for the Collation or reading before Compline (the last service of the monastic day), and an unusual and interesting survival. The west range, of which only fragments remain, would have housed the lay brothers, usually locally recruited by Cistercian houses to carry out the manual work on the monastery. These low-born brethren were kept apart from the 'choir-monks' and would have used the nave of the church for their services.

In the old school building at the entrance to the site is a small exhibition with some of the artefacts found during excavations of the abbey. The Cistercians were lovers of simplicity, but that is not to say that their churches were devoid of all decoration. The finely decorated stonework from window, door and roof helps us to visualise some of the ornament now missing from the abbey ruins.

Appendix: Sites of Further Interest

This a list of fine sites which lie on private land, or which are on open ground but are remote and difficult of access. Permission should be sought before visiting sites marked R. It is often difficult to trace the owners of sites, and it is usually best to seek help and information from the owners of the nearest house to the site in question.

Palaeolithic Period

Little Hoyle Cave, Tenby
OS 158   SS 112999   R4
Small cave in which Upper Palaeolithic and early Christian material has been found. There are three entrances on the north, one on the south.

Nanna's Cave, Caldey
OS 158   SS 146970   R4
A shallow cave in which Upper Palaeolithic Creswellian tools and later artefacts have been found.

Potter's Cave, Caldey
OS 158   SS 144971   R4
A cave with two entrances, in which Upper Palaeolithic and later material has been found.

Priory Farm Cave, Pembroke
OS 158   SM 979018   R4
Cave at the base of a low cliff above Pembroke estuary. Upper Palaeolithic and Mesolithic flint tools have been excavated there.

Neolithic Period

Garn Gilfach, Llanwnda
OS 157   SM 909390   R4

A large capstone is supported by a number of small sidestones with a partly subterranean chamber.

Cerrig Llwydion, Cynwl Elfed
OS 145   SN 374326   R4
A very ruined tomb, with a number of large stones, many displaced. This must originally have been a very impressive site.

Colston, Little Newcastle
OS 157   SM 983281   R4
The tomb, in a hedge bank, consists of a capstone supported by two slumped sidestones. The mound around the chamber may be the remains of a cairn.

Mountain, Mynachlog Ddu
OS 145   SN 166328   R4
A ruined burial chamber consisting of a large capstone slumped on to four or five large prostrate stones surrounded by a low circular mound.

Parc y llyn, Wolf's Castle
OS 157   SM 982266   R4
A ruined burial chamber consisting of a capstone and four small sidestones. Around the chamber are what may be the remains of an encircling cairn.

Penrhiw, Llanwnda
OS 157   SM 943391   R2

The capstone of this tomb rests on three sidestones to form a rectangular chamber, and was re-erected some years ago.

Tre Ffynnon, Croesgoch
OS 157   SM 854286   R4

This box-like tomb consists of a rectangular chamber formed of three uprights, one on each side save the open north side, with a displaced capstone.

Tre-Walter Llwyd, Mathry
OS 157   SM 868317   R4

The massive capstone of this tomb rests partly on the ground and partly on one slumped sidestone, and the chamber is incorporated into a hedgebank.

Castell Garw, Maenclochog
OS 145   SN 147269   R4

An eroded circular enclosure with a low bank which may be the remains of a henge, related perhaps to the nearby embanked stone circle of Meini Gwyr (no. 25)

Ffynnon Newydd, Nantgaredig
OS 159   SN 495212   R2

An oval enclosure, about 80m by 90m, with a bank and internal ditch, and an entrance on the south-east, within which lie a pair of standing stones. The west side of the site is built over.

Bronze Age

Hirfaen Stone, Lampeter
OS 146   SN 624464   R4

This fine standing stone is 4.5m high. Splendidly carved graffiti on one side reads: SDC NOV 5 1874 DIES IRAE (*Day of wrath*).

Lan Round Barrows, Llanboidy
OS 145   SN 207247   U/R1

A fine linear group of five mounds with one outlier to the north. A further barrow lies just to the north at SN 202268. Most are visible from the road.

Maen Pica and Capel Nebo Stones, Efailwen
OS 145   SN 131252 and 138254   R2

Both standing stones are about 2m high. The Capel Nebo stone is used as a gatepost.

Round Barrows, Llangeler
OS 145   SN 391335 (centre)   R/U4

There are many round barrows in this area: Crug Tarw (372347), Crug Perfa (355341), Crug y Gorllwyn (351342), Nant Sais (344339) and Moelfre (327361). Open access to Carn Wen (399339), Crug Bach (394337) and Crug Glas (391335).

Llech Gron, Cross Inn
OS 146   SN 542648   U/R1

The standing stone is 4m high, and 3m thick at the base. It is visible from the road.

Cefn Gwernffrwd, Rhandirmwyn
OS 146   SN 737494   U4

This circle is 24m in diameter and consists of 20 small stones. Nearby are a number of cairns and standing stones.

Sythfaen Llwyn Du, Llanwrda
OS 159   SN 675244   R4

A standing stone, almost 3m high, on which signs of tooling are faintly visible.

Dyffryn Syfynwy, Maenclochog
OS 145   SN 059284   R4

A stone circle, composed of 12 uprights and other, fallen, stones set around a roughly oval mound, 22m by 19m and 1m high. The stones are up to 2m in height.

Freni Fawr Round Cairns, Crymmych
OS 145   SN 202349   U4

A fine group of three round barrows on the summit of Freni Fawr.

Mabesgate, St Ishmaels
OS 157   SM 828076   R2

This spectacular standing stone is, at 2.7m, one of the tallest in the county.

Iron Age

Caer Pencarreg, Lampeter
OS 146   SN 589442   R4
A very fine hilltop enclosure of 1.2ha, defended by a single bank and ditch with a simple entrance on the south-east.

Castell Cogan, Llansteffan
OS 159   SN 328140   R4
A defended farmstead, with a single subcircular bank and ditch and a second defence on the west. Excavations revealed wooden houses in the interior.

Craig Gwrtheyrn, Llandyssul
OS 146   SN 433403   R4
A fine hillfort, defended by a single bank and ditch, and scarping on the west. The entrance has a magnificent twin hornwork and a *cheveaux de frise*.

Caer Cadwgan, Lampeter
OS 146   SN 622480   R4
A hilltop enclosure, with a single bank and ditch, an entrance and outer bank on the south, and a large annexe. Excavations have shown a complex history.

Caer Lletty Llwyd, Talybont
OS 135   SN 651882   R3
A triangular hilltop fort, with a double bank-and-ditch system on the two long sides, and an impressive triple system around the entrance.

Castell Fflemish, Tregaron
OS 146   SN 654632   R4
A strongly defended enclosure with two banks on the north, and one on the south, an inturned entrance, and another bank on the south-east.

Gaer Fawr, Llanilar
OS 135   SN 649719   R4
A fine hillfort with a double bank and ditch on the north and west, a single bank elsewhere and inturned entrances on the east and west.

Pen y Bannau, Pontrhydfendigaid
OS 135   SN 742669   R4
A narrow hilltop settlement, with a single bank supplemented on the north by triple defences around the inturned entrance.

Sunnyhill Wood Fort, Tregaron
OS 146   SN 687602   R4
A rocky hillock cut off on the gentler east by a well-preserved double bank-and-ditch system which protects the entrance.

Bayvil Enclosure, Nevern
OS 145   SN 112418   R2
This small, circular farmstead enclosure, defended by a single bank and ditch, was found, on excavation, to have been reused as an early Christian cemetery.

Bucket Camp, Fishguard
OS 157   SM 950310   R2
A fine circular enclosure, with a single bank and remains of a ditch, and curving outer earthworks on the west to protect the entrance.

Llanychaer Enclosure, Fishguard
OS 157   SM 987353   U1/R2
A simple hill-slope enclosure, with a single bank-and-ditch defence, and a short length of outer bank on the north-west. It is visible from the road.

Roman's Castle, Haverfordwest
OS 157   SM 895106   R2
A small enclosure with a double bank and ditch on all sides save the west. The entrance is on the west, and there is an additional outer bank on the south.

Rosemarket Rath, Milford Haven
OS 157   SM 953080   R2
A low-lying oval enclosure, with a single bank and ditch, supplemented on the flatter north side by an additional outer bank.

Woodbarn Rath, Haverfordwest
OS 157   SN 017170   R4

A small, circular enclosure, defended by a single bank and ditch, with an outer bank and ditch on the east. Excavations revealed timber round-houses.

Holgan Fort, Narberth
OS 158   SN 074182   R4

A fine inland promontory fort defended on the west by a double bank-and-ditch system. Small-scale excavations revealed traces of a pre-fort occupation.

Roman Period

Llanio, Tregaron
OS 146   SN 644564   R1

An auxiliary fort (*Bremia*) on the Roman road between Trawscoed and Pumpsaint. Excavations have revealed the bath-house and civilian buildings.

Trawscoed, Aberystwyth
OS 135   SN 671727   U1/R4

The large auxiliary fort, on the Roman road between the forts at Pennal (Gwynedd) and Llanio is cut by (and is visible from) the B4575, but retains some earthworks. Excavations have revealed the '*vicus*', or civil settlement, adjacent.

Sarn Helen
This Roman road, which linked Pumpsaint, Llanio, and Trawscoed is still followed by: the Ffarmers road (SN 648425–648458 and SN 646483–635505); the B4578 (SN 642570–643635) and, less faithfully, the A485 to Lledrod. The road name (Sarn = road) may derive from the legendary Welsh wife of Magnus Maximus.

Llandovery–Brecon Road
Parts of the Roman road from Brecon to Llandovery (*Alabum*) is followed by a road from Trecastle (SN 873291) to Hafod fawr (SN 816311). This road continued from Llandovery to Carmarthen, and parts lie beneath the modern A40.

Cwmbrwyn, St Clears
OS 158   SN 254122   R4

A rectangular farmstead with a bank and ditch, and a single entrance on the east. Excavations revealed a long rectangular building, with outbuildings of the 2nd to 4th century.

Castell Flemish, Ambleston
OS 158   SN 007268   R3

A rectangular enclosure surrounded by a bank and ditch, and now bisected by the modern road. Excavations showed it to have Romanised buildings in the interior.

Early Medieval Period

Carmarthen Museum, Abergwili
The museum has a number of good Christian stones, including the Voteporix, Cynwyl Gaeo, Bivadus and Newchurch Stones. The Voteporix stone commemorates, with a Latin and Ogam inscription, the Demetian ruler of the mid-6th century, and has a incised ring-cross. One of the Cynwyl Gaeo stones has a Latin inscription which translates as: *Preserver of the Faith, constant lover of his country, here lies Paulinus, the devoted champion of righteousness.* Paulinus is probably the saint of that name, the teacher of St David. The Bivadus stone has a Latin and Ogam inscription and a probably later incised ring-cross. The Newchurch stones have Latin inscriptions and one has a later incised Latin cross.

Henllan Amgoed, Whitland
OS 158   SN 177198   R3

A fine 6th-century pillar-stone with a Latin inscription which translates as: *(The stone) of Quenvendanus, son of Barcunus.*

Penbryn, Aberporth
OS 145   SN 289514   R4

A 5th- or 6th-century stone with a Latin inscription which translates as: *(The stone) of Corbalengus. (Here) he lies, an Ordovician.*

This suggests the continuing existence of the north-Wales tribe of that name known in the Roman period.

Cilgerran, Cardigan
OS 145   SN 190431   U1

A 6th-century stone with Ogam and Latin inscriptions which translate as: *(The stone) of Trenegussus, son of Macutrenus*. It stands in the churchyard.

Llandissilio, Narberth
OS 158   SN 119219   U1

Four inscribed stones built into the external face of the nave wall of the church. Three have Latin inscriptions dating to the 5th or 6th century and translate as: *(The stone) of Clutorix, son of Paulinus Marinus of Latium; (The stone) of Evolenggus, son of Litogenus. He lies here*; and 'RIAT' (untranslatable). Latium is an area in Snowdonia or perhaps Brittany. The fourth has an incised Maltese cross, of the 7th–9th century. A fifth stone in the church has a Latin inscription: 'CARANTACUS' and a later incised cross.

Newport
OS 145   SN 058388   R1/U1

Two 7th–9th-century stones. One with a cross with four dots in the interspaces stands in a garden at SN 059388. The outer, with an incised Latin ring-cross, stands in the churchyard.

Clawdd Mawr, Cynwyl Elfed
OS 145   SN 378333 (centre)   R4

This dyke consists of a bank with a ditch on the eastern, downhill side, running north–south along a ridge for about 3km. Best preserved is the northern 1km stretch adjacent to the road, which runs from Nant Clawdd Uchaf to an area of marsh on the north. The bank generally survives to a height of about 3m. The dyke may have acted as an early medieval tribal boundary.

Medieval Period

Whitland Abbey, Whitland
OS 158   SN 207182   R1

Low grassy footings of the church ruins are all that survive of this great Cistercian house, founded in 1140, which moved to this site in about 1150.

Llawhaden Hospital
OS 158   SN 067173   R2

The plain stone-vaulted building behind the village hall is probably the remains of the chapel of the medieval hospital founded in 1287 by Thomas Bek.

Paterchurch Tower, Pembroke Dock
OS 158   SM 957035   R4

A vaulted tower with three floors, and a newel stair in a circular turret on one corner.

Angle Tower, Angle
OS 157   SM 866030   R1

A small machicolated medieval tower.

Cardigan Castle, Cardigan
OS 145   SN 177459   U1 (exterior only)/ R4 (interior)

The much-repaired south curtain wall and towers of this important castle are visible from the road. A house was built in the 19th century on the remains of the keep.

Narberth Castle, Narberth
OS 158   SN 110144   R2

Three round towers and fragments of another, the remains of the hall and a vault survive from this castle, built soon after 1257.

Newport Castle, Newport
OS 145   SN 057389   R1

The double-towered gatehouse on the north was converted into a house in the 19th century, and the curtain wall with towers rings the garden of the house.

Cenarth, Newcastle Emlyn
OS 145   SN 269414   R2

A well-preserved motte, probably succeeded by the site at Newcastle Emlyn.

Llanfihangel Abercywyn, Laugharne
OS 159   SN 297136   R2

A fine motte with a small, well-preserved bailey.

Caer Penrhos, Llanrhystud
OS 135   SN 552695   R4

A magnificent ringwork and bailey, with well-preserved earthworks on a strong site. Probably a Welsh foundation, built 1149.

Rhyd y Felin, Aberystwyth
OS 135   SN 585790   R4

A fine ringwork and bailey at the end of a high ridge. It is probably the original Aberystwyth Castle, built in 1110.

Castell Meurig, Llangadog
OS 146   SN 709276   U1/R4

An imposing motte with well-preserved bailey earthworks. There is a modern house in the bailey. The castle is referred to in 1203, 1208 and 1209 as being captured during the Welsh–English struggles. It may be viewed from the road and from a public footpath nearby.

Twmpath, Burry Port
OS 159   SN 466026   R4

A well-preserved motte, overlooking a steep, sloping valley.

Eglwyswrw, Cardigan
OS 145   SN 139384   R4

A well-preserved ringwork on a steeply-sloping site.

Parc y Castell, St Davids
OS 157   SM 744251   R4

A fine, well-preserved ringwork and bailey.

Walwyn's Castle, Haverfordwest
OS 157   SM 872111   R4

A complex site, probably Iron Age in origin, then adapted to form an earthwork castle of two wards. It formed part of the same lordship as Laugharne Castle.

Castlemartin, Pembroke
OS 158   SR 915984   U1/R4

Large ringwork and bailey with a well-preserved bank, partially visible from the road.

Sentence, Narberth
OS 158   SN 110116   R4

A small motte, the predecessor of Narberth. It is first mentioned in 1116 when it was taken by the Welsh.

Eastington, Pembroke
OS 158   SM 901026   R1

A fine medieval strong-house, with later features due to its conversion into an agricultural building, but still retaining much good medieval stonework.

Eglwyscummin Deserted Medieval Village, Laugharne
OS 158   SN 231107   U1

The church is surrounded by a circular graveyard and the earthwork remains of houses, gardens and fields.

Hodgeston Moated Site, Pembroke
OS 158   SS 029995   U1/R4

A square, rather overgrown but well-preserved moated site with the earthworks of the surrounding moat still evident. It is visible from the road.

Summary of Dates

Prehistoric monuments in this book are ascribed to archaeological periods based on the conventional three-age system of Stone Age, Bronze Age and Iron Age. This system of classification has served archaeology well through the years, but has recently been criticised for giving too great an emphasis to the materials with which implements were made. Our study of settlements and burial places now makes us realise that the periods of greatest change and upheaval in society do not necessarily coincide with the adoption of new technological improvements.

Accordingly, archaeologists now tend, when they can, to use absolute chronology for descriptive purposes. This has been made possible by the use of radiocarbon dating. Every living thing contains carbon 14, which, after death, decomposes at a known rate. This dating technique measures the amount of carbon 14 remaining in an organic substance, such as charcoal from a burial mound, to give a date for its death – the felling of the tree, for instance. Unfortunately, we now know that radiocarbon dating gives results that are too young, and dates are therefore corrected or 'calibrated' on a set calculation to give a 'calendar' rather than a 'radiocarbon' date.

But the calculation for correcting radiocarbon dates is by no means accepted by all archaeologists, and the very accuracy of radiocarbon dating itself has received criticism in recent years. For this reason, it was decided to retain the conventional three-age system for the basic classification of the monuments in the book. The date given for each monument in the site heading is designed only to be a rough guide. When a radiocarbon date is given in the text, it is specifically described as a radiocarbon date, is normally given uncorrected in years BC and is therefore too young in calendar years. From the Roman period onward, radiocarbon dating is not normally appropriate, and calendar years are always given.

The following table is designed to outline the basic chronology over the time span covered by the book, and may help explain some of the terms used in the text.

Summary of Dates

Approximate Date	Archaeological Period	Characteristic Features
225,000 BC	Lower Palaeolithic (Old Stone Age)	Warm interglacial within Pleistocene Ice Age. First evidence of man in Wales.
100,000 BC	Middle Palaeolithic	Mousterian hand-axes deposited in Coygan Cave, Dyfed.
26,000 BC	Early Upper Palaeolithic	First evidence of *Homo sapiens* in Dyfed caves. Aurignacian tool types used. Onset of final glaciation.
15,000 BC	Late Upper Palaeolithic	Ice retreats. Increasing evidence for man's activity in Dyfed caves. Creswellian tool types appear.
10,000 BC	Early Mesolithic (Middle Stone Age)	Nomadic hunter-gatherers use finely worked microlithic flints to tip arrows and spears for hunting.
6,000 BC	Late Mesolithic	Seasonal settlements established, especially in coastal areas, by regionalised groups of peoples. Some evidence for manipulation of environment.
3,500 BC	Early Neolithic (New Stone Age)	First farmers arrive. Megalithic tombs built in fertile, low-lying parts of Dyfed. Pottery first used; stone axes of Preseli dolerites used. Much forest clearance.
2,500 BC	Late Neolithic	Communal tombs decline in importance. Ceremonial henges built. Farming activity spreads to marginal uplands.
2,000 BC	Early Bronze Age	Beaker pottery and first metal objects appear. Burial mounds and cairns, stone circles and standing stones erected in upland and lower areas in Dyfed.
1,300 BC	Late Bronze Age	Population pressures, deterioration of climate, and soil degradation lead to abandonment of uplands. Defensive settlements first appear in Dyfed.
600 BC	Iron Age	Hillforts and small, circular defended farms built in increasing numbers. Iron tools first appear. Regionalised groups of people emerge, including Dyfed tribe of Demetae.

Dyfed

Approximate Date	Archaeological Period	Characteristic Features
AD 43	Roman Period	Wales conquered by Romans. Auxiliary forts established. Roads built and Moridunum (Carmarthen) established as capital of region. Dyfed far less Romanised than SE Wales or England.
AD 410	Early Medieval Period	Roman withdrawal. Irish invaders establish dynasty in Dyfed. Kingdom of Dyfed emerges. Spread of Christianity. Viking raids. Hywel Dda and, later, Gruffudd ap Llywelyn establish short-lived unity over parts of Wales.
AD 1066	Medieval Period	Normans invade Wales and establish lordships in southern Dyfed. Welsh remain independent in 'pura Wallia' on upland areas to north, subject to overlordship of English king; Welsh rulers of principality of Deheubarth (south-west Wales) recognised. Continental-style monasteries founded.
1276–83		Edwardian conquest of Wales crushes independent Wales.
1400–10		Owain Glyndŵr leads Welsh rebellion.
1485	Post-Medieval Period	Henry VII becomes first Tudor monarch.
1536–40		Dissolution of the Monasteries by Henry VIII.
1536–43		Acts of Union, whereby a unified Wales merges politically with England.
1642–8		Civil War between Royalists and Parliament brings many medieval castles back into use for the last time.

Glossary

Aisle A lateral division of the nave or chancel of a church, usually separated off by columns, and lying to one or both sides.

Apse Semicircular or polygonal end to a chancel, chapel or aisle.

Apsidal Apse-shaped.

Arcade A row of arches usually supported on columns.

Arrowslit, arrowloop A narrow vertical slit in masonry used by archers.

Ashlar Fine masonry, using stones dressed to a regular shape, and laid in thin-jointed courses.

Augustinian Communities of clerics, often known as 'Regular Canons', who adopted the Rule of St Augustine.

Bailey The defended outer courtyard or 'ward' of a castle.

Barbican An outer defence protecting a gateway.

Barrow A mound of earth or earth and stones used, most often during the Bronze Age, to cover burials.

Batter The sloping part of a wall, usually at the bottom of the exterior face of a tower or curtain wall.

Battlements The parapet of a wall or tower equipped with openings ('crenelles') and solid walling ('merlons') and used for defence by archers. Battlements are also known as crenellations.

Bellcote A structure to hold bells, usually built on to the gable end or junctions of roofs of churches.

Benedictine The oldest of the monastic orders. The monks followed the Rule of St Benedict and wore black habits.

Berm A strip of ground between the base of the curtain wall and the ditch.

Bifid Double-ended or two-footed, especially used to describe terminals on the arm-ends of crosses.

Boss A decorative knob, often on vaulting ribs or on sculptured crosses.

Burgage plot A plot of land, usually long and narrow, forming the unit of property in a medieval borough.

Burgess A property owner in a medieval borough who usually held rights in that town.

Burin A type of flint implement.

Buttery Store-room for wine and other beverages.

Buttress Projecting mass of masonry giving additional support to a wall, often on corners of churches.

Cairn Mound of stones. Used to cover burials in the Neolithic and Bronze Ages, and often had additional ceremonial functions. Clearance cairns are mounds created by clearing agricultural fields of stones.

Cantref The main Welsh administrative unit of land division, used in pre-Norman and later times.

Capital The top or head of a column, often decorated.

Chancel The eastern part of the church, which usually housed the high altar and which was reserved for the clergy.

Chapter house The room in which monks met daily to discuss business and to hear a chapter of the monastic rule.

Cheveaux de frise Rows of small stones set upright in the ground usually in front of the entrance to a hillfort, to impede an enemy attack.

Chi-Rho A monogram formed from the two initial letters X (*chi*) and P (*rho*) of the name of Christ written in Greek.

Choir The part of the church where services were sung, containing the choir stalls.

Cist A stone-lined or slab-built grave.

Cistercian A movement of reformed Benedictine monks, established at Citeaux in 1098. The 'White Monks', named after their white habits, were especially successful in Wales.

Cistern A storage tank for water.

Civitas An area or unit of tribal land under the Romans.

Clas A community of clergy in the pre-Norman Welsh church.

Cloister A four-sided enclosure, usually at the centre of a monastery, with a covered walk along each side, used for study.

Commote A Welsh administrative unit of land division, a subdivision of a cantref.

Constable The governor of a castle.

Corbel A projecting stone used for support, often for floor or roof timbers.

Counterscarp Outer defence, a wall or slope of a ditch.

Crossing The central space at the intersection of the east–west axis and north–south transepts of a church. The tower often stands above.

Crosslet The crossing of incised arm-ends of crosses to create additional crosses.

Cross-slab A shaped stone slab on which is, in relief, a cross and often other ornament.

Cruciform Cross-shaped.

Curtain The wall, often strengthened with towers, which encloses the courtyard of a castle.

Decorated The style of Gothic architecture which flourished *c.*1280–1340.

Dormitory The sleeping quarters of a monastery.

Drawbridge A wooden bridge across the ditch to the entrance or gateway of a castle. It could be raised or lowered for defensive purposes.

Drystone wall Stone wall built without mortar or clay.

Embrasure A splayed opening, either in a parapet for defensive use by archers, or in walls for windows.

Exchequer The finance officer of a castle.

Forebuilding A projection from the front of a keep as an extra protection for the entrance, usually over the stair.

Fret-pattern Typical Celtic motif of classical derivation, and used for decoration on early Christian crosses.

Gunloop, gunport The opening in a wall for a gun.

Hall The room in a castle used for administration of estates and justice, and for entertainment on important occasions. Many castles would also have a smaller hall for less formal everyday use.

Henge A non-defensive circular earthwork with a bank and ditch and one or more entrances, apparently used for ceremonial purposes during the late Neolithic period.

Hoard A timber fighting platform projecting from the outside of the top of a castle keep or tower for extra defence.

Interlace A favourite Celtic decorative motif derived from late classical art. Continuous interlacing patterns frequently used on crosses include plaitwork and knotwork.

Jamb The straight side of a doorway or window.

Justiciar The chief minister of the king in the medieval period.

Keep The main, strong, usually free-standing, tower of a castle.

Key-pattern A decorative motif of classical derivation, used on early Christian crosses.

Knotwork see *interlace*.

Lancet A plain slender window with a pointed arch.

Latin cross An upright cross with the lower arm longer than the others, distinguished from the equal-armed Greek cross.

Lavatorium A bowl for monks to wash their hands before meals.

Leat A channel for conveying water.

Lintel A supporting wooden beam or stone over an opening in a wall.

Lordship   The area ruled by a lord under the supremacy of the king.

Louvre   The opening in the roof to allow smoke to escape.

Machicolation   Openings in the floor of a projecting structure, often in front of a castle gatehouse, through which missiles could be dropped on to attackers. See also *murder hole.*

Maltese cross   A cross with strongly-splayed arms often curved or indented at the ends.

Marches   Border or frontier, especially used for the south and east areas of Wales under Norman control.

Megalith   Large stone or a structure built of large stones (from the Greek *mega* (great) and *lithos* (stone)). Neolithic chambered tombs are often known as megaliths.

Merlon   see *battlement.*

Mortise   Socket in which a projection or 'tenon' is placed. This device is used to join two pieces of stone or wood, as on a composite cross.

Motte   A mound of earth constructed to support a tower and palisade.

Mullion   The vertical bar between window openings.

Murage toll   Charges exacted for the purposes of building medieval town defences.

Mural tower   A tower built on a curtain wall.

Murder hole   A hole, often in the vault of a castle gate passage, through which missiles could be dropped on to attackers, or for water to extinguish castle timbers set on fire during an attack. See also *machicolation.*

Nave   The part of a church extending from the crossing to the west end.

Newel stair   A spiral stair with a central support or 'newel'.

Ogam   A system of writing invented in Ireland before the 5th century AD, comprising 20 letters represented by groups of notches, and often used for early medieval inscriptions on stone.

Oriel window   A projecting, curved or polygonal window.

Palisade   A strong timber fence.

Pent roof   A lean-to roof.

Piscina   A basin with a drain, usually set into the church wall by the altar, used for washing vessels during Mass.

Plaitwork   see *interlace.*

Portal stone   The stone at the front or entrance to a chambered tomb.

Portcullis   Wood and iron gate which could be raised or lowered in grooves in the wall of a castle gate-passage, for defensive purposes.

Postern   A small gateway, subsidiary to the main entrance.

Premonstratensian   An order of canons founded by St Norbert at Prémontré and following the Rule of St Augustine.

Presbytery   The part of the church around the high altar, to the east of the choir.

Pulpitum   A screen wall dividing the nave from the choir.

Redan   An outwork, usually of a castle or fort, consisting of two faces forming an outward-projecting angle.

Revetment   Timber- or stonework built to give support to the side of a bank or ditch.

Ringwork   A type of early castle consisting of a defensive enclosure, usually circular, with a surrounding bank and external ditch.

Rule   The code of religious life followed by a religious order. The two most important in medieval Europe were the Rules of St Benedict and St Augustine.

Sacristy   The room for the storage of vestments and sacred vessels.

Sedile   The seat for the clergy, usually set into the south wall of the chancel.

Shell-keep   A defensive stone wall built around the perimeter of a motte.

Slight   Damage or destroy a castle.

String course   A projecting horizontal decorative band of masonry running around a building.

Tironensian A monastic order founded by St Bernard at Tiron.

Tithes A tax payable to the church, comprising one-tenth of agricultural produce.

Tracery Decorative stonework in the upper parts of windows or on walls.

Transept The transverse, short arms of a cruciform church, orientated north–south.

Transom A horizontal bar across the lights of a window.

Trifid Three-footed.

Triquetra A triangular ornament formed of three interlaced arcs.

Triskele A symbolic figure consisting of three legs radiating from a common centre.

Vault An arched stone roof. A barrel-vault is a vault of semicircular section.

Vine-scroll A decorative motif of east-Christian (Syrian) derivation, and adopted for use on early Christian stones, especially in the north of England.

Wall-walk A passage behind the parapet of a castle or town wall, used for defence.

Ward A courtyard within the walls of a castle.

Wheel-head cross A type of cross on which the head has an inset wheel joining the arms.

Bibliography

Guidebooks

The monuments in the care of Cadw and other conservation bodies often have guidebooks which give a more detailed history and tour of the site. Most of the monuments listed below will have the guides for sale at reception areas, but some of the older official guides to Cadw sites may now be out of print; these are due to be replaced by new Cadw guides in the near future.

Carew Castle   Official Guidebook, Pembrokeshire Coast National Park Authority.
Carew Cross   R Turner, Cadw Guidebook (Cardiff 1991).
Carreg Cennen Castle   J M Lewis, Cadw Guidebook (Cardiff 1990).
Carreg Coetan Arthur   J B Hilling, Cadw Guidebook (Cardiff 1992).
Carswell Old House   R Turner, Cadw Guidebook (Cardiff 1991).
Castell Henllys   H Mytum, Official Guidebook.
Cilgerran Castle   J B Hilling, Cadw Guidebook (Cardiff 1992).
Dolaucothi   Official Guidebook, National Trust.
Kidwelly Castle   J R Kenyon, Cadw Guidebook (Cardiff 1990).
Lamphey Bishop's Palace   R Turner, Cadw Guidebook (Cardiff 1991).
Llansteffan Castle   D J C King, Official Guidebook (Cardiff 1979).
Llawhaden Castle   R Turner, Cadw Guidebook (Cardiff 1991).
Manorbier Castle   Official Guidebook (Llandeilo).
Pembroke Castle   Official Castle Guidebook.
Pentre Ifan Burial Chamber   J B Hilling, Cadw Guidebook (London 1992).
St Davids Bishop's Palace   J W Evans, Cadw Guidebook (Cardiff 1991).
St Dogmael's Abbey   J B Hilling, Cadw Guidebook (Cardiff 1992).
St Non's Chapel   W Evans, Cadw Guidebook (Cardiff 1991).
Skomer Island   J G Evans, *Prehistoric Farmers of Skomer Island: An Archaeological Guide*. West Wales Trust for Nature Conservation (Haverfordwest 1986).
Strata Florida   C Platt and D M Robinson, Cadw Guidebook (Cardiff 1992).
Talley   C Platt and D M Robinson, Cadw Guidebook (Cardiff 1992).

Further Reading

This is a very selective list of general books which give further information about aspects of Welsh history and archaeology.

Prehistory

Bradley, R, *The Prehistoric Settlement of Britain* (London 1978).
Burl, A, *The Stone Circles of the British Isles* (London 1976).

225

Cunliffe, B, *Iron Age Communities in Britain* (London 1974).
Daniel, G E, *The Prehistoric Chamber Tombs of England and Wales* (Cambridge 1950).
Darvill, T, *Prehistoric Britain* (London 1987).
Forde-Johnston, J, *Hillforts* (Liverpool 1976).
Hogg, A H A, *Hill-Forts of Britain* (London 1975).
Megaw, J V S and Simpson, D D A, (eds), *Introduction to British Prehistory* (Leicester 1979).
Taylor, J A (ed.), *Culture and Environment in Prehistoric Wales* (Oxford 1980).
Williams, G H, 'Recent work on rural settlement in later prehistoric and early historic Dyfed', *Antiquaries Journal, LXVIII* (1988), pp 30–54.

Roman

Frere, S S, *Britannia: A History of Roman Britain*, 3rd edn (London 1987).
Margary, I D, *Roman Roads in Britain* (London 1973).
Jarrett, M G and Nash-Williams V E, *The Roman Frontier in Wales*, 2nd, revd edn (Cardiff 1969).
Todd, M *Roman Britain 55 B.C.–A.D. 400* (London 1981).
Webster, G *The Roman Imperial Army* 3rd edn (London 1985).

Early Medieval

Davies, W *Wales in the Early Middle Ages* (Leicester 1982).
Edwards, N and Lane, A (eds), *Early Medieval Settlements in Wales AD 400–1100* (Bangor and Cardiff 1988).
Nash-Williams, V E *Early Christian Monuments of Wales* (Cardiff 1950).

Medieval

Butler, L and Given-Wilson, C *Medieval Monasteries of Great Britain* (London 1979).
Davies, R R *Conquest, Coexistence and Change: Wales 1063–1415* (Oxford 1987).
Kenyon, J R, *Medieval Fortifications* (Leicester 1990).
King, D J C *The Castle in England and Wales* (London 1988).
Knowles, D and Hadcock, R N, *Medieval Religious Houses: England and Wales*, revd edn (London 1971).
Renn, D *Norman Castles in Britain*, 2nd edn (London 1973).
Smith, P *Houses of the Welsh Countryside: A Study in Historical Geography*, 2nd edn (London 1988).
Williams, G, *The Welsh Church from Conquest to Reformation*, 2nd edn (Cardiff 1976).

General Reference

The Royal Commission on Ancient and Historical Monuments in Wales publishes county volumes or 'inventories' which give detailed descriptions of all monuments known at the time of publication. Two inventories have so far been published for Dyfed, those for the old counties of Carmarthenshire and Pembrokeshire. Both volumes are now old and require revision, but are still useful and may be found in good reference libraries.

An Inventory of the Ancient Monuments in Wales and Monmouthshire: V – County of Carmarthen (London 1917).
An Inventory of the Ancient Monuments in Wales and Monmouthshire: VII – County of Pembroke (London 1925).

Gazetteer References

This is the full list of references added to the relevant site entry in the gazetteer. They are designed to help the interested visitor find out more about a specific monument.

Annels, A E and Burnham, B C, 1986, *The Dolaucothi Gold Mines*, National Trust monograph.

Avent, J R, 1988, 'Laugharne Castle excavations, 1976–1988', *Archaeology in Wales 28*, pp 25–7.

Baring Gould, S, 1899, 'Exploration of the stone camp on St David's Head', *Archaeologia Cambrensis*, 5th series, *XVI*, pp 105–31.

Baring Gould, S, 1900, 'Exploration of Moel Trigarn', *Archaeologia Cambrensis*, 5th series, *XVII*, pp 189–221. An interpretation of Foel Trigarn (no. 49).

Benson, D G and Williams, G H, 1987, 'Dale Promontory Fort', *Archaeology in Wales*, *27*, p 43.

Burnham, B C and Burnham, H B, 1986, 'Recent survey on the fort and vicus at Pumsaint', *Carmarthenshire Antiquary*, *XXII*, pp 3–13.

Burnham, B C and Burnham, H B, 1989, 'Excavations at Pumsaint, 1989: interim report', Interim Reports and Occasional Papers, no. 11, St David's University College, Lampeter.

Caple, C, 1990, 'The castle and lifestyle of a 13th-century independent Welsh lord; excavations at Dryslwyn Castle 1980–1988; *Chateau Gaillard. Etudes de Castellologie medievale*, *XV*, pp 47–59.

David, A, 1989, 'Some aspects of the human presence in west Wales during the Mesolithic', in Bonsall (ed.), *The Mesolithic in Europe*, Edinburgh, pp 241–53.

Davies, J L, 1971, 'The hut-settlement on Gateholm, Pembrokeshire', *Archaeologia Cambrensis*, *CXX*, pp 102–10.

Drewett, P L, 1987, 'An archaeological survey of Mynydd Preseli, Dyfed', *Archaeology in Wales*, *27*, pp 14–16.

Evans, J, 1986, *Prehistoric Farmers of Skomer Island: An Archaeological Guide*, West Wales Trust for Nature Conservation, Haverfordwest.

Evans, W and Worsely, R, 1981, *St Davids Cathedral*, St Davids.

Forde, C D et al, 1963, 'Excavations at Pen Dinas, Aberystwyth', *Archaeologia Cambrensis*, *CXII*, pp 125–53.

Fox, C and Grimes, W F, 1928, 'Corston Beacon: an early Bronze Age cairn', *Archaeologia Cambrensis* 7th series *LXXXII*, pp 137–74.

Grimes, W F, 1939, 'Notes on Excavations', *Proceedings of the Prehistoric Society*, *V*, p 258.

Grimes, W F, 1949, 'Pentre Ifan Burial Chamber, Pembrokeshire', *Archaeologia Cambrensis*, *C*, pp 3–23.

Grimes, W F, 1963, 'The stone circles and related monuments of Wales', in I LL Foster and L Alcock (eds), *Culture and Environment*, London.

Guilbert, G, 1974, 'Llanstephan Castle: 1973 interim report', *Carmarthenshire Antiquary*, *X*, pp 37–48.

Hogg, A H A, 1973, 'Gaer Fawr and Carn Ingli: two major Pembrokeshire hill-forts', *Archaeologia Cambrensis*, *CXXII*, pp 69–84.

Hogg, A H A, 1974, 'Carn Goch, Carmarthenshire', *Archaeologia Cambrensis*, *CXXIII*, pp 43–53.

Hogg, A H A, 1977, 'Two cairns at Aber Camddwr, near Ponterwyd, Cardiganshire', *Archaeologia Cambrensis*, *CXXVI*, pp 24–37.

James, H, 1978, 'Excavations at Church Street, Carmarthen, 1976', in G C Boon (ed), *Cambrian Archaeological Association Monographs and Collections, I: Roman Sites*, pp 63–112.

James, H, 1982, *Roman West Wales*, Carmarthen.

James, T A, 1980, *Carmarthen: An Archaeological and Topographical Survey*, Carmarthen.

James, T A, 1989, 'Medieval Carmarthen and its burgesses', *Carmarthenshire Antiquary*, *XXV*, pp 9–26.

Jones, G D B, 1966, 'Ystradfellte and Arosfa Garreg: two Roman marching camps', *Bulletin of the Board of Celtic Studies*, *21*, (1964–6), pp 174–8.

Jones, G D B, 1968, 'The Roman Camps at Y Pigwn'. *Bulletin of the Board of Celtic Studies*, *23*, (1968–70), pp 100–3.

Jones, G D B and Little, J H, 1973, 'Excavations on the Roman fort at Pumpsaint, Carmarthenshire: interim report, 1972', *Carmarthenshire Antiquary*, *IX*, pp 3–32.

Jones, G D B and Little, J H, 1974, 'Excavations at Pumpsaint 1973: interim report', *Carmarthenshire Antiquary*, *X*, pp 3–16.

King, D J C, 1978, 'Pembroke Castle', *Archaeologia Cambrensis*, *CXXVII*, pp 75–121.

King, D J C, 1983, 'Notes on the Castle of Saint Clears', *Carmarthenshire Antiquary*, *XIX*, pp 5–7.

King, D J C and Cheshire, M, 1982, 'The town walls of Pembroke', *Archaeologia Cambrensis*, *CXXXI*, pp 77–84.

King, D J C and Perks, J C, 1951, 'Castell Nanhyfer, Nevern (Pemb)', *Archaeologia Cambrensis*, *CI*, pt 2, pp 123–8.

King, D J C and Perks, J C, 1962, 'Carew Castle, Pembrokeshire', *Archaeological Journal*, *CXIX*, pp 270–307.

King, D J C and Perks, J C, 1970, 'Manorbier Castle, Pembrokeshire', *Archaeologia Cambrensis*, *CXIC*, pp 83–118.

Laws, E, 1896, 'Notes on the fortifications of medieval Tenby', *Archaeologia Cambrensis*, 5th series, *XIII*, pp 177–92, 273–89.

Lethbridge, T C and David, H, 1930, 'Excavation of a house-site on Gateholm, Pembrokeshire', *Archaeologia Cambrensis*, *LXXXV*, pp 366–74.

Lewis, J M, 1974, 'Excavations at Rhos-y-Clegyrn prehistoric site, St Nicholas, Pembs', *Archaeologia Cambrensis*, *CXXIII*, pp 13–42.

Lewis, J M, 1976, 'A survey of early Christian monuments of Dyfed, west of the Taf', in G C Boon and J M Lewis (eds), *Welsh Antiquity*, National Museum of Wales, Cardiff, pp 177–92.

Little, J H, 1971, 'The Carmarthen Amphitheatre', *Carmarthenshire Antiquary*, *VII*, pp 58–63.

Lynch, F, 1972, 'Portal dolmens in the Nevern Valley, Pembrokeshire', in F Lynch and C Burgess (eds), *Prehistoric Man in Wales and the West*, Bath, pp 67–84.

Lynch, F, 1975, 'Excavations at Carreg Samson megalithic tomb, Mathry, Pembrokeshire', *Archaeologia Cambrensis*, *CXXIV*, pp 15–35.

Lynch, F, 1976, 'Towards a chronology of megalithic tombs in Wales', in G C Boon and J M Lewis (eds), *Welsh Antiquity*, National Museum of Wales, Cardiff, pp 63–79.

Marshall, E and Murphy, K, 1991, 'The excavation of two Bronze Age cairns with associated standing stones in Dyfed: Parc Maen and Aber Camddwr II', *Archaeologia Cambrensis*, *CXL*, forthcoming.

Mytum, H C, 1989, 'Excavations at Castell Henllys, 1981–89: the Iron Age Fort', *Archaeology in Wales*, *29*, pp 6–10.

Mytum, H C and Webster, C J, 1989, 'A survey of the Iron Age enclosure and *chevaux de frise* at Carn Alw, Dyfed', *Proceedings of the Prehistoric Society*, 55, pp 263–7.

Nash-Williams, V E, 1950, *The Early Christian Monuments of Wales*, Cardiff.

O'Neil, B H St J, 1946–7, 'Castell Gwallter motte', *Archaeologia Cambrensis*, *XCIX*, pp 156–7.

Parry, C, 1987, 'Survey and excavation at Newcastle Emlyn Castle', *Carmarthenshire Antiquary*, *XXIII*, pp 11–27.

Savory, H N, 1956, 'The excavation of "Twlc-y-Filiast" Cromlech, Llangynog (Carm.)', *Bulletin of the Board of Celtic Studies*, *16* (1954–6), pp 300–8.

Bibliography

Savory, H N, 1973, 'Excavations at the Hoyle, Tenby, in 1968', *Archaeologia Cambrensis, CXXI*, pp 18–34.

Smith, P, 1988, *Houses of the Welsh Countryside*, Royal Commission on Ancient and Historical Monuments in Wales, London.

Thomas, W G, 1962, 'Tenby town walls', *Archaeological Journal, CXIX*, pp 324.

Turner, H M, 1970, *Town Defences in England and Wales: An Architectural and Documentary Study, AD 900–1500*, London.

Wainwright, G J, 1971, 'Excavations at Tower Point, St Brides, Pembrokeshire', *Archaeologia Cambrensis, CXX*, pp 84–90.

Ward, A H, 1976, 'The cairns on Mynydd Llangyndeyrn', *Carmarthenshire Antiquary, XII*, pp 3–21.

Ward, A H, 1983, 'Excavations around two standing stones on Mynydd Llangyndeyrn, Dyfed', *Archaeologia Cambrensis, CXXXII*, pp 30–48.

Ward, J, 1918, 'Some prehistoric sepulchral remains near Pendine, Carmarthenshire', *Archaeologia Cambrensis, XVIII*, pp 35–79.

Williams, A, 1952, 'Clegyr Boia, St David's (Pemb): excavations in 1943', *Archaeologia Cambrensis, CII*, pt 1, pp 20–47.

Acknowledgements

I have been helped in the writing of this book by innumerable friends and colleagues. The director of Cadw, John Carr, has given unwavering support for the project from the beginning and my colleagues in the publications department of Cadw, David Robinson and Diane Williams, have been of great assistance with advice and suggestions for the editing and illustration of the volume. The staff of the Welsh Office cartographic drawing office undertook the work of production of the line drawings with laudable speed, often working with my rather sketchy field plans and notes. The text has benefited immeasurably from the suggestions of many friends who gave up their time to read chapters or individual site entries: Richard Avent, Stephen Briggs, David Browne, Barry Burnham, Andrew David, Stephen Green, Heather James, John Kenyon, John Lewis, Francis Lynch, Bill Manning, Harold Mytum, David Robinson, Jack Spurgeon, Gwyn Thomas, Rick Turner and George Williams. I am very grateful to Peter Humphries, Ken Murphy, Harold Mytum, Rick Turner and Anthony Ward who kindly gave me photographs of individual sites for illustration, and to colleagues in the Dyfed Archaeological Trust, National Monuments Record, National Museum of Wales and the National Trust who provided numbers of photographs either at cost or free of charge. Lynn Hughes deserves my thanks for his encouragement at the very beginning of the project, for without him I might never have begun writing at all. The professionalism of Ruth Bowden and Philip Glover of HMSO has been of immense assistance during the production of the volume, and it is a pleasure to record my gratitude here.

I would also like to pay tribute to the pioneering work of my predecessors in the Inspectorate, especially Oswin Craster, without whose dedicated field work in Dyfed some of the sites here described might not have survived until today. Staff of the Dyfed Archaeological Trust deserve thanks also for their continuing role in guarding the remains of our built heritage. Innumerable discussions with them through the years have considerably influenced and assisted my own work.

My greatest thanks go to my family, my husband, Richard Avent, for his support, encouragement and tolerance throughout the project, and my children, Cerian and Tomos, who remained stoically understanding, companiable and good even in the most trying situations, and Rhydian, whose many hours of helpful slumber concentrated my mind wonderfully. This book is dedicated to all four of them, for without their different forms of kindness, it would never have been completed.

Sources of Illustrations

Most of the line drawings were produced by staff of Cartographic Services, Welsh Office. Many were redrawn with amendments using plans published elsewhere: nos 105, 109, 117, 118, 119, 123, 124, 133, 135, 140, 146, 149 and 150 (Crown copyright plans from Welsh Office or Cadw guidebooks); nos 6 and 8 (Lynch 1972) no. 13 (Lynch 1975); no. 22 (Lynch 1976); nos 49, 58 and 79 (Hogg 1975 – see Further Reading); no. 50 (Mytum and Webster 1989); no. 52 (Hogg 1973); nos 56 and 76 (Hogg 1974); no. 60 (Williams 1952); no. 67 (Evans 1986); nos 70 and 73 (Forde-Johnston 1976 – see Further Reading); no. 84 (Burnham and Burnham 1989); no. 93 (Davies 1971); no. 106 (King and Perks 1951); no. 112 (King 1978); no. 113 (King and Perks 1962); no. 114 (King and Perks 1970); no. 120 (James 1989); no. 122 (Caple 1990); no. 126 (Kenyon 1990 – see Further Reading); no. 127 (O'Neil 1946–7).

I am most grateful to the National Museum of Wales and the University of Wales Press for permission to reproduce from Nash-Williams, 1950: nos 85, 88, 89, 90, 91 and 101; to the editor of *Archaeologia Cambrensis* for permission to reproduce from the same volume: nos 87, 94, 95, 99, 100, 102, 103 and 104, and from *Archaeologia Cambrensis*, 1868: no. 33; and 1872: nos 4, 12, 14, 18 and 20; and 1978: no. 2; and to the National Museum of Wales for permission to reproduce the six reconstruction drawings in the introductory sections to chapters 1, 2 (Casseli) 3 (Jenkins) 4 (Hughes) and 6 (Sorrell). The reconstruction drawings in chapters 5 (Banbury), 7 (Ball, Derbyshire and Lloyd) and 8 (Ball) are the copyright of Cadw, Welsh Historic Monuments.

Copyright acknowledgements are due to the following photographic sources: National Monuments Record collection in the Royal Commission on Ancient and Historical Monuments in Wales: nos 19, 81*, 91, 98, 114*, 115*, 126, 131, 142, 143 and 148 (* indicates photographs from the Aerial Photography section of the NMR). National Museum of Wales: 1, 23 and 34. Dyfed Archaeological Trust Ltd and Cadw, Welsh Historic Monuments: nos 44, 47, 53, 57, 64, 67, 70, 72, 75, 82, 83, (twice), 105, and 123. Dyfed Archaeological Trust: nos 69 and 78. Clwyd Powys Archaeological Trust: no. 80. Cadw, Welsh Historic Monuments: nos 109, 110, 119, 120 and 129. National Trust: no. 84 (photo: Kathy de Witt). Roger Worsley: nos 63, 66 and 86. Andrew David: no. 3. Anthony Ward: no. 39. Harold Mytum: no. 51. Peter Humphries: no. 118. Welsh Tourist Board: nos 112, 113, 117 and 124.

Index

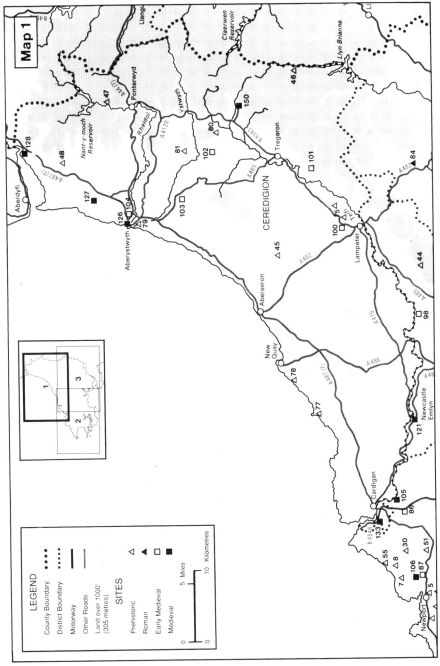

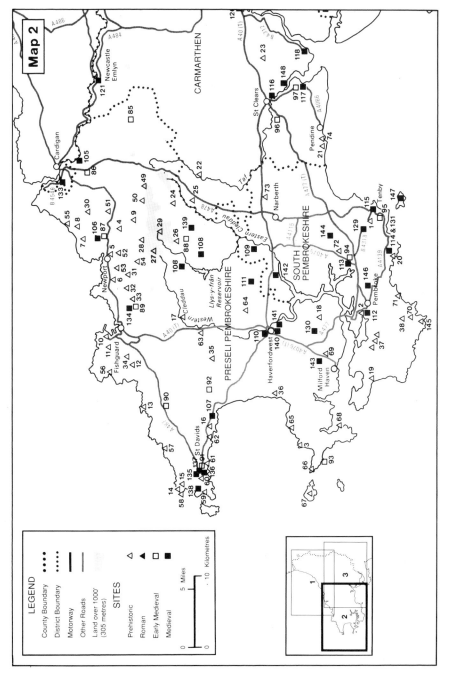

Map 2

LEGEND

County Boundary
District Boundary
Motorway
Other Roads
Land over 1000'
(305 metres)

SITES

Prehistoric △
Roman ▲
Early Medieval □
Medieval ■

0   5 Miles
0   · 10 Kilometres

CARMARTHEN

SOUTH PEMBROKESHIRE

PRESELI PEMBROKESHIRE

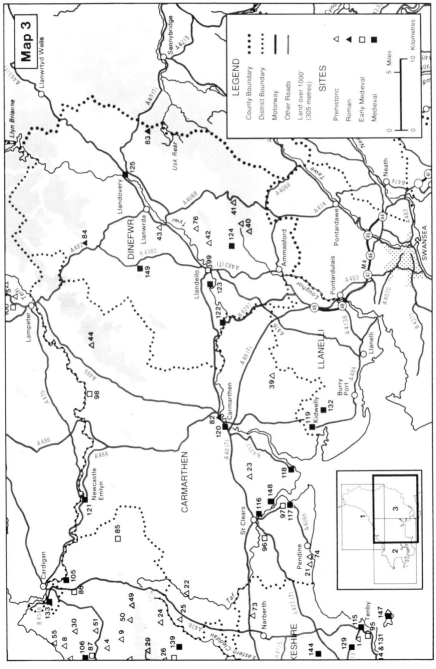

Map 3

LEGEND

County Boundary
District Boundary
Motorway
Other Roads
Land over 1000'
(305 metres)

SITES
△ Prehistoric
▲ Roman
□ Early Medieval
■ Medieval

0 — 5 Miles
0 — 5 — 10 Kilometres

241